ARCHITECTURE

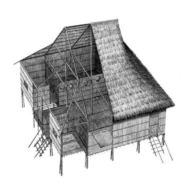

PATRON

Dato' Seri Dr Mahathir Mohamad

SPONSORS

The Encyclopedia of Malaysia was made possible thanks to the generous and enlightened support of the following organizations:

DRB-HICOM GROUP

GEC-MARCONI PROJECTS (MALAYSIA) SDN BHD

MALAYAN UNITED INDUSTRIES BERHAD

MALAYSIA NATIONAL INSURANCE BERHAD

MINISTRY OF EDUCATION MALAYSIA

PERNAS INTERNATIONAL HOLDINGS BERHAD

PETRONAS BERHAD

RENONG BERHAD

STAR PUBLICATIONS (MALAYSIA) BERHAD

SUNGEIWAY GROUP

TENAGA NASIONAL BERHAD

UNITED OVERSEAS BANK GROUP

YAYASAN ALBUKHARY

YTL CORPORATION BERHAD

© Editions Didier Millet, 1998
Published by Archipelago Press *an imprint of* Editions Didier Millet Pte Ltd
121, Telok Ayer Street, #03-01, Singapore 068590
Tel: 65-6324 9260 Fax: 65-6324 9261 E-mail: edm@edmbooks.com.sg

Kuala Lumpur Office:
25, Jalan Pudu Lama, 50200 Kuala Lumpur, Malaysia
Tel: 03-2031 3805 Fax: 03-2031 6298 E-mail: edmbooks@edmbooks.com.my

Websites: www.edmbooks.com • www.encyclopedia.com.my

First published 1998
Reprinted 1999, 2001, 2003, 2005, 2007

Colour separation by Overseas Colourscan Sdn Bhd (236702-T)
Printed by Tien Wah Press (Pte) Limited
ISBN 978-981-3018-43-3

ACKNOWLEDGMENT

The Encyclopedia of Malaysia was first conceived by Editions Didier Millet and Datin Paduka Marina Mahathir. The Editorial Advisory Board, made up of distinguished figures drawn from academic and public life, was constituted in March 1994. The project was publicly announced in October that year, and eight months later the first sponsors were in place. By 1996, the structure of the content was agreed; later that year the appointment of Volume Editors and the commissioning of authors were substantially complete, and materials for the work were beginning to flow in. By late 1998, five volumes were completed for publication, and the remaining ten volumes fully commissioned and well under way.

The Publishers are grateful to the following for their contribution during the preparation of the first five volumes:
Dato' Seri Anwar Ibrahim,
who acted as Chairman of the Editorial Advisory Board;
and the following members of the Board:
Tan Sri Dato' Dr Ahmad Mustaffa Babjee
Prof. Dato' Dr Asmah Haji Omar
Puan Azah Aziz
Dr Peter M. Kedit
Dato' Dr T. Marimuthu
Tan Sri Dato' Dr Noordin Sopiee
Tan Sri Datuk Augustine S. H. Ong
Ms Patricia Regis
the late Tan Sri Zain Azraai
Datuk Datin Paduka Zakiah Hanum bt Abdul Hamid

SERIES EDITORIAL TEAM

PUBLISHER
Didier Millet

GENERAL MANAGER
Charles Orwin

PROJECT COORDINATOR
Marina Mahathir

EDITORIAL DIRECTOR
Timothy Auger

PROJECT MANAGER
Noor Azlina Yunus

EDITORIAL CONSULTANT
Peter Schoppert

EDITORS
Alice Chee
Chuah Guat Eng
Elaine Ee
Irene Khng
Jacinth Lee-Chan
Nolly Lim
Kay Lyons
Premilla Mohanlall
Wendy (Khadijah) Moore
Alysoun Owen
Amita Sarwal
Tan Hwee Koon
Philip Tatham
Sumitra Visvanathan

DESIGN DIRECTOR
Tan Seok Lui

DESIGNERS
Ahmad Puad bin Aziz
Lee Woon Hong
Theivanai A/P Nadaraju
Felicia Wong
Yong Yoke Lian

PRODUCTION MANAGER
Sin Kam Cheong

VOLUME EDITORIAL TEAM

EDITORS
Noor Azlina Yunus
Philip Tatham

DESIGNERS
Theivanai A/P Nadaraju
Yong Yoke Lian

ILLUSTRATORS
Anuar bin Abdul Rahim
Chai Kah Yune
Julian Davison
Stephen Dew
Kerry Elias-Moore
Domitille Héron-Huge
Ishak bin Hashim
Sui Chen Choi
Tam Hoe Yen
Tan Hong Yew
Wee Siew Hock
Wong Swee Fatt
Yeap Kok Chien

THE ENCYCLOPEDIA OF
MALAYSIA

Volume 5

ARCHITECTURE

Volume Editor
Chen Voon Fee
Architectural Consulting Services

ARCHIPELAGO PRESS

Contents

Introduction

This volume traces the development of Malaysia's architecture from the simplest built shelters to the mega projects of the late 20th century. Although no 'Golden Age' in Malaysia's history produced the equivalent of a Borobudur or an Angkor Wat, the country's geographical location has always opened it to ideas and influences from both East and West, resulting in an architectural mosaic of great diversity, artistry, sophistication and cross-cultural influences.

Malay houses in Kelantan and Terengganu (above) show Thai and Cambodian influences in the curved roof form and in the use of heavier wall panels. In contrast, houses with a *bumbung Perak* (below)—a hipped roof with gable-like ends—raised on masonry columns are found extensively along the west coast of the Malay Peninsula.

Indigenous buildings

As early as the 3rd century BCE, Indian chroniclers knew of the existence of the Malay Peninsula, and in the 5th and 6th centuries CE, a number of trading kingdoms were established. Although structures from these times have not survived, their forms are evident in the buildings of Malaysia's indigenous peoples and in those of other parts of Southeast Asia, such as Thailand and Indonesia.

By the time the Portuguese conquered Melaka in 1511, the Malays had developed a highly sophisticated architecture for their houses embodying modern-day principles of standardization, prefabrication, site assembly and expansion. Characterized by pitched roofs, post-and-beam construction, and built from timber and other jungle produce, the houses were eminently suited to the hot, wet tropics. Although the roof forms evolved along different lines on the east and west coasts of the Peninsula—strongly influenced by the kingdom of Patani in southern Thailand and by the Minangkabau from southeastern Sumatra—they all afforded the occupants comfortable ventilation and filtered light. The same construction techniques and materials were employed by the Malays in their palaces and mosques, by the indigenous peoples of Sabah and Sarawak in their longhouses, and by the immigrant peoples in their dwellings.

Foreign influences

Although the Portuguese and later the Dutch occupied Melaka on the west coast for over 300 years, their different architectural styles had no lasting influence. They did, however, introduce previously unknown building types, such as forts and churches, and techniques as well as a change in the scale of buildings and the materials used. Town planning was also used to lay out streets and assign quarters of the town to different communities.

Agreement between the Dutch and the British at the end of the Napoleonic Wars led the British to set up the Straits Settlements of Penang, Melaka and Singapore in 1826. Thereafter followed a hundred years of peace which allowed a great transformation in Malaysia's architecture. Towns such as Melaka, George Town in Penang and Kuching in Sarawak, created out of colonial occupation and commercial interests, paved the way for modern, urban infrastructure. Tin mining, initially a cottage industry along the estuaries of the west coast, changed in scale and moved upriver and inland. Following the large-scale planting of rubber in the early 1900s, the interior of the Peninsular west coast was effectively opened up, leading to the founding of tin-mining centres. Chinese and Indian settlers, brought in to work the mines

The domes of the Ubudiah Mosque in Kuala Kangsar, Perak (left), show the influence of Persian and northern Indian styles of mosque architecture. In contrast, this five-storey shophouse (right) in Jalan Cheng Lock, Kuala Lumpur, displays features of early Modernism couched in a mainly Classical composition.

The 88-storey Petronas Twin Towers is among the world's tallest buildings. The retiform, Islamic-inspired plan is extruded into two tapering, multifaceted gleaming spires in glass and stainless steel. The bridge link between the towers is an engineering feat in itself.

and plantations, enriched their new homeland with their distinctive buildings.

The rise of Western industrialization created world markets for Malaysia's tin and rubber, the profits from which financed the infrastructure of roads, railways and ports. Prosperity and confidence enabled the erection of imposing administrative and commercial buildings, mainly in the Western Neoclassical style, and of other buildings in a mixture of European styles. Kuala Lumpur, the capital of the Federated Malay States from 1896, enjoyed a brief but enduring period of the imported Mogul style, which was copied all over the country, especially for mosques. Tin and rubber wealth lined the shady avenues of Penang, Ipoh, Melaka and Kuala Lumpur with spacious villas. In the northern and eastern parts of the Malay Peninsula, where colonial influence was minimal, Malay urban centres evolved from clusters of kampongs grouped around the rulers' palaces and the main mosques, into the royal capitals of Alor Setar, Kota Bharu, Kuala Terengganu and Arau.

In the period between the two world wars, Malaysia's architecture reflected the prevailing trends from the West. Art Deco marked the transition from the traditional vernacular and Western Neoclassical styles to early Modernism and the International Style. Most buildings were now designed by professionally qualified architects, mostly expatriate. Building activities became institutionalized; the introduction of building by-laws required 'qualified persons' to submit building plans within town limits.

Post-Independence developments

The greatest architectural transformation followed Merdeka, or Independence, in 1957. Kuala Lumpur was transformed from a colonial town into the new nation's capital. Proud symbols of nationhood were expressed in new and daring forms, often the work of overseas trained Malaysians. Innovative construction techniques and industrialized components changed the scale of commercial buildings and enabled the erection of the first skyscrapers. Shophouses were replaced by shopping arcades, then by mega malls. Townhouses made way for multifunction complexes. Later, condominiums with centralized facilities replaced bungalows and apartments. Large-scale housing estates of repetitive single- and double-storey link houses created suburban centres and townships.

In the ongoing search for a Malaysian architectural identity, indigenous cultural forms vie with the International Style, the results of which are not always compatible. The sunshading devices of the early skyscrapers have been discarded in favour of anonymous, all-enveloping tinted, heat-resisting glass. Only occasionally are tropical elements such as elevated planting and new screening devices introduced.

The overbuilding of the 1980s caused a slowdown in the property market. This coincided with increasing public awareness of the need to protect prewar buildings and saw the birth of the country's first non-governmental organization for heritage conservation. In contrast, a near decade of uninterrupted economic growth in the 1990s stimulated the pace of building, culminating in a number of mega projects: the Petronas Twin Towers, among the world's tallest office towers; the Kuala Lumpur International Airport, a state-of-the-art airport set in a man-made forest; the Multimedia Super Corridor, designed to place Malaysia at the forefront of chip and fibre optics technology; and Putrajaya, the nation's 21st century seat of government.

On the threshold of the new millennium, Malaysian architecture faces tremendous challenges in a technological world. Greater urbanization will demand more environmentally responsive solutions to the way Malaysians live and work. To this end, it is imperative to conserve Malaysia's early buildings and to draw from them valuable lessons on scale and usage for a better quality of life in the 21st century.

The first permanent shophouses in the Straits Settlements were designed by immigrant Chinese master builders from Guangdong. The narrow street frontage, the interior airwells that provide light and ventilation, the symmetrical arrangement of the louvred windows and the doors, and the clay tiles on the roof are typical features of this imported form.

A booming economy in the last decade of the 20th century, coupled with increased personal wealth, has encouraged more Malaysians to buy their own homes. This has stimulated a rapid growth in the building of single- and two-storey link houses, bungalows and condominiums in housing estates on the outskirts of cities and towns. Although such housing estates offer a well-ordered lifestyle, they have also introduced commuting as a way of life for many Malaysians.

7

Chronology

PRE-16TH CENTURY

c. 40000–2500 BCE: The earliest inhabitants of the region (the Orang Asli Negritos) build temporary shelters of saplings and palm leaf thatch, the prototype of the first indigenous dwelling. Caves and rock shelters are probably also used as habitation sites as evidenced by cave burials.

Pebble tools are produced at stone tool workshops at Kota Tampan in Perak and at the Niah Caves in Sarawak. Later, more sophisticated bifacial stone tools, used for hunting and planting, as well as for making shelters, are made at Tingkayu in Sabah.

c. 2800–500 BCE: Polished stone tools, used for hunting and planting and for making shelters, and earthenware, are used at cave and open sites on the Malay Peninsula. Pottery is made in Sabah and Sarawak. Cave paintings appear.

Houses built on posts are probably introduced to Sabah and Sarawak via Austronesian sea migrations. The houses of the Orang Asli Senoi on the Peninsula are constructed with poles, bamboo, palm thatch and rattan.

c. 500 BCE–500 CE: Bronze drums and bells are found at Peninsular sites along with iron implements, including adzes, axes and long-shafted knives.

The port site of Kuala Selinsing in Perak (c. 200 BCE) and the inland sites of the Bernam Valley (100–800 CE) are connected by trade routes to the east coast. Stumps found at Kuala Selinsing indicate pile dwellings made of wood.

By 200 BCE, long-distance sea trade in bronzeware, beads, pottery and iron tools begins with mainland Southeast Asia, India and China. Highly valued imported objects are deposited at grave sites.

500–1300 CE: The earliest Malay kingdom appears in the Bujang Valley in southern Kedah (5th century). Polities are established at Santubong in Sarawak and Chi tu in Kelantan in the 7th century. There is increasing use of iron for agricultural tools, and technical skills evolve for the construction of architecture in stone.

Hindu–Buddhist beliefs, introduced through trade contacts, are incorporated into existing indigenous beliefs. Permanent architecture in brick, stone and laterite blocks appears in the Bujang Valley and at Santubong in the form of Buddhist (from 500 CE) and Hindu shrines (after the 11th century). The upper parts are made of wood and only the bases survive. The best known is Candi Bukit Batu Pahat (Temple on the Hill of Cut Stone) in the Bujang Valley. Domestic dwellings continue to be built in perishable materials.

The early port kingdoms evolve into entrepôts and conduct trade with China, India, West Asia and Southeast Asia under the suzerainty of Srivijaya (7th–13th centuries). Tributary relations with China are established.

1300–1500: Mass production of metalware and pottery begins. Craftsmen are attached to royal courts which operate as ceremonial centres and loci of economic activity.

The arrival of Islam in the 14th century, confirmed by the Islamic laws inscribed on the Terengganu Stone (1303 CE), greatly influences Malay culture and tradition.

In c. 1403, a refugee prince from Sumatra, Parameswara, establishes a new state on the west coast of the Peninsula—the Melaka Sultanate—to challenge the pre-eminence of Srivijaya. The state embraces Islam and attracts large numbers of Indian Muslim merchants. It becomes an important centre of culture and statecraft.

Chinese and Portuguese accounts describe wooden palaces, watch towers and palisades on the hill (later named St Paul's) which commands a strategic position overlooking the Melaka River and Strait. The *Sejarah Melayu* (Malay Annals) describes the 15th-century wooden palace of Sultan Mansur Shah (r. 1459–88) in Melaka, later destroyed by fire.

16TH CENTURY

1500: The Majapahit Empire supplants the Malay kingdom of Srivijaya, the overlord of vast areas in Sumatra, Java and the southern Malay Peninsula from the 7th century to about the 13th century, and a centre of Malay culture and Buddhist religion.

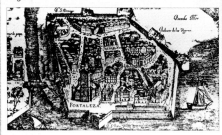

The settlement at the mouth of the Melaka River grows rapidly as the most convenient collecting point in the Malay Archipelago for the valuable spices produced in the Spice Islands (the Moluccas) of the eastern archipelago. It develops into a vast, cosmopolitan trading centre in which Tamils, Arabs, Chinese, Persians, Javanese and others live, each in their own quarter of the town. For nearly 150 years, Melaka remains the pivot around which the east–west trade revolves.

In the countryside, the houses of the Malays are raised off the ground on tree trunks or bamboo posts. The residences of rulers or village chiefs stand on elaborately carved wooden pillars. Immigrants and traders from the Minangkabau region of Sumatra bring their house-building techniques and forms, particularly the curved roof. Chinese settlers introduce traditional elements such as courtyards and masonry staircases. On the east coast of the Peninsula, immigrants from the kingdom of Patani in southern Thailand introduce their artistic traditions and house styles, including high-pitched roofs.

1511: Melaka's political domination is short-lived. It attracts the attention of the Portuguese who are seeking alternative routes to the Spice Islands following the closure of the traditional overland trade routes in the aftermath of the fall of Constantinople to the Ottoman Turks. In 1511, the city-port falls to the Portuguese and becomes the centre of their eastern trading empire.

The Portuguese build a substantial fort, A Famosa, on the site of the Malay fort and royal compound on St Paul's hill, to protect their settlement. Inside the walls are palaces, assembly halls, churches and hospitals. Only one of the four gateway bastions, Porta Santiago, remains.

European architecture, in the style of Manuelino Gothic (the last phase of Gothic architecture in Portugal), named after King Manuel I (1495–1521), is for the first time transplanted to the East. It is characterized by square-shaped, barn-like structures.

1521: The Portuguese build St Paul's Church on the crown of the hill with stones from the demolished foundations of the Melaka Sultanate palace. In 1566, the Jesuits enlarge the building to its present size and in 1590 add a tower. The Dutch later pull down the roof. Around the walls of the roofless St Paul's are several massive tombstones dating from Dutch times.

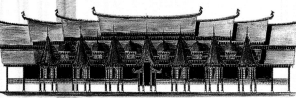

17TH CENTURY

Religious movements result in significant shifts of power and influence in Europe. Holland and England, champions of Protestantism, supplant the Catholic powers of Spain and Portugal in Europe and wrest control of their eastern possessions and trade routes.

1641: Continuous assaults by the Dutch out of Batavia (Jakarta) culminate in their conquest and subsequent destruction of the Portuguese settlement of Melaka, which they control until 1824 as a trade emporium. The Portuguese withdraw into their enclaves of Goa, Timor and Macao.

The Dutch repair the fort (adding the Dutch East India Company's coat of arms and the date 1670 above the Santiago Gate), rebuild the town and bring their style of architecture to Melaka.

The best example of Dutch architecture is the three-storey Stadthuys (Town Hall), built between 1641 and 1660, whose gable walls can be found in Dutch-style buildings in Indonesia and other outposts of their empire. It is the oldest Dutch building extant in Southeast Asia. In front of the

Stadthuys, the Dutch build a replica of the clock tower put up earlier by the Portuguese. A century later, they build Christ Church next to the Stadthuys.

Sporadic attempts by the Dutch to expand inland are repulsed. The Dutch East India Company decides to employ their resources of men and armour to colonize and exploit the enormous riches of the future Indonesia.

A permanent settlement of shopkeepers, craftsmen and farmers from southern China establishes itself in Melaka in the early 17th century although Chinese traders came and settled as early as the 14th century. Many of these early settlers come without their families and form marriage and working ties with the local population. They develop a distinctive brand of the Malay language, dress, food and customs, but maintain the traditional Chinese urban house form.

The earliest types of townhouses, or 'row houses', in Melaka are built during the Dutch occupation of the town, including some of the houses in Jalan Tun Tan Cheng Lock (Heeren Straat). They are much deeper than elsewhere in the country, and often extend from one street back to the next.

c. 1650: The leader of the Chinese community in Melaka, the Kapitan China Lee Wei King, founds the Cheng Hoon Teng Temple to commemorate the visit made by Admiral Cheng Ho two and a half centuries earlier. It is the oldest Chinese place of worship in Malaysia (the main hall is not built until

1704) and is home to the three Eastern religious philosophies of Buddhism, Taoism and Confucianism. It is a fine example of traditional Chinese temple architecture and craftsmanship, shaped by symbolism, mythology and geomancy.

Mosques proliferate and take on a focal position and role in the life of villages and among small communities of Muslims. They are probably simple structures, consisting of a wooden structure on stilts with a thatched roof.

18TH CENTURY

The Dutch continue to rule over the vast Malay Archipelago. They build substantial palaces, mansions and churches, from Aceh in northern Sumatra to the Bandas and the Moluccas in the easternmost parts of the archipelago. Many buildings exhibit Dutch architectural features, such as thick walls, Dutch-style gables and double-sash windows.

1710: The original Protestant fervour gives way to commercial interests. The Melaka Portuguese regroup and prosper. In 1710, they build St Peter's Church, the oldest Christian church still in use in the Malay Peninsula, in a mixture of indigenous and Manueline styles.

early 1700s: The Kampung Laut Mosque, the oldest surviving large wooden mosque in Malaysia, is built at the mouth of the Kelantan River, purportedly by seafarers from Java who model it on the Agung Mosque at Demak, near Semarang, the prototype of many mosques in Java, which are characterized by a square plan and a multi-tiered roof.

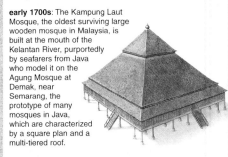

c. 1728: A 'Melaka-style' mosque emerges, the earliest examples being the Terengkera Mosque and the Kampung Hulu Mosque. The Melaka mosque retains the Javanese-style square plan but timber walls are replaced by stone and brick. Chinese influences are evident in the rooftop ornament, pagoda-like multi-tiered roof and minaret.

1741–53: The Dutch build Christ Church in Melaka in the style of classical Dutch architecture, using bricks shipped specially from Holland. It is Malaysia's oldest Protestant church.

1786: Captain Francis Light founds Penang, an island off the coast of Kedah, whose Sultan cedes it to the East India Company in return for protection against claims of suzerainty by Siam. This signals the start of British involvement in the Malay Peninsula, which is to have a profound influence on the political system, administration, architecture and lifestyle of the country. In return for free land, people from many nations settle on the island, each introducing their own way of life and style of buildings.

The Malayan 'bungalow' emerges, a mixture of European and local features, such as timber posts and thatched roofs. A handful of grand garden houses, such as Francis Light's 'Suffolk House', are built in a mixture of English and Indian architecture.

1795: By the end of the 18th century, Europe is in turmoil. Following the French invasion of the Netherlands, a government in exile takes refuge in England. In 1795, the British disembark in Melaka where they establish a joint Anglo-Dutch administration. Melaka goes into a decline as Penang and Singapore emerge as trading posts.

19TH CENTURY

1824: Following the Napoleonic Wars, the British sign an agreement with the Dutch, now free of the French occupation of their country, dividing the region into spheres of influence separated by the Strait of Melaka. The Dutch are assigned Indonesia while the British set up the Straits Settlements of Penang, Melaka and Singapore in 1826 and continue their process of expansion in the country. The Malay States remain essentially self-governing kingdoms under their local rulers. The British take little interest in their affairs and little development or construction of buildings takes place.

1841–1941: Across the South China Sea, a dynasty of White Rajahs—the Brookes—exercise benevolent rule over the Sarawak peoples and transform Kuching into a modern town. Further east, the British North Borneo Company obtains most of the land of today's Sabah from the Sultan of Brunei and acquires the rest by extending its influence over the indigenous chiefs of the country.

1842: A revival of Malay architecture results in a number of royal palaces, mainly on the east coast of the Peninsula, including Istana Balai Besar in Kota Bharu, the only extant east coast wooden palace.

1869: Business and trade accelerate with the advent of steamships and the opening of the Suez Canal. The massive demand for tin for canned goods in America and elsewhere transforms the business climate in Malaya.

New tin mines open in Perak and Selangor and lead to the growth of small towns. Following repression by the Manchu rulers in China, there is mass migration of Chinese labourers to the tin mines, who bring with them their traditional dwelling design. Two-storey shophouses become common in all new towns, along with clan associations and temples, the latter built in the styles of the Chinese provinces from which the immigrants come.

1877: Rubber saplings are brought to Malaya, and by the early 1900s the country is the world's leading exporter. Indentured labourers from South India and Ceylon (Sri Lanka)

are brought in to work on rubber plantations. Hindu temples with elaborate gate towers spring up in towns and on estates.

1885: The first railway line, between Taiping and Port Weld, helps to further open up the Peninsular west coast.

The narrow-fronted townhouse becomes the prototype house of the urban Chinese in Penang, Melaka and Singapore. The concept spreads to Kuala Lumpur and other towns. In 1884, Frank Swettenham, the British Resident in Selangor, introduces formal building by-laws, including the provision of a 'five-foot way' in front of shophouses.

1896: The British group four of the Malay States to form the Federated Malay States, with Kuala Lumpur as its capital. Tremendous growth and a building boom ensues, partly due to the efforts of the colonial government and partly as a result of private enterprise.

The British 'Raj' or Mogul style from India is adopted for a number of government buildings as being appropriate to an Islamic country. The Secretariat Building, now the Sultan Abdul Samad Building, is built at one side of the Padang in 1894–7, setting the style for other civic buildings in Kuala Lumpur and elsewhere and contributing to one of the largest collections of colonial buildings left standing throughout the British Empire. Most buildings, both public and private, are elaborate and ornate, in keeping with an age when manpower is cheap, and contain a mixture of architectural styles: Renaissance, Palladian, Neoclassical and revived Gothic. New materials, such as cast iron, make their appearance.

Although solid masonry replaces timber and thatch in the towns, the Malays and indigenous groups of the Peninsula, Sabah and Sarawak continue to live in their own style of housing. Civil servants and colonial entrepreneurs live in spacious wooden bungalows raised on brick piers.

20TH CENTURY

1909: The remaining five 'Unfederated' Malay States join the four Federated Malay States to form the Colony of British Malaya. Sarawak continues to be ruled by the Brooke Dynasty, and Sabah to be under the supervision of the North Borneo Company.

1910s: Malaya is relatively unaffected by World War I and continues to export commodities. The last of the colonial edifices are built, including Kuala Lumpur's third Railway Station (1911) and the Ubudiah Mosque (1913–17) in Kuala Kangsar, Perak, built in a mixture of Mogul and Moorish styles.

1920s–1930s: The demand for rubber for assembly-line manufacturing of automobiles ensures a further flow of wealth into Malaya. Banks build new headquarters in a mixture of styles, while the European and Chinese merchants, the nouveaux riches of the time, build vast, opulent mansions.

Ornate facades are grafted onto traditional Chinese shophouses. But a decrease in public expenditure signals an era of more modest architectural design for civic buildings.

Art Deco enjoys a brief popularity and represents an early break from the hitherto dominant Classical style of architecture. Most urban dwellers live in modest linkhouses, and in most rural areas, timber dwellings continue to reflect local styles.

1940s: Construction comes to a standstill during World War II, and its aftermath. Nearly 10 per cent of the population is resettled into New Villages during the Emergency period.

1950–1960s: The advent of true Modernism and the International Style begins to shape the nation's new skyline. The rise of nationalism, culminating in Independence (Merdeka) in 1957, spurs a spate of public building, including Parliament House (1963) and the National Museum (1963), to portray the country's vernacular heritage as well as its young, forward-looking status. The National Mosque (1965) combines Islamic and Modernist principles. Architects employ energy conservation devices, such as sunshading. Mass migration to the cities results in the creation of a number of 'new towns'.

1970s: Concrete monuments, such as Bank Negara in Kuala Lumpur (1970) and the Dewan Tunku Canselor in Universiti Malaya (1972), are heavily influenced by the architect Le Corbusier. Developments in concrete technology invite increasingly advanced building designs.

1980s–1990s: Malaysia joins the ranks of the 'Asian economic miracle' countries. Office towers and high-rise residential buildings follow the dictates of international architecture, employing glass facades and curtain walling. New building types, such as condominiums, shopping complexes and resort hotels, make their appearance. In reaction, Islamic, indigenous and regional elements are grafted onto buildings, such as the Dayabumi Complex (1984), Putra World Trade Centre (1985) and Central Plaza (1996) in Kuala Lumpur.

Increased urban migration and a growing middle class result in a demand for mass residential housing on the outskirts of towns. The traditional urban shophouse is eclipsed.

In the 1990s, the latest technological innovations are incorporated into mega projects such as the Petronas Twin Towers (1998), Kuala Lumpur International Airport (1998) and Telekom Tower (1999 projected).

Malaysia's simplest vernacular structures, such as the Dusun house (1), may be constructed entirely of bamboo, or, as in traditional houses in Perak (2), of a combination of woven bamboo strips and timber. Traditional Malay palaces (3) were usually constructed of timber and had shingle roofs. The veranda running the length of an Iban longhouse (4) is laid with strips of split bamboo and is used for drying crops.

ABOVE LEFT: This *rumah penghulu* (headman's house), originally located in Kampung Sungai Kechil, Kedah, has been relocated to Kuala Lumpur and lovingly restored by the Badan Warisan Malaysia. Typically, it is built of timber and raised above the ground. Rows of large windows with carved fanlights above provide good ventilation and give the house its open, airy quality.

FAR LEFT: The traditional Orang Asli dwelling, located in deep jungle, is designed to last from a few months to a few years. Roofs are commonly made of woven palm fronds and the walls and floors of flattened bamboo.

LEFT: The clusters of houses in riverine and estuary settlements in Malaysia reflect the culture and way of life of the people. The houses are built on stilts above the high water level and are connected to each other by wooden boardwalks.

VERNACULAR HOUSES OF THE INDIGENOUS COMMUNITIES

Vernacular houses refer to the everyday dwellings of the local people. The word 'vernacular' is derived from the Latin *vernaculus*, meaning 'domestic' or 'indigenous'. Thus, this type of architecture focuses mainly on the styles of local houses, the ways in which they are built and the types of materials used. It has been estimated that such dwellings form two-thirds of all the man-made structures in the world. In Malaysia, these include the homes of the Orang Asli—the first indigenous people of the Peninsula—as well as of the indigenous groups of Sabah and Sarawak and of the Malays who belong to the Austronesian group of people.

With the exception of the simple makeshift lean-to shelters of small nomadic groups, Malaysia's vernacular houses are basically post-and-beam structures raised on stilts, with gabled roofs, which have been designed and built by the people themselves to suit their socioeconomic, cultural and environmental requirements. Not only do they offer near perfect solutions to accommodating Malaysia's tropical climate, but they incorporate flexibility in their design and in the use of space.

Although the most developed of Malaysia's vernacular houses belong to the Malays—reflected in the range of construction methods and building materials employed—the houses of the Orang Asli have a raw, organic charm which derives from the use of building materials from the immediate surroundings. The common house form in Sabah and Sarawak, the longhouse, in which many families live in separate apartments under one roof, is a response to climatic and environmental conditions as well as to a unique social structure and way of life. All of these vernacular house forms, while specific to different cultural and environmental settings, are the result of long-term modification and adaptation, shared experience and innovations approved by the community.

A search for the origins of vernacular architecture in Malaysia reveals houses with similar features throughout island Southeast Asia and as far afield as Micronesia and Madagascar. The roof forms, in particular, share common origins dating back at least 6,000 years.

Although the rationale behind Malaysia's vernacular houses differs completely from that of modern houses—the environmentally respectful versus the nature conqueror, and basic needs versus luxury needs—the design superiority and relevance of Malaysia's simple but elegant vernacular houses will ensure their continued survival, albeit in modified form.

The traditional Orang Asli dwelling requires over 1,000 pieces of woven *bertam* leaf for the roof.

Orang Asli forest dwellings

The Malay term Orang Asli means 'original people'. At least 18 distinct Orang Asli groups, comprising about 100,000 people, live on the Malay Peninsula, mostly in the forests. There are three main groups: the Negritos in the north, the Senoi mainly in the centre, and the Proto-Malays in the south. Collectively, the Orang Asli have maintained their cultural identity despite the pressures of rapid modernization. Many continue to live in traditional dwellings, though increasing numbers have moved to zinc-roofed structures on the fringes of small towns.

Distribution of Orang Asli groups in Peninsular Malaysia

Perlis
Kedah
Kensiu
Kintak
Jahai
Mendriq
Lanoh
Pulau Pinang
Bateq
South China Sea
Temiar
Kelantan
Perak
Terengganu
Semai
Pahang
Semoq Beri
Che Wong
Jahut
Strait of Melaka
Selangor
Semelai
Temok
Mah Meri
Temuan
Jakun
Negeri Sembilan
Melaka
Johor
Orang Kanaq
Orang Kuala
Orang Seletar

0   150 km

Negritos
Senoi
Proto-Malays

Living in the forest

Before industrial logging and urbanization reduced their hunting and gathering range to mere hectares, the Orang Asli regarded the forests as their real home. Their dwellings were designed for basic shelter, not for the storing of material goods. As such, house building was never seen as a specialized activity requiring professional skills. Every able-bodied male was capable of constructing his own house before he married, and help was always at hand from family members, if not the entire settlement.

Basic house structures

Orang Asli house structures have evolved only minimally over the centuries, from nomadic to semi-permanent settlements. Among persistently nomadic groups, shelters are designed to last only a few years. Occasionally, small groups of hunters and gatherers, such as the Bateq and Jahai—members of the Negrito group—can still be encountered in deep jungle, staying no more than a week in makeshift lean-tos made of leafy branches and bamboos lashed together with vines.

Two of the largest Senoi groups, the Semai and the Temiar, and the Proto-Malay Temuan, are among the groups that have struck a tenuous balance between tradition and modernity. In a typical village, one will find zinc-roofed houses of grey brick and planks interspersed with bamboo and wooden huts.

The coastal groups, such as the Orang Kuala and Orang Seletar of Johor, have mastered the art of building over water or mangrove swamp (see 'Coastal and riverine settlements'). Their dwellings are supported on *nibong* palm trunks which become more durable as they become waterlogged. While lowland groups tend to inhabit clusters of small huts within communal

Unlike the Senoi and the Negritos, the Proto-Malays live in village-like settlements in fairly accessible areas.

A Negrito putting a roof on his shelter.

compounds or clearings, the highland and riverine groups often live in modular houses that can shelter up to 30 members of an extended family.

The parts of a house

Young hardwood trees, such as *cengal* and *petaling*, are used for the standing poles because they are not vulnerable to termites. Poles are driven into the ground to a depth of approximately 40 centimetres measured from elbow to fingertips. Edge beams and roof joists are lashed to the standing poles with *rotan* (cane), although sometimes nails are used. Once the ridge piece has been fixed to the ridge poles, the rafters and purlins—usually cut from saplings—are lashed in place. The framework is complete when the floor beams and joists are added, and the entire structure reinforced where necessary with right-angled wedges or brackets called *kukut tupai* (after the squirrels they resemble).

Some wild palms produce fronds that can be woven into thatch roofing, generically known as *atap*. The Semai and Temuan favour the leaves of the thorny *bertam* because the species grows profusely in

A log fire not only makes a simple dwelling feel cosier, but also keeps away nocturnal animals, mosquitoes and other insects.

Geometric precision and symmetry are not crucial criteria in Orang Asli structures, hence the raw organic charm of these Semai houses.

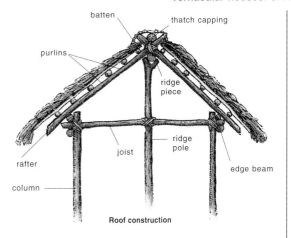

batten — thatch capping
purlins
ridge piece
rafter — joist — ridge pole — edge beam
column

Roof construction

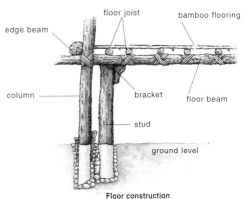

edge beam — floor joist — bamboo flooring
column — bracket — floor beam
stud
ground level

Floor construction

Building materials from the forest

Mengkuang leaves are used for weaving decorative wall panels.

Rotan is stripped to make strings for tying together bamboo strips.

Bamboo is cut into mat-like strips for flooring while it is still green and flexible.

Bertam leaves are used for making *atap* roofs. With regular fumigation from kitchen fires, a well-made thatched roof can last five or more years.

Cengal trees produce hardwood for house posts.

the foothills of the Main Range where they live. The average dwelling requires well over a thousand pieces of woven bertam leaf, which are lashed to the rafters in tight layers starting from the eaves and finishing at the top. Traditionally, a *perabong* (thatch capping), consisting of bertam leaves held in place by a triangular framework of thin sticks, was used to seal the peak of the roof, but zinc sheets are now commonly used. Thatch roofs have a minimum pitch of 45 degrees to allow torrential rain to run off quickly during the rainy season.

Usually the floor beams are supported by hardwood studs 1–4 metres above the ground, driven into the earth to a depth of 35 centimetres. A high floor effectively produces a two-storey structure with ample covered space below for storage and cottage industries to be carried out, such as the making of bamboo skewers for Chinese prayer candles and joss sticks. Nevertheless, lower floors are preferred for easy access.

Floor joists are lashed at right angles to the beams and overlaid with strips of *buluh picap* (flattened bamboo) aligned at right angles to the joists. With regular use and wood smoke fumigation, the bamboo *lantai*, or flooring, acquires a sturdy resilience and pleasing sheen. Such floors facilitate the free circulation of air, are damp-proof and easily maintained, and can last up to five years if protected from driving rain.

The ubiquitous bamboo is also commonly used for the walls. Some Temiar huts have walls made from the bark of the bertam palm. Other groups prefer the decorative effect of wall panels woven from *mengkuang* (screw pine) leaves. As a rule,

structures raised high above the ground often boast large windows, giving them the appearance of watchtowers, while those built close to the ground tend to feature only bunker-like slits for windows, if they have windows at all. This is most likely a vestige of the days when a great many more animals roamed the rainforests of the Peninsula.

Orang Asli huts traditionally had only one door, made of bark panels or sackcloth, so that the occupants had to enter and leave through the same opening. With exposure to the structure of Malay houses, many Orang Asli dwellings now feature two doors, including a back door for women to enter and leave the kitchen when there are male visitors in the house.

A Semai man making an *atap* roof.

The *tangga*, or ladder, is an essential feature of huts raised high above the ground. This is usually made of two hardwood beams about 8 centimetres thick, with 9–10 logs serving as steps lashed or nailed to the beams, and reinforced with kukut tupai. To prevent the steps from rotting in the rain, the ladder is usually placed under a roof.

Orang Asli dwellings, apart from those located on river banks, generally include an open-air *mandi*, or bath house, which can be communal or private, depending on the water supply. Lavatory facilities, however, are usually absent since the *belukar* (secondary forest) is always within a short distance of the house.

13

The Austronesian house: Ancient antecedents

Vernacular dwellings in Malaysia, in all their diversity and subtle variation, share certain recurrent features which can be found throughout island Southeast Asia and as far afield as Micronesia and Madagascar. A search for the origins of these styles takes us back to the Austronesian-speaking seafarers whose migrations through the archipelago into the Pacific began at least 6,000 years ago. Who were the Austronesians and how much can we discover about the way they built their houses?

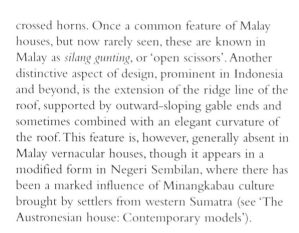

Ilanun houses built on stilts in Kampung Mengkabong, Sabah, feature pairs of crossed horns on the gable ends of their roofs.

Crossed-horn finials at the gable ends of houses are common throughout Southeast Asia. On Minangkabau-style houses in Negeri Sembilan they are usually referred to as *silang gunting* or 'open scissors'.

The stubs of these house posts, preserved in waterlogged conditions in the Zhejiang Province Museum in Hangzhou, China, were excavated in Hemudu, 25 kilometres south of Hangzhou Bay on a site which dates between 5200 and 4900 BCE. The stubs came from Neolithic houses built of timber and raised on rows of small timber posts. The origins of Austronesian houses can probably be traced to South China where some archaeologists believe Austronesians came from as long ago as 10,000 years.

Austronesian migration

Linguistic evidence suggests that Proto-Austronesian, the dialect (or more likely group of dialects) from which all modern Austronesian languages derive, developed on the island of Taiwan at least by 4000 BCE. The speakers of this dialect were a Mongoloid population, presumed to have spread from a homeland somewhere in southern China, in a process that may have begun as long ago as 10,000 years. From Taiwan they migrated down through the Philippines around 3000 BCE, and thence into western and eastern Indonesia. The colonization of Oceania probably began sometime after 2000 BCE, while the Malay Peninsula and Vietnam were reached in a movement back from the western islands of Indonesia sometime after 1000 BCE. Austronesian speakers settled in Madagascar around 400 CE, introducing a number of characteristic cultural features to that island, at about the same time that, thousands of kilometres away, other descendants of the original Austronesians were setting out from the Tahitian islands towards New Zealand. This, then, is the world's biggest language family, extending halfway around the world's circumference. The Austronesians were clearly accomplished and daring seafarers. By contrast with already existing Australoid populations in Southeast Asia, who specialized in hunting, gathering and fishing, linguistic reconstructions show them also to have been cultivators and domesticators of pigs, dogs and chickens. Austronesians proceeded to displace Australoid populations, not without much intermingling. One must imagine also much back and forth movement by the Austronesians themselves, who like their present-day descendants viewed trade as an important incentive for travel.

House posts and gable horns

Perhaps the most characteristic and pervasive of the architectural features shared by the Austronesians is the almost universal use of post construction. Another is the extension of the rafters at the gable ends to form decorative gable finials in the shape of crossed horns. Once a common feature of Malay houses, but now rarely seen, these are known in Malay as *silang gunting*, or 'open scissors'. Another distinctive aspect of design, prominent in Indonesia and beyond, is the extension of the ridge line of the roof, supported by outward-sloping gable ends and sometimes combined with an elegant curvature of the roof. This feature is, however, generally absent in Malay vernacular houses, though it appears in a modified form in Negeri Sembilan, where there has been a marked influence of Minangkabau culture brought by settlers from western Sumatra (see 'The Austronesian house: Contemporary models').

Looking for prehistoric clues

The wide distribution of these elements throughout Austronesian-speaking areas in itself provides one of the clues to the origin of this style of building. Yet, to find archaeological evidence of early architecture is very difficult in a tropical climate, where timber buildings with post foundations neither last very long nor are likely to leave any excavable trace behind—even when posts rest on stones, as is often the case. In the face of these limitations, linguistic reconstruction has become a valued tool for prehistorians. Reconstructions of Proto-Malayo-Polynesian (the dialect from which the largest subgroup of Austronesian languages has developed) include those for ridge pole, rafter, thatch, house post, notched-log ladder, hearth and storage rack above the hearth. This already tells us quite a lot about the house: that it was raised on posts, the floor being reached by a ladder, and that it had a pitched roof, for example. The interior box-like hearth, filled with earth, with a rack above, is still a ubiquitous feature of Southeast Asian kitchens today.

Archaeological evidence

Some of the earliest surviving images of post-built houses with extended ridge lines are the engraved pictures on bronze drums of the Dongson culture, which had its heartland in North Vietnam and flourished between approximately 400 BCE and 100 CE. The saddle-roofed houses represented on

This 500 BCE bronze sarcophagus made in the shape of a saddle-roof house with extended beams was found in western Yunnan, China, in 1964. Similar house styles seen throughout Southeast Asia today suggest an origin that goes back to the Neolithic period in southern China.

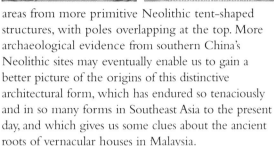

areas from more primitive Neolithic tent-shaped structures, with poles overlapping at the top. More archaeological evidence from southern China's Neolithic sites may eventually enable us to gain a better picture of the origins of this distinctive architectural form, which has endured so tenaciously and in so many forms in Southeast Asia to the present day, and which gives us some clues about the ancient roots of vernacular houses in Malaysia.

1. A bronze drum from the island of Sangeang in eastern Indonesia (c. 100–300 CE), shows a woman in a post-built house with animals occupying the under-floor level.

2. and 3. Dongson drums from North Vietnam (c. 500 BCE–300 CE) show saddle-roof, post-built houses with birds perched on the roofs. The main floor is occupied by people, the under floor by domestic animals. This division of space is still practised in present-day dwellings throughout Southeast Asia.

the Dongson drums (luxury goods widely traded throughout Southeast Asia) were probably examples of an Austronesian style which was already well developed by this time. Houses of similar style were also represented on Dongson bronze drums found on the islands of Sangeang and Salayar in eastern Indonesia. Other interesting evidence comes from bronze objects of the 5th–1st century BCE excavated in Yunnan, southern China, and engraved bronze objects excavated in Japan, dating to the 1st–2nd centuries CE. Gaudenz Domenig (1980) has suggestively explored some ways in which post building, extended ridge lines and crossed-horn gable finials could all have evolved together in these

A hill tribe house near Hoa Binh in North Vietnam. The saddle roof, gable horns and timber posts are typical of the houses of Southeast Asia. In Malaysia, the gable horns are known as *silang gunting*, or 'open scissors'. Note the similarity of the house form to that of the bronze sarcophagus, which was probably modelled on a Neolithic house in Yunnan, China.

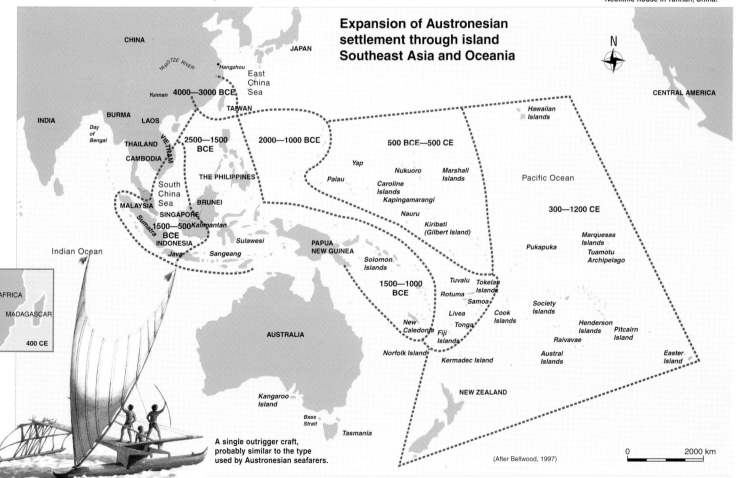

Expansion of Austronesian settlement through island Southeast Asia and Oceania

A single outrigger craft, probably similar to the type used by Austronesian seafarers.

(After Bellwood, 1997)

0   2000 km

The Austronesian house: Contemporary models

Parallel with the historical evidence linking Malaysian vernacular architecture with others in the region are the styles of houses and the methods of house construction. The post-and-beam method and the roof form, in particular, provide concrete evidence to connect the Malaysian house with those of neighbouring peoples.

The roof is the most dominant feature of indigenous houses. The tent-shaped roof of the Rungus house covers almost the entire structure.

Foreign influences on house design

Other sources of similarity between the architectures of Malaysian and neighbouring peoples may be the borrowing of certain elements originating elsewhere. In Kelantan, for example, the use of (1) Thai roof tiles and (2) heavier wood wall panels in the Thai style are common; (3) louvred shutters (*jendela*) may have been borrowed from the Portuguese whose historical presence in the region dates back several centuries; (4) the courtyard arrangement of some Melaka houses may also show Portuguese, or possibly Chinese, influence.

Common features in Southeast Asian houses

Indigenous architectures of Southeast Asia share certain underlying principles of construction, to which Malaysian vernaculars are no exception. They are based on a post-and-beam method of construction, the posts running from the ground to the roof, while the beams supporting the floor platform are mortised through the posts and held firmly by wooden wedges (see 'The Malay house: Materials and construction'). In this system, the roof is the dominant aesthetic element, while walls are rarely load-bearing. They are often screens prepared separately—woven from split bamboo, for example—and then attached to the structure. All the parts of the house can be prefabricated and then assembled with relatively little labour. Even very large structures, such as the longhouses of Sarawak, are built according to the same principles and make extensive use of cooperative village labour.

In many Austronesian house styles, the roof is such a dominant element that it entirely encloses the house platform, making walls unnecessary. These houses are commonly windowless and dark inside, serving their occupants mainly as a place to sleep and store their heirloom valuables. But some peoples, especially in lowland areas, like the Bugis, Makassarese or Acehnese, have traditionally built their houses very similar to the Malay style, open and airy, with large, shuttered windows designed for maximum ventilation. Skilled woodcarving, from the beautiful carved shutters, friezes and panels of old houses in Terengganu, to the exuberance of carved beams and doorways in a Kayan longhouse, bear witness to

the creative talents of indigenous carpenters and find their echoes across the archipelago in the dwellings of other Austronesian peoples.

Bringing a house to life

Throughout the Southeast Asian world, people have traditionally believed that power or vitality, being distributed throughout the cosmos, was shared not only by people and other living things, but also by entities that in other cultures might be considered inanimate. Thus, the Malays, in common with other peoples of the region, regarded trees (particularly the large, hardwood trees often favoured for house timbers) as having their own share of vitality, often referred to by the term *semangat*. Such trees traditionally could not be cut without the performance of appropriate rituals; the main posts of a house were supposed to be cut from a single trunk and arranged in the same relation to each other that they had within the tree. Another universal rule, which seems to be distinctively Austronesian, is that house posts must not be inverted, but 'planted' with the 'base' or trunk end down and the 'tip' up, otherwise misfortune will befall the occupants. N. Annadale (1903), writing about the Patani Malays in the early 20th century, recorded that 'the semangat rumah, or "house soul", comes automatically into existence as the various parts of the walls and roof are fitted together'; as elsewhere, the vitality and well-being of the house and of its occupants are regarded as interdependent. The rituals traditionally connected with house building are well described by Phillip Gibbs (1987) and bear many comparisons not only with societies in Indonesia, but also with Thailand, where ideas about *khwan* or 'essence of life' closely parallel those concerning semangat in the Malay World.

A Malay house-building ritual

In the ceremony, 'Searching for the base of the house', the *bomoh* (shaman) places incense in a burner filled with embers and blesses the site chosen for the house.

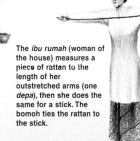

The *ibu rumah* (woman of the house) measures a piece of rattan to the length of her outstretched arms (one *depa*), then she does the same for a stick. The bomoh ties the rattan to the stick.

Incense is burnt again and prayers are recited by the bomoh.

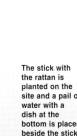

The stick with the rattan is planted on the site and a pail of water with a dish at the bottom is placed beside the stick.

16

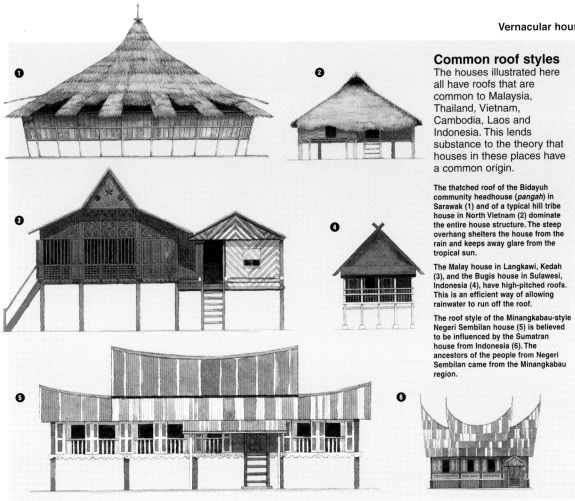

Common roof styles

The houses illustrated here all have roofs that are common to Malaysia, Thailand, Vietnam, Cambodia, Laos and Indonesia. This lends substance to the theory that houses in these places have a common origin.

The thatched roof of the Bidayuh community headhouse (*pangah*) in Sarawak (1) and of a typical hill tribe house in North Vietnam (2) dominate the entire house structure. The steep overhang shelters the house from the rain and keeps away glare from the tropical sun.

The Malay house in Langkawi, Kedah (3), and the Bugis house in Sulawesi, Indonesia (4), have high-pitched roofs. This is an efficient way of allowing rainwater to run off the roof.

The roof style of the Minangkabau-style Negeri Sembilan house (5) is believed to be influenced by the Sumatran house from Indonesia (6). The ancestors of the people from Negeri Sembilan came from the Minangkabau region.

Mystical beliefs surrounding house posts

Following the principle of 'one tree, one house', the *tiang* (posts) are always positioned in the house in exactly the same way as they were extracted from the tree. Like the trees they come from, house posts are regarded as live items imbued with spirits.

The black cloth placed at the top of each post to ward off evil spirits represents mysterious powers; the red cloth, life and courage; and the white cloth, purity.

The interconnectedness of houses and their occupants is made more pronounced by the traditional system of measuring house timbers based on proportions of the human body. Old Malay books which give instructions for house building stipulate that certain measurements be taken from the woman of the house; she must also place her hands on the main house post as it is being erected. Similar practices are observed in parts of Indonesia.

Warding off evil forces

Like many other post-built houses of the region, Malay houses are splendidly designed for natural ventilation, so that they seem to 'breathe'. In another sense, the flow of forces in and out of the building connects with cosmological ideas. The house with its many door and window openings and spaces under the roof is also penetrable by dangerous forces from which the occupants need protection; it is also particularly vulnerable to penetration at the joints. Therefore, one often finds pieces of Islamic

calligraphy set above the doors and windows, where they serve a protective as much as a decorative function in warding off evil influences.

Communal living

In Sarawak, some Malay house forms seem to resemble the Minangkabau style and layout, being very long and large, with an open section in front onto which give a row of rooms, each occupied by a married daughter. The most recently married daughter takes the room furthest from the kitchen; occupants rotate through the rooms as each younger daughter marries, the oldest women of the household often ending in the kitchen. Other peoples of Sabah and Sarawak, such as the Iban, Kayan and Kenyah of Sarawak or the Rungus Dusun of Sabah, have maintained a tradition of longhouse dwelling which is perhaps the most famous of the numerous forms of multifamily living arrangements once common in Southeast Asian communities but increasingly rare today.

Prayers are recited by both the ibu rumah and the bomoh.

The next morning at dawn, the ibu rumah measures both the stick and the rattan. The water is also checked. If the rattan or stick has lengthened during the night, or if the water has overflowed onto the plate, the site is chosen.

The site becomes the exact spot where the *tiang seri* (main post) will be erected. It is believed that the *semangat rumah* (spirit of the house) lives in the column.

The kampong

The Malay village, known as a kampong, is visible all over rural Malaysia, and is usually sited near the source of the villagers' livelihood. Fishing villages are found close to the sea while inland villages are usually located near paddy fields or small holdings of rubber trees or oil palm.

Early postcards of Malay villages show houses made entirely of thatch (*atap*) roofing and woven bamboo walls, situated close together below a canopy of coconut trees.

Kampong surroundings

A kampong comprises several Malay houses and their compounds. The houses are usually organized in family clusters, each house being occupied by a family and each cluster belonging to related families. Every house has a compound which is demarcated by trees, usually coconut or fruit trees, at the corners of the compound.

There are no physical boundaries, such as fences, in a Malay kampong, so the concept of trespassing on someone else's property is alien. The openness of the kampong—and the impression that all external spaces are communal—is enhanced by a network of paths leading from house to house and from the houses to the various public buildings. Life in a kampong focuses not only on the individual household but also on the community. The public buildings in a village comprise the mosque or *surau* (prayer house), *kubur* (cemetery), school and shop, and these are regarded as communal rather than formal public places.

A kampong does not develop according to a plan. Instead, the sites of houses are usually selected according to traditional beliefs. House-building rituals are important in Malay society, for the Malays believe that the spirit of a site must be appeased in order that the house be peaceful and the well-being of the occupants assured. Unlike in modern housing

estates where the infrastructure and services determine the siting of houses, in the kampong electricity and water supplies, drainage systems and telephone lines are installed only after the kampong has developed into a substantial settlement. An access road leading into the kampong might also then be built by the local authorities.

In remote rural areas where piped water is not available, wells, rivers, streams and springs in the foothills are the common means of water supply. Wells and rivers provide not only water resources, but also act as focal points for villagers to meet socially. Children bathe and play in the shallow streams while the womenfolk gather to collect water for their household chores, to bathe and to do their washing. The menfolk, of course, supplement the family's diet by fishing in the river.

The social organization of a kampong

The comparatively random layout of a Malay kampong, and the lack of physical barriers, gives the kampong an informal and open atmosphere which is conducive to communal activities. These include such activitiess as *takbir* (visiting neighbours on festive occasions) and *gotong-royong* (sharing work with others in the community). In the kampong, no household exists as an isolated unit, and special occasions, such as a wedding, become communal affairs with the whole village joining in to prepare for and celebrate the occasion.

The concepts of sharing and cooperation, which are fundamental to the Malay culture and to the traditional Malay lifestyle, as well as the general preference for community intimacy over personal privacy, are partially encouraged by the design of the Malay house. Its wide, open *serambi* (veranda), large windows, minimal partitions and open spaces below the house foster neighbourliness and satisfy the communal needs of the residents.

In many kampongs, coconut palms not only provide an essential food item but also screen houses from the glare of the sun. Traditionally, the Malays plant a coconut palm after the birth of each of their children.

The layout of a typical kampong

1. *Masjid* (mosque)
2. *Kubur* (village cemetery)
3. *Rumah Penghulu* (Headman's house)
4. School and playing field
5. Village shop
6. Paddy fields
7. Stream and water gate
8. Clusters of houses surrounded by coconut palms and fruit trees
9. Resting hut

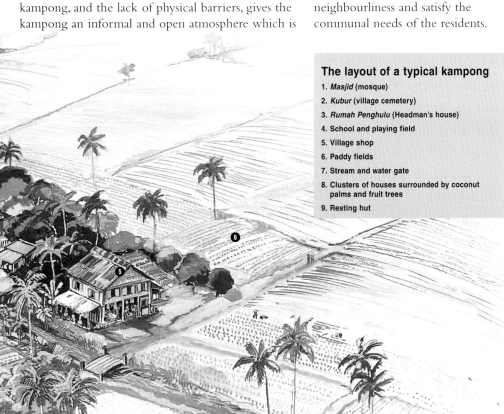

In paddy-growing areas, houses may be located amidst coconut palms and fruit trees and completely surrounded by paddy fields.

Fishing villages, like this one at Marang, Kuala Terengganu, are located along the beaches and sandbanks. The houses are usually more densely grouped than in inland kampongs.

The mosque is the centre of religious activities in a kampong and is usually centrally located. Shown here is the Quariah Mosque at Ulu Beranang, Selangor.

19

The basic Malay house

Malay house styles, particularly the design of the roof, vary from state to state in Peninsular Malaysia, but the basic house form and construction methods are similar.
In the tradition of vernacular houses, the Malay house is not professionally designed but has evolved over a period of time using readily available local materials, which suited the local climatic and environmental conditions. The design of the house has also been dictated by the social mores of the Malays, such as the provision of a private space for the womenfolk and a public space for the entertaining of male guests, because the Malay house is always considered a unit of a larger community in the village.

In a modern Malay house, a zinc roof often replaces thatch even though it is not as effective as an insulator.

Extending the house

The traditional Malay house is modular in concept. Extensions can be made in response to increasing family size and prosperity.

rumah ibu (main house)

serambi gantung (back veranda)

selang and *dapur* (covered passageway and kitchen)

lepau (extension)

anjung (porch)

Main features of the Malay house

The traditional Malay house not only reflects the creative and aesthetic skills of the Malays, but also meets their socioeconomic, cultural and environmental needs.

Set in a compound with a small, open space in front skirted by plants, a variety of fruit trees planted around the sides, and a well at the back for drawing water for drinking, bathing and washing, the house is distinguished by its roof form, raised floor construction, flexible addition of spaces, and the materials from which it is built. The basic design of the Malay house and its construction methods give it great flexibility so that extensions to the house can be carried out whenever necessary.

A distinctive feature of the vernacular Malay house is its high, steeply sloping roof with gables at both ends. The roof is covered with *atap*, a lightweight and excellent thermal insulator made from the fronds of the *nipah*, *rumbia* or *bertam* palm, which holds little heat during the day and cools down at night. The gables are fitted with screens (*tebar layar*), which provide protection from driving rain while allowing ventilation.

Another distinctive feature is the practice of raising the houses on posts above the ground. Since many early settlements were built along rivers and the coastline, the raised floor construction was an ideal solution for coping with ground dampness in the hot and humid tropical climate and with the heavy rains that frequently resulted in flash floods. In settlements that were built within the thick, virgin rainforest, the raised floor system secured the house from the attacks of wild animals. The system also allowed the house to be ventilated through cracks in the raised floor.

Traditional Malay houses have at least two entrances by steps, the main entrance at the front for

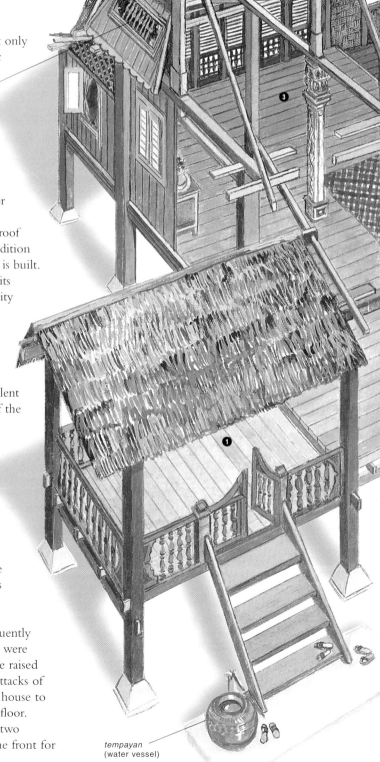

tebar layar (gable screen)

3

1

tempayan (water vessel)

Interior spaces in the Malay house

One of the most congenial aspects of the Malay house is its openness. The house is divided into areas, rather than rooms, for various social and household activities. A noticeable feature in the traditional house is the absence of partitions or solid ceiling-height walls separating the different areas.

A single-unit house, known as a *rumah dangau* or *teratak*, is the earliest vernacular form and is rarely found now, except in the poorest rural areas. It has only a single main space with a small kitchen area and sometimes a porch extending from the roof of the main house. Much more widespread in Peninsular Malaysia is the house consisting of three main areas—the *serambi* (veranda), *rumah ibu* (main house) and *rumah dapur* (kitchen)—which are formed by slight floor level changes and the positioning of doorways to separate the different areas.

The *serambi* is the open, airy area adjacent to the main house. This is where guests are entertained.

Public spaces

The stairs at the front of the house lead to the *anjung* (1), a covered porch where guests are greeted and where family members can also relax. The anjung leads to the long, narrow serambi (2), or reception area, where social and religious functions involving non-family members mainly take place. Its ceiling-to-floor windows allow for good ventilation and also a good view outside.

Private spaces

The rumah ibu (3), adjacent to the serambi, is the core area of the house and the most private and sacred part. Here, the occupants pray, sleep and perform household chores such as sewing and ironing. In the absence of wooden partitions, parts of the rumah ibu may be screened off by cloth to provide private sleeping areas for different members of the family. An attic space, called a *loteng*, can sometimes be found in the roof space under the gables of the rumah ibu. A closed passageway, known as the *selang* (4), links the rumah ibu to the rumah dapur and provides an effective firebreak between the front and back portions of the house. The rumah dapur (5), which is always situated facing the back of the house compound, is mainly where the women congregate and where they do their cooking, although it may also be where the family dines, seated on mats on the floor. The cooking area usually consists of a simple wooden firebox. Sometimes a *pelantar*, an open platform for washing clothes and dishes and for preparing food for cooking, is attached to the rumah dapur.

The space underneath the house is a utility area, serving as storage and 'workshop' space.

The kitchen in a Malay house is rather basic. The cooking is often done over a wooden firebox and dishes are placed on wall racks.

In some houses a *pelantar*, an open timber platform, is added on to the kitchen for washing clothes and preparing food for cooking.

The main areas

1. *Anjung* (covered porch)
2. *Serambi* (veranda)
3. *Rumah ibu* (main house)
4. *Selang* (passageway)
5. *Rumah dapur* (kitchen)

visitors and males and the one at the back mostly for women and children. Sometimes women visitors enter the back entrance to join the womenfolk in the kitchen. At the bottom of the steps is a slab of stone or timber where people leave their footwear, and a clay water vessel (*tempayan*) with a water gourd (*gayong*) where they wash their feet (for hygienic and religious reasons) before ascending the stairs to the house.

1. An illustration of a Chinese miner's house from Isabella Bird's *The Golden Chersonese* (1883).

2. A Chinese house in Pantai Klebang, Melaka, with a typical central door and side windows. The large roof overhang provides protection from the sun and rain.

An adaptation of the Malay house

In the early 19th century, when Chinese labourers arrived in large numbers to work in the tin mines in Perak, Selangor and Pahang, a unique house form developed to accommodate the workers. Some of the features of these early Chinese houses resemble the Malay house and could have been constructed by Malay builders: 'The structure could be as high as 30 feet resembling a huge thatched roof. Walls are fabricated of split timber or split bamboo assembled in a simple and primitive construction. There is one entrance into the structure, which is closed at night by a rough plank door' (Kohl, 1984). Similar to the Malay *serambi*, the house also features a covered veranda '. . . which runs along the front of the house, and a doorway leads from the veranda into the main inner hall giving access to other parts of the building' (Kohl, 1984). The veranda, being the most public area, was the place where hawkers, such as cake sellers, pork vendors, and other pedlars, gathered. To prevent an outbreak of fire, cooking usually took place in a separate kitchen hut. The cooking range was a brick hearth with a large iron rice-pan or wok.

Today, similar style Chinese shophouses and private dwellings can still be seen in rural areas. The main difference between the Chinese and Malay vernacular houses is that the Chinese build their houses on the ground with floors made of compacted earth or cement.

The Malay house: Materials and construction

The traditional Malay house is primarily a timber structure, built off the ground using the post-and-beam method by local carpenters or by the owners themselves. Its walls are usually made of timber, although bamboo is still used in certain areas. Numerous full-length windows line the walls, providing both ventilation and a view outside. The high-pitched, gabled roof, which dominates the house, was traditionally covered with thatch but is now more often covered with galvanized iron.

The construction of a Malay house is often a village affair, combining colourful rituals and cooperative labour.

Materials

The main structure of the traditional Malay house—the posts, crossbeams, tie beams or girts and roof structure—are made of hardwood, such as *cengal* (*Neobalanocarpus heimii*), *belian* (*Eusideroxylon zwageri*), *merbau* (*Intsia palembanica*) or *resak* (*Vatica* spp.), while the secondary structure of the house—the rafters, floor joists, wall studs, window frames and door frames—are usually made of a moderately hard timber, such as *meranti* (*Shorea* spp.) and *jelutong* (*Dyera costulata*).

The posts, called *tiang*, which carry the weight of the roof directly to the ground, measure at least 12 centimetres square. The crossbeams supporting the floor are mortised through the posts and secured by timber wedges, while girts and tie beams at the top of the posts hold the posts in position and form the base of the roof. Various types of joints and connectors have been developed by Malay carpenters to allow the house to be built in stages, and also to allow it to be dismantled and re-erected elsewhere.

Building materials with low thermal qualities, such as woven bamboo for walls and thatch for roofs (above), have been largely replaced by timber and galvanized iron (below).

The walls of the earliest Malay houses were formed of bamboo, woven into panels using traditional patterns and reinforced with timber studs. The floors were laid with strips of bamboo. More frequently, the wall- and floorboards of the Malay house are made of a moderately strong wood, such as the various types of *meranti* (*Shorea* spp.). The wallboards are arranged either vertically, diagonally or horizontally, or in combination. On the external walls are rows of shuttered openings, made of solid timber panels or timber louvres, which are kept open during the day and closed at night. Carved or latticed panels above and below the windows and doors allow air and light into the Malay house. The balustrades behind the shuttered windows, made from carved wooden strips or perforated planks, perform both an aesthetic and safety function. The roof and floor edges are often covered with decorative wooden fascia boards, adding to the beauty of the house.

The traditional roofing material of the Malay house is *atap*, made by splitting fronds of the *nipah*,

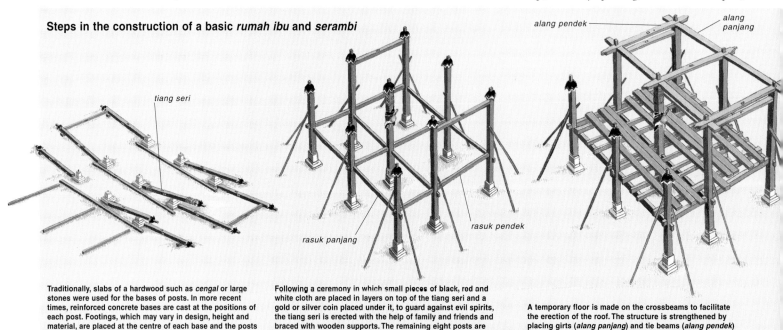

Steps in the construction of a basic *rumah ibu* and *serambi*

tiang seri

rasuk panjang

rasuk pendek

alang pendek

alang panjang

Traditionally, slabs of a hardwood such as *cengal* or large stones were used for the bases of posts. In more recent times, reinforced concrete bases are cast at the positions of each post. Footings, which may vary in design, height and material, are placed at the centre of each base and the posts laid in their respective positions on the ground, with the main column (*tiang seri*) in the centre.

Following a ceremony in which small pieces of black, red and white cloth are placed in layers on top of the tiang seri and a gold or silver coin placed under it, to guard against evil spirits, the tiang seri is erected with the help of family and friends and braced with wooden supports. The remaining eight posts are erected similarly. At floor level, crossbeams (*rasuk panjang* and *rasuk pendek*) are pushed through slots in the posts and secured with wooden wedges.

A temporary floor is made on the crossbeams to facilitate the erection of the roof. The structure is strengthened by placing girts (*alang panjang*) and tie beams (*alang pendek*) at the top of the posts. These also form the base of the roof.

rumbia or *bertam* palm and reinforcing the spine with a bamboo or timber batten. Each piece of atap, about 2 metres by 0.5 metre, is lashed to the roof structure in overlapping, horizontal layers. However, because such roofing needs to be regularly maintained and renewed every few years, and because it is increasingly difficult to obtain a constant supply of palm, most traditional houses on the Malay Peninsula have now had their atap roofs replaced with sheets of galvanized iron, popularly called 'zinc', or asbestos-cement sheets, although the traditional roof form has been retained. Similarly, non-traditional materials such as bricks and concrete are used in the construction of some walls.

  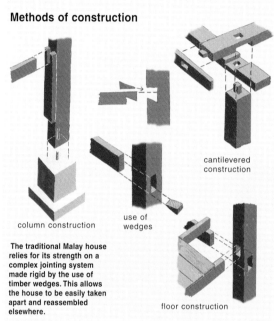

Wallboards may be arranged vertically, horizontally or diagonally, or in combination (1). The many voids in the Malay house, for example, in the gable screens (2) and the full-length shuttered windows (3), reflect the importance given to ventilation.

Construction

Most Malay houses are constructed by local carpenters and, occasionally, by the owners themselves. The components of the house, such as the posts, beams, trusses, wall panels and screens, are prefabricated in a workshop or at the site prior to erection using simple hand tools. Before the actual construction of the house begins, the owner will identify a suitable site within his compound. Neither the site nor the orientation of the house will depend on the presence of a road or water and electricity supply, but rather on a complex framework of geomancy and ritual to ensure that wandering spirits are appeased and the house will be harmonious and tranquil for its occupants. Careful consideration is also given to the selection of timber for all the components of the house.

The construction of the house starts with the erection of the main house (*rumah ibu*). The other parts of the house, such as the entrance porch (*anjung*), veranda (*serambi*) and kitchen (*rumah dapur*) may be added later, depending on the resources of the owner and the needs of a growing household. Sometimes the rumah ibu is converted into a kitchen if the owner decides to build a bigger house. Because these additions take place over a period of time and in a variety of arrangements, a kampong usually consists of houses in various stages of construction and arrangement.

Methods of construction

column construction   use of wedges   cantilevered construction   floor construction

The traditional Malay house relies for its strength on a complex jointing system made rigid by the use of timber wedges. This allows the house to be easily taken apart and reassembled elsewhere.

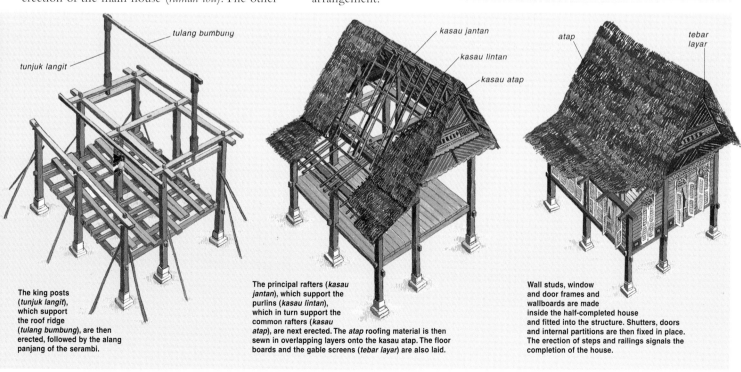

tunjuk langit — *tulang bumbung*

The king posts (*tunjuk langit*), which support the roof ridge (*tulang bumbung*), are then erected, followed by the alang panjang of the serambi.

kasau jantan — *kasau lintan* — *kasau atap*

The principal rafters (*kasau jantan*), which support the purlins (*kasau lintan*), which in turn support the common rafters (*kasau atap*), are next erected. The *atap* roofing material is then sewn in overlapping layers onto the kasau atap. The floor boards and the gable screens (*tebar layar*) are also laid.

atap — *tebar layar*

Wall studs, window and door frames and wallboards are made inside the half-completed house and fitted into the structure. Shutters, doors and internal partitions are then fixed in place. The erection of steps and railings signals the completion of the house.

The Malay house of the Peninsular west coast

There are many variations of the traditional Malay house on the west coast of Peninsular Malaysia although the basic component, the **rumah ibu** *(the main living area), is common to the whole region and, indeed, to the whole of the Peninsula. The main distinguishing feature is the roof. On the west coast, the two major roof forms are the indigenous* **bumbung panjang** *(long ridge roof) and the foreign-influenced* **bumbung lima** *(hipped roof).*

The eight west coast states of Peninsular Malaysia.

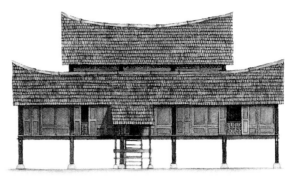

The Negeri Sembilan roof is a visual analogy of a bull's head and horns, purportedly honouring the buffalo for the role it played in winning an important battle in Sumatra.

The bumbung panjang house

The bumbung panjang house is the oldest and most widespread house type on the Peninsula. It has an elegant, steeply inclined roof with a long, central ridge supported by a number of posts (depending on the size of the house) which carry the weight of the roof to the ground. Triangular-shaped decorative gables (*tebar layar*) on either end of the roof assist ventilation of the roof space. The simple construction of the roof allows various types of extensions and additions to be made to the house. However, the low headroom of the house—acceptable in the past when the house had minimal furniture and the occupants sat on the floor—has led to a decline in popularity of this roof type.

Regional variations of the bumbung panjang house

In the northern west coast states of Perlis, Kedah, Penang and Perak, the bumbung panjang house is plain and functional. It usually consists of either a basic rectangular rumah ibu with a front veranda with rows of shuttered openings and an enclosed rear veranda, or two structures separated by a *selang* (passageway), placed parallel to each other or at right angles or end-to-end. The selang, which has a dropped floor and a roof that fits under the eaves of the adjacent structures, not only provides a convenient way of adding to an existing form by avoiding merging roof forms, but serves to demarcate the 'living' and 'working' areas of the house. It also provides a private entrance for women and a place for them to socialize. This house style is commonly called *rumah selang*.

A variation of the two-structure form is the *gajah menyusu* house, so-called because it resembles a baby elephant suckling its mother (*gajah* means 'elephant' and *menyusu* 'to suckle'). The *rumah dapur* (kitchen), which is a smaller version of the main house, is placed end-to-end and the difference in their status is indicated by

The *bumbung panjang* is the most common roof form on the west coast.

Three-dimensional view of the bumbung panjang and anjung.

The *gajah menyusu* house, so-called because of its resemblance to a suckling elephant, is the easiest way of extending the basic house form.

drops in the floor level and in the ridge of the roof. An additional space, called a *lepau*, may be added to the front of traditional houses in Kedah and Perlis, giving rise to the name *rumah lepau*. In all the houses, a small, open gable entrance may be added at the front. Simpler houses may be entered by wooden steps covered with a lean-to roof.

The increasingly rare traditional bumbung panjang house known as *rumah kutai*, found in central Perak in areas around Kuala Kangsar, Kampung Gajah, Bota Kanan and Bota Kiri, has walls, and sometimes floors, made entirely of bamboo matting and a roof constructed of *atap* (thatch). The interior is undivided and on the same level, although the kitchen may be a separate structure and reached by a selang. Because of the small window and door openings, the interior of the house is often very dark.

The Negeri Sembilan house is the only traditional house on the Malay Peninsula to have a curved roof reminiscent of the Minangkabau roof of Sumatra, though the house itself is much smaller, the curve of the roof less pronounced, and the gable ends vertical rather than tapered inwards. The roof may be covered in atap or shingles or the more modern corrugated iron ('zinc'). An elongated *serambi gantung* (hanging veranda), located lower than the rumah ibu but with a similarly curved roof, low windows and a central entrance covered by a lean-to roof, contributes to the formality and symmetry of the house. In some houses in Negeri Sembilan, the roof of the rumah ibu is raised and an additional floor added to form a one-and-a-half or two-storey building. When necessary, further extensions may be added to the back of the house.

This house comprises two *bumbung panjang* structures joined by a covered passageway *(selang)*. The stairs to the selang provide private access for women. In the front structure, the lower section of the roof covers the veranda.

The *bumbung lima*, or 'five ridge roof', which allows greater height within, derives from European house styles of the colonial period. The space below is often used as a garage or for storage.

The bumbung lima house

The *bumbung lima*, literally 'five ridge roof', is a hipped roof comprising one main ridge across the top of the rectangular floor plan and four descending corner ridges. The roof, which covers the main areas of the house, including the *rumah ibu* and the *serambi*, completely envelops the eaves of the roof, providing protection to the walls. An *anjung*, protruding from the serambi, forms another hipped roof and may be built at the same elevation as the main house. Believed to have been influenced by British and Dutch house styles, the roof's greater height allows the introduction of furniture and explains its popularity among less traditional and more urban families. The concrete staircase and masonry columns—further evidence of Malay response to foreign influence—and shuttered full-length windows contribute to the sturdy appearance of the house. The bumbung lima house and its variations are mostly found in the states of Penang, Perak, Selangor and Johor.

Three-dimensional view of the bumbung lima and anjung.

The *bumbung Perak* is also known as the *bumbung potongan Belanda*, or 'Dutch-style roof ridge'. Its more complex gable ends dictate the use of modern roofing materials.

Regional variations

The *bumbung Perak* is a gambrel roof—a hipped roof with gable-like ends—which has evolved in response to the use of modern roofing materials, particularly zinc, since World War II. The anjung of the bumbung Perak house, attached to the serambi, has its own gambrel roof. The roof of the anjung may continue downwards to cover the staircase, which is enclosed by railings and decorated with timber latticework.

In Johor, the bumbung lima is usually tiled and the fascia boards decorated with carved patterns. Because the roof is shorter, the walls are more dominant. The space below the house may be enclosed with a timber lattice.

Masonry columns and stairs and full-length shuttered windows are features of the Johor-style house.

One of the most beautiful Malay houses is the Melakan courtyard house, which is formed by two parallel bumbung panjang house forms—the rumah ibu and the rumah dapur—separated by a raised, open courtyard, a versatile yet private work space. The side of the rumah dapur facing the courtyard may be left open, forming a pavilion. The roofs of the two structures are pointed and high-pitched and the ridges usually straight, with sometimes a subtle curve. A combination of atap and corrugated iron is the most common roofing material although clay tiles are frequently used. An attic under the roof provides additional storage and sleeping space. The long outer wall of the serambi—located at a lower level in front of the house—may be partly closed with windows but is most often left open and bordered with a railing. The *anjung* (porch) attached to the left of the serambi is an excellent space in which to relax and to entertain male guests. Unique to Melaka is the elaborate concrete staircase covered with colourful ceramic tiles that leads to the *anjung*.

The house style in Johor is influenced by the Bugis of Sulawesi, Indonesia, who migrated to Peninsular Malaysia in the 17th century. Its dominant features are its steeply inclining roof, which terminates in a *butan* (finial), and the two-tiered gable end which faces the entrance of the house. The walls are generally punctuated by three full-length windows. The anjung, at one side of the serambi, is surrounded by railings.

The bamboo walls and *atap* roof of the *rumah kutai* in the Kuala Kangsar district of Perak allow natural ventilation and reduce glare.

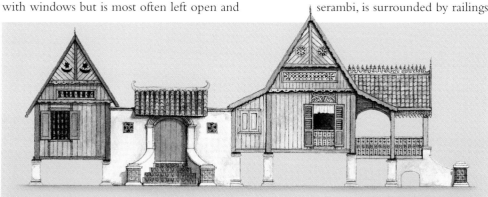

The Melakan courtyard house

The Melakan courtyard house evinces a mixture of architectural influences. The raised courtyard, formed of masonry walls ventilated by large, green, Chinese 'air' bricks, and entered by a roofed doorway, is a feature adopted from the traditional Chinese house. Clay tiles are frequently used on the roof, as are galvanized iron roof ridges and finials. The beautiful stairs at the front, and sometimes at the entrance to the courtyard (the latter used mainly by women), are elaborately ornamented with tiles imported from Europe and China. Such tiles are also found on the facades and interiors of Melakan townhouses.

Ornamental glazed tiles are a favourite decorative device on the staircases of Melakan houses. Flowers are a common motif.

The Bugis-style long ridge house is found mainly in the the regions of Pontian and Batu Pahat in Johor.

25

The Malay house of the Peninsular east coast

Much of the east coast of Peninsular Malaysia is culturally and architecturally different from the west coast. Strong Thai and Cambodian influences have shaped the culture of the east coast for many centuries, and have created what some consider to be the richest cultural heritage of the Peninsular Malay states.

For hundreds of years, the east coast of Peninsular Malaysia had an active trading relationship with the neighbouring countries of Thailand and Cambodia in the north and Indonesia in the south. This influenced the house styles and construction methods in the area.

The east coast tradition

It is believed that the early ancestors of the Malays came from the ancient civilization of Kemboja (Cambodia) and Champa in Indochina and settled along the east coast of the Peninsula. Later, when trade flourished in the region, the cultural influences from these countries were further reinforced.

From the 2nd to the 16th century, much of the area (Kelantan, Terengganu, and Patani in southern Thailand) was part of the Malay kingdom of Langkasuka. Many of the traditional Malay art forms known today originated there, including Wayang Kulit (shadow puppet theatre), Mak Yong and Menora (dance), and *sobek* (filigree-like woodcarving). Out of this rich tradition arose an architectural vocabulary distinctive to the east coast.

Traditional house types in Kelantan and Terengganu

In Kelantan and Terengganu, houses are described by the number of *tiang* (posts) holding up the roof structure of the *rumah ibu* (main house), and can be classified into two distinct types. The smaller of the two is called the *rumah bujang* (bachelor house) or *rumah tiang enam* (house with six posts). The larger is almost twice as large, and is called *rumah serambi* (veranda house) or *rumah tiang duabelas* (house with twelve posts). Besides the main posts there are also intermediate floor supports which are known as *tongkat*, but these are not included when a house is referred to as six or twelve tiang. The tiang and tongkat raise the house nearly 2.5 metres off the ground, and give the impression of an animal with many legs. With its high walls and steeply pitched roof, a large rumah serambi can stand over 10 metres.

Smaller stuctures

Both types of houses are often attached to a number of smaller structures along one or both of the long sides of the rumah ibu. If this structure is roofed and runs the full length of the house it is called a *selasar*. Its floor is always lower than the rumah ibu. This is the place where male visitors are entertained. Tall window panels, just broad enough to admit an adult, are sometimes built into a side wall, opening onto the selesar. An unroofed structure, projecting from a side door with a flight of steps leading to the ground, is called a *lambor*. The kitchen (*rumah dapur*) is sometimes contained in a separate structure, linked to the rumah ibu by a *selang* (passageway or open platform).

Inside the house there are few partitions, but decorative screens of split bamboo, plaited to create foliated or geometric patterns, are sometimes added.

Regional influences and common features

A Kelantanese house in the grounds of Wat Kok Seraya in Chabang Empat, near Kota Bharu. The three-tiered roof of the gateway and the finials on the roof ridge are features also seen in Thai houses.

The evolution of the architectural styles of the east coast houses must have derived from several influences brought about by migration and trade. What has developed shows homogenous features peculiar to Kelantan, Terengganu, Cambodia and Thailand. These include steep, tiered roofs with curved gable ends, a feature not found on houses on the west coast of Peninsular Malaysia; rhomboid-shaped terracotta roof tiles which are Thai in origin but have long been made locally; and walls made of timber panels which are slotted into grooved frames. This technique accentuates the rectangular pattern of the panels, a decorative feature popular in Thailand as well as in Cambodia.

Curved gable ends on a Thai house are also common on the east coast.

The structure of this simple Cambodian timber house is similar to the houses in Terengganu and Kelantan.

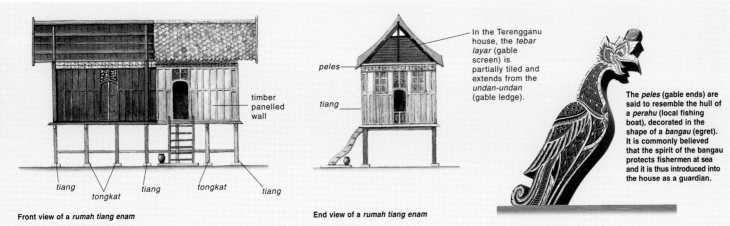

tiang   tongkat   tiang   tongkat   tiang

timber panelled wall

Front view of a *rumah tiang enam*

peles

tiang

In the Terengganu house, the *tebar layar* (gable screen) is partially tiled and extends from the *undan-undan* (gable ledge).

End view of a *rumah tiang enam*

The *peles* (gable ends) are said to resemble the hull of a *perahu* (local fishing boat), decorated in the shape of a *bangau* (egret). It is commonly believed that the spirit of the bangau protects fishermen at sea and it is thus introduced into the house as a guardian.

singhorra tiles   rumah dapur

lambor

tiang

Side view of a *rumah tiang duabelas*

tiered roof

The use of the sunbeam motif on the gable screens of Kelantanese houses symbolizes the beginning and the end of a day.

timber panelled wall

End view of a *rumah tiang duabelas*

Roof styles

The roofs of Kelantan and Terengganu houses are usually covered with *singhorra* tiles, named after the town, Songkhla, in southern Thailand where the tiles originate. Gently curved *peles* (gable ends) are fitted to the ends of the roof overhangs, giving the houses their distinctive appearance. Thai houses have a similar form which is supposed to represent the *naga* (water dragon), an aquatic symbol pervasive in Thai rites and rituals.

Pahang, to the south of Terengganu, may have been part of this cultural development, although today little evidence exists to suggest that link. There is rumour of a great Khmer city buried at the bottom of Tasik Chini in Pahang, and the local aborigines speak a language with some similarities to that of the ancient Khmer civilization (c. 800–1370 CE), renowned for its architecture.

Adopting a house style

In the 13th-century, the Chinese traveller Ma Touan Lin recorded that the houses in Tchin La (Cambodia) resembled those in a country further south which he called Chi tu. This area, the 'Red Earth Land', has been tentatively identified as inland Kelantan.

Today, this description still holds true. The oldest examples of traditional houses in Kelantan and Terengganu—those older than 100 years—are very different from the house styles of other states, and features similar to Thai and Cambodian houses are still very much in evidence. While the planning and layout of these dwellings are similar to other houses on the Peninsula, they are set apart by their detailing, the construction of the walls and roof, in particular, and the intricate carvings.

Like most houses throughout Southeast Asia, houses on the east coast are raised off the ground, allowing for ample air circulation, protection from floods and wild animals, and the storage of livestock, boats and tools under the house. However, unlike most Thai houses, which tend to be arranged around a central courtyard or a raised platform, east coast houses are usually individual, free-standing buildings linked by a series of walkways or covered porches. Traditionally, the main door of the house does not face west because the direction of sunset marks the coming of the darkness of night and black symbolizes death. Houses are therefore usually orientated along a north–south axis.

Solid panelled walls are often finely carved along the top to admit light and air. This form of carving employs the piercing techniques known as *tebuk terus* (direct piercing), *tebuk separuh* (semi-piercing) and *tebuk timbul* (embossed piercing).

The Pahang house

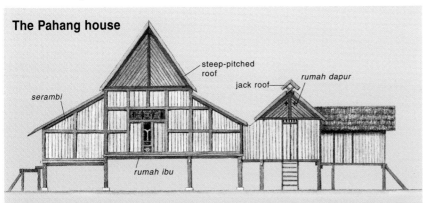

serambi

steep-pitched roof

jack roof

rumah dapur

rumah ibu

Architecturally, houses in Pahang have more in common with those of the west coast states than with their northern neighbours, perhaps because many of the earliest houses were built by the Bugis, a seafaring people from Sulawesi who settled along much of the Peninsular coastline. The houses are typically lower to the ground, use smaller timbers and are less elaborately carved. The above shows the main house, a closed veranda and a kitchen with a jack roof to allow smoke to escape.

The sliding lock device for opening and shutting windows and doors.

Coastal and riverine settlements

The earliest settlements in Malaysia developed along river basins because rivers were the only means of transportation into the interior of the country and because their estuaries provided a safe haven for seafarers and fishermen. Major towns such as Melaka, Kota Bharu, Kuala Terengganu, Kota Kinabalu and Kuching all began as river settlements. But with advances in modern transport systems, the importance of coastal and riverine settlements receded and today waterfront settlements are mostly fishing villages. In Sabah and Sarawak, numerous coastal villages, known as kampung air *(water villages), can be seen spreading out along the coastlines of both states.*

Living above water

Generally, two types of houses are built in waterfront settlements: houses built on rafts known as *rumah rakit*, and houses built on stilts known as *rumah tiang seribu* (house on a thousand stilts). These houses are typical of fishing villages in Peninsular Malaysia as well as Sabah and Sarawak.

The rumah rakit is a house that sits on a raft made of dried bamboo. The house is tied to the raft to hold it in position and the raft is anchored to the sea bed to keep it from being swept away by strong currents. Clusters of rumah rakit can be seen along the Kelantan River, especially in Kota Bharu and Kuala Krai. This unique form of housing is also found in parts of Pahang. Rumah rakit dwellers

A *rumah rakit* (raft house) is built on a structure made of dried bamboo which is light and buoyant. Nowadays, oil drums or plastic containers are also used to help keep the raft afloat.

In Sabah, the sea gypsies are the Bajau Laut who make their homes in boats. Each boat shelters a single family. Enclosed by sideboards, its decked mid-section, covered by a pitched roof that can be taken down when required, forms the living quarters.

often have a floating fish farm nearby but nowadays many earn their living working in towns, despite their proximity to the sea.

The tiang seribu houses are built on very tall stilts which are erected on the river or sea beds. These houses appear as if they have risen from the water supported precariously on wooden stilts. They are, however, quite sturdy and

The beach houses in a Malay fishing village are similar in construction and layout to a typical Malay house (see 'The basic Malay house'). An open veranda is a common feature and is used for drying clothes and fishing nets.

can withstand tropical storms and strong waves. The houses are linked to one another by wooden boardwalks. Jetties are built far out into the sea so that fishermen can get in and out of their boats easily. Most of the houses are made of wood or are half-plank and half-brick. The traditional thatch is often replaced with roof tiles or zinc sheets. The timber stilts are made from *bakau* or *nibong*, which are available from the mangrove swamps nearby, although concrete columns are increasingly used for their durability.

Riverine settlements are usually crowded as the houses are built in tight clusters within a limited sheltered area. The communities living in such settlements are usually close-knit and many of their houses are built by communal effort, known as *gotong-royong*.

A *kampung air* (water village) exists cheek by jowl with the hub of modern Kota Kinabalu in Sabah.

A fishing village in Perlis on the northwest coast of Peninsular Malaysia. Fishing is still an important livelihood for many rural people.

A *rumah tiang seribu* is built on stilts to prevent water from entering the house during high tide. The raised floors also ensure good ventilation.

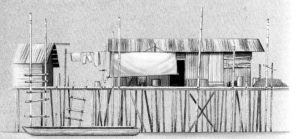

The houses of the Orang Kuala are constructed on stilts like the houses in the fishing villages, but are smaller and are usually made of cheaper building materials.

Houses on the beach are also built on stilts but are not as tall as the rumah tiang seribu because they are not so affected by the fluctuations of the tides. The houses are usually oriented towards the sea, with the living room facing the waterfront so that the sea breeze cools the living room during the day and the land breeze cools the bedrooms at night.

People of the sea

Apart from the fishing communities, there is a minority group of Orang Asli known as Orang Laut ('people of the sea') who also live by the estuaries. The Orang Laut are made up of two distinct groups: the Orang Kuala, who are people of the river mouth, and the smaller group, the Orang Seletar, often called 'sea gypsies', who live their entire lives on small boats. They rarely stay in any one place longer than a day or two. The river is the Orang Seletar's highway and the sea their workplace.

The Orang Kuala always build their houses at a river mouth (*kuala*) to ensure a supply of fresh water. They are mainly found along the west coast of Johor. The villagers make a living by catching fish, large crabs and shellfish, and most of them build their own boats.

Although the houses built in these villages are not sophisticated, they are a demonstration of the dwellers' innovative response to their immediate environment and are also suited to their livelihood.

Keeping houses above the water

Coastal and riverine settlers have developed effective techniques for building houses that can stand the battering of tides and tropical storms. The trunk of the *nibong* palm is traditionally used for stilts, especially as nibong trunks become more durable when waterlogged.

Stilts are erected by sinking nibong trunks into the river bed. Timber boards are then lashed to them with strips of rattan.

Some beach houses have posts resting on clay pots to prevent them from sinking into the sand.

Settlement types of Sabah and Sarawak

Throughout Sabah and Sarawak, traditional settlement types are linked to both cosmological beliefs and features of the natural terrain. Mountains and sea coasts are seen to be separated by an intermediate zone of rivers, and in most indigenous cosmologies this intermediate area is considered the pre-eminent dwelling place of human beings.

Mount Kinabalu is regarded as a sacred place, its summit considered by many Kadazandusun as the abode of the dead. Houses, as here in Kundasang, are often oriented towards it.

Seaward and landward zones

In Sarawak, at the coast and along major river mouths, trading and fishing communities, mostly Muslim and Malay-speaking, predominate. Moving inland, sea lanes give way to river passages, and here, over most of Sarawak's interior, the main rivers and streams are home to numerous indigenous groups.

Sabah is to some degree exceptional. Here, the riverine zone, so prominent elsewhere in Borneo, tends to be constricted. Instead, an island-fringed, deeply embayed sea coast creates a disproportionately large and varied maritime zone, while inland, the mountainous ranges of Borneo converge to produce a rugged interior of upland plains and narrow valleys separated by steep hills and mountains, culminating in the towering granite peaks of Mount Kinabalu.

Spatial orientations within this coastal zone are characteristically defined by 'landward' and 'seaward' directions, or by location 'at sea' or 'ashore'. These distinctions have also human equivalents. Thus, along the east coast of Sabah, sea nomads historically formed a small minority of the larger Bajau population. Known to outsiders as Bajau Laut, these nomads distinguished themselves as 'people of the sea' (*a'a dilaut*). Making their homes in boats, they subsisted exclusively by fishing and inshore gathering, collecting among other things, shellfish and trepang (sea cucumbers), the latter for trade.

Inland, Kadazandusun people predominate and are divided between upland groups practising shifting cultivation and more populous lowland, valley and plains people growing principally wet rice. Along the western coastal plains, Kadazandusun villages typically stand, like raised islets, amid palms and fruit trees, in loosely nucleated clusters, surrounded by seasonally flooded paddy fields. In the wet rice growing areas of Tuaran, Papar and Penampang, Kadazandusun settlements tend to be more dispersed, with individual houses scattered among rice fields (see map in 'Traditional houses of Sabah'). Scattered settlements are also characteristic of the interior Tambunan and Ranau plains. In the Kota Belud district, houses were traditionally oriented so that the two end walls faced 'seaward' and 'landward'. As with the Bajau Laut, the direction of the rising sun (east) was associated with life and its beginnings; the setting sun (west) with death.

Longhouse settlements

In the past, a few upland Kadazandusun groups, like the Rungus, lived in longhouses, as did most of the inland Murut who inhabit the rugged southern interior of Sabah. The Lundayeh, another upland people of the southern Sipitang, Tenom and Keningau districts, also lived in longhouses until about the 1930s.

Each Lundayeh longhouse was like a village in which the whole community lived under one roof. The house itself was surrounded by a well-tended clearing, setting it apart from the fields and forests beyond. The house and its environs comprised a series of bounded spaces, each the physical location for different kinds of activities, both mundane and sacred. While the more

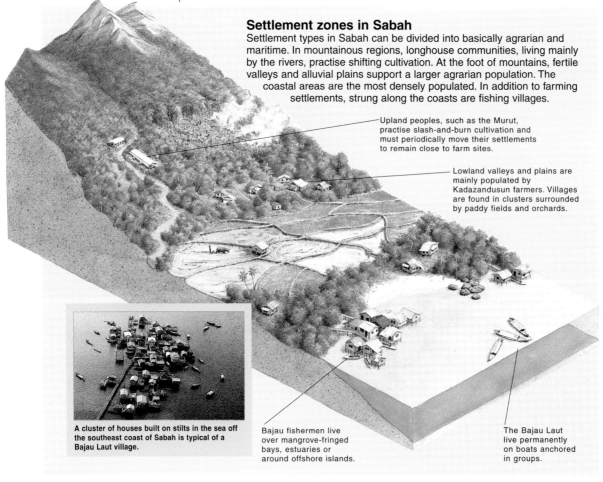

Settlement zones in Sabah
Settlement types in Sabah can be divided into basically agrarian and maritime. In mountainous regions, longhouse communities, living mainly by the rivers, practise shifting cultivation. At the foot of mountains, fertile valleys and alluvial plains support a larger agrarian population. The coastal areas are the most densely populated. In addition to farming settlements, strung along the coasts are fishing villages.

Upland peoples, such as the Murut, practise slash-and-burn cultivation and must periodically move their settlements to remain close to farm sites.

Lowland valleys and plains are mainly populated by Kadazandusun farmers. Villages are found in clusters surrounded by paddy fields and orchards.

A cluster of houses built on stilts in the sea off the southeast coast of Sabah is typical of a Bajau Laut village.

Bajau fishermen live over mangrove-fringed bays, estuaries or around offshore islands.

The Bajau Laut live permanently on boats anchored in groups.

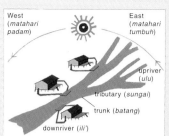

Longhouse dwellers refer to the location of their house as upriver or downriver. The river also defines neighbourhood boundaries.

Longhouse orientation in Sarawak

The upriver–downriver orientation of the traditional Saribas Iban longhouse is associated with botanical imagery. Like a living tree, each longhouse is regarded as a 'trunk', with the arrangement of its parts mirroring the 'base' and 'tips' of a tree. During house construction, timbers are placed so that their natural base is down or towards the chief 'source' of the house; while their natural tip is up, or towards its outer 'tips', reflecting the original orientation of the wood as part of a once-living tree. The *tiang pemun* (source post) acts as the primary 'base' (*pun*) of the structure, while its lateral tips (*ujung*) remain, as with a living tree, points of continuing growth to which, from each end of the house, families may add new apartments.

Most Iban longhouses are built near a river or stream with their main axis oriented in an upriver–downriver direction. The two sides of the house face, if possible, east and west. The *tanju* (open deck), which is used for drying, ideally faces east to catch the morning sun.

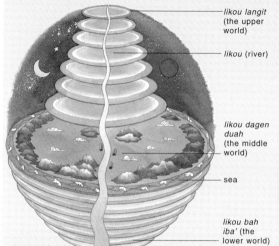

The middle world consists of the village surrounded by sago palms, orchards and rice fields on the river banks. This territory is known as the *uma*.

likou langit (the upper world)

likou (river)

likou dagen duah (the middle world)

sea

likou bah iba' (the lower world)

The Melanau's cosmos

In the traditional Melanau view, the universe was made up of a number of worlds, of which a riparian middle world, between the sky and the underworld, was considered the realm of human beings. This was called the 'country (or river) in between' (*likou dagen duah*). Here, man's proper place was in the village.

Concepts of space and the universe

Rivers formed the central axis of this middle world and dominated Melanau views of space. Thus, the main directions were upriver and downriver, and secondarily, of the river and away from the river. Humankind shared this middle world with spirits, animals and plants, each of which had its own proper place. Beyond the village, cultivated areas were only half-domesticated. Here, other beings had rights and human beings had therefore to take care when working their fields and gardens. For traditional Melanau, *adet* (a principle of order) provided a guide to the proper behaviour that should be displayed towards these beings. Superimposed upon this river-centred middle world were upper and lower worlds, each consisting of seven layers called *susun* (layers) or *lapih* (stratas), which, taken together, comprised, in traditional Melanau belief, a roughly egg-shaped universe surrounded by water, beyond which were the sun, the moon and the stars.

Although most Melanau live today in coastal or river bank villages, in the past they lived in longhouse settlements.

public of these took place on the gallery, spaces within the family apartments provided privacy for shared meals and family conversation. In its construction, the longhouse expressed ideals of both equality and difference. Beneath a common roof, each family's apartment was the same size, yet apartments were constructed of different materials and displayed inside their walls inherited property signifying differences of wealth and status. With the construction of individual houses, this expression of difference is given greater scope. Yet, despite the dramatic changes registered in settlement design signalled by the move to individual houses, many of the ideas expressed in traditional architecture persist. Internal space within each house is still organized as before. Most houses now face onto a central clearing (*padang*), a well-groomed space with a village chapel (*sidang*) at its centre, forming, like the traditional gallery, the communal focus of village social and ritual life, while their back walls, like the rear walls of the former longhouse, are set against the surrounding forest, delineating human from non-human domains. The layout of a modern Lundayeh village thus expresses both change and a more enduring scheme of values.

Settlements in Sarawak

Apart from small numbers of hunter-gatherers who live in temporary camps erected deep inside the forest, most indigenous groups construct their settlements along the open banks of rivers and streams. The Iban are the most populous of these

groups. An egalitarian, expansive people, the Iban live chiefly in longhouse settlements built mainly along the major rivers and more accessible tributaries, notably those of the Batang Lupar, Saribas and Rajang river systems. Until recently, these rivers afforded the only practical means of communication and travel; in the past, they defined the lines separating warring groups.

Above the Iban, in the upper rivers and interior highlands, live a number of more remote groups—Kenyah, Kayan, Kelabit and others—known collectively as Orang Ulu. Unlike the Iban, most are stratified and live in villages composed of one, or occasionally several, longhouses. Longhouse architecture mirrors social structure; the central apartments belonging to aristocratic families are typically larger and more spacious than others, their roofs rising above the apartments of lesser nobles and commoners which flank them on each side.

Below the Iban, in the Oya and Mukah districts of Sarawak, live the Melanau. Here, in swampy areas along slow-moving rivers, the Melanau cultivate sago palms and rice. Although most Melanau live today in coastal or riverine villages, in the past they constructed massive houses, like longhouses in their spatial arrangement. Each village comprised 2–3 houses, some enormous structures as much as 130 metres long and standing 8–16 metres above the ground.

A nomadic group, the Penan live in temporary shelters in the interior forests of Sarawak. They are mainly found in the upper reaches of the Baram, Limbang and Rajang rivers.

A modern Lundayeh village in Long Pasia, Sabah. The houses face the chapel on the village green (*padang*), which is the focus of village social and ritual life.

Traditional houses of Sabah

The traditional houses of Sabah reflect not only the diverse ways in which people have adapted to their environment, but also their lifestyles, which are governed by rituals and beliefs. The house is regarded as a microcosm of the world of spirits and the universe. The site of a house and its spatial organization may therefore be influenced by omens and dreams as well as physical factors, such as the orientation of the sun and the river and a fresh supply of water.

The wide expanse of roof on a Rungus house acts like a sunshade, keeping the house cool even during the hottest part of the day.

Distribution of traditional houses in Sabah

N

South China Sea

BALAMBANGAN ISLAND · BANGGI ISLAND
Kudat · Pitas
Matunggong ·
Kota Belud · Kota Marudu
Tuaran ·
Kota Kinabalu · ▲ MOUNT KINABALU
Penampang ·
Papar · · Ranau
· Tambunan
· Keningau
Tenom ·
· Sipitang · Nabawan
Kemabong · Sapulut

BRUNEI

Sulu Sea

Sabah

Semporna
SIPADAN ISLAND

0   200 km

INDONESIA

Celebes Sea

▮ Rungus longhouse	▮ Bamboo house
▮ Bonggi house	▮ Lotud house
▮ Bajau house	▮ Bajau houseboats
▮ Murut house	

Types of traditional houses

Although the ethnic peoples of Sabah comprise several diverse groups, their traditional dwellings share many features in their design and construction. The houses are generally built on stilts, have pitched roofs, are well ventilated and are constructed of timber and other local materials. Purpose-built granaries, ritual ceremonial huts and mortuary houses may be constructed of a similar design but on a smaller scale. The traditional houses can be classified into two major types: communal houses, such as the Rungus longhouse and the Murut longhouse, and individual houses, such as the Bajau house of Kota Belud, the Bonggi house on Banggi and Balambangan islands, the bamboo house of Tambunan, and the Lotud house in the Tuaran district.

One roof, one community

Although the layout of a longhouse may vary, its spatial organization reveals the close relationship between a family and the longhouse community.

A longhouse is designed to provide domestic and private spaces for each family as well as a public and social space for the whole community. The Murut longhouse consists of several family apartments (*sulap*) at the rear of the house and a communal veranda (*saloh*) at the front. Each sulap contains an earthen fireplace (*rapuan*) and a sleeping area for a couple and their unmarried daughters. Boys, bachelors and guests sleep outside on the saloh.

Unique to the Murut longhouse is the *lansaran*, a trampoline-like dance platform which is constructed in a central area on the saloh. It is used during festive occasions in which the whole community participates in singing and dancing, and also for jumping competitions.

The spatial arrangement of the Rungus longhouse reflects similar principles to the Murut longhouse but differs in construction techniques. The public space (*apad*) and the rear domestic space (*ongkob*) form one domestic unit. The slanting walls, made of timber poles, are a distinctive feature. The spaces between the timber poles allow for good ventilation, and the walls also provide a convenient back rest for the occupants when they sit on the floor. The Rungus always orientate their houses towards Mount Kinabalu, which is considered sacred. It is also customary for the Rungus to sleep with their heads at right angles to the mountain.

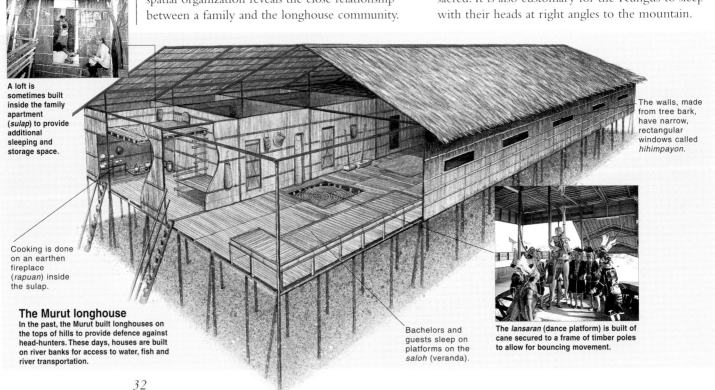

A loft is sometimes built inside the family apartment (*sulap*) to provide additional sleeping and storage space.

The walls, made from tree bark, have narrow, rectangular windows called *hihimpayon*.

Cooking is done on an earthen fireplace (*rapuan*) inside the sulap.

The Murut longhouse
In the past, the Murut built longhouses on the tops of hills to provide defence against head-hunters. These days, houses are built on river banks for access to water, fish and river transportation.

Bachelors and guests sleep on platforms on the *saloh* (veranda).

The *lansaran* (dance platform) is built of cane secured to a frame of timber poles to allow for bouncing movement.

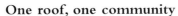

The individual house: A living and ritual entity

The Bajau house: An open-plan concept

The Bajau house of Kota Belud reflects the structure and social organization of traditional Bajau family life. The house is divided into three parts. The biggest section is the living area. The other parts—the kitchen and porch—are built separately, each with its own roof. Each of these parts is different in its construction, elevation and use of materials. A distinctive feature is the open-plan concept of the living area. Here, curtains are placed around the sleeping areas at night to provide privacy.

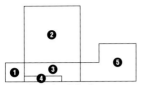

Plan of a modern Bajau house:
1. *Pantaran* (porch)
2. *Keoyoon* (living area)
3. *Kalimantong* (passageway)
4. *Meja rehat* (platform for resting)
5. *Serudong* (kitchen)

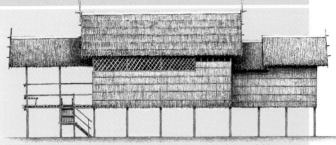

A pitched roof with crossed horns (*layang layang*) at the ends of the roof ridge characterizes the Bajau house. The number of house posts indicates the size of the house, and thus the wealth and status of the owner.

The Lotud house: A symbolic, ordered space

A traditional Lotud house, consisting of a veranda, kitchen and dining area, elevated sleeping and living area and storage attic, is said to replicate the houses in the spirit world of the Lotud belief system.

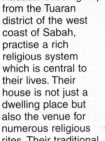

The Lotud, a Kadazandusun group from the Tuaran district of the west coast of Sabah, practise a rich religious system which is central to their lives. Their house is not just a dwelling place but also the venue for numerous religious rites. Their traditional house, which is long and made of timber, is divided into five sections: a veranda (*soliu*); the inner house (*soriba*), which is the kitchen and dining area; an elevated space (*kawas*), which serves as a living and sleeping area; an attic (*tilud*) above the soliu and soriba, which is a storage space for rice and other farm produce; and the *olod-olod*, a passageway between the soliu, soriba and kawas.

Ritual activities, such as the house-warming ceremony (*mohlukas*), begin at the veranda and proceed to the inner house. Fertility rites are performed in the tilud to invoke spirits to provide protection and to ensure good harvests.

The Lotud believe that the attic (*tilud*) represents the realm of the good spirits.

The bamboo house: Adapting to the environment

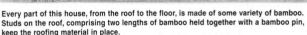

Every part of this house, from the roof to the floor, is made of some variety of bamboo. Studs on the roof, comprising two lengths of bamboo held together with a bamboo pin, keep the roofing material in place.

An attic, called a *loteng*, serves as an extra bedroom.

The bamboo house found in Tambunan shows how well the Kadazandusun people in the interior have adapted to their environment. Abundant supplies of no fewer than nine species of bamboo found in the district provide a good stock of versatile construction materials for dwellings. Local wisdom handed down from generation to generation has taught the Kadazandusun several ways of using the bamboo. Bamboo articles such as household utensils, musical instruments and traps are also widely used.

The Bonggi house: Permanence in a shifting culture

The Bonggi live on Banggi and Balambangan islands in the Kudat district of Sabah. Because they practise shifting cultivation, the Bonggi lead a semi-nomadic life. In the past, they built houses to last a couple of years. It was also customary for them to abandon a house whenever there was a death in the family. However, with the introduction of galvanized iron sheets as a roofing material, the Bonggi now tend to maintain their houses on a more permanent basis. Instead of shifting from field to field, they erect tower-like huts called *londukng* in or adjacent to their fields from which they guard their crops from pests.

Most Bonggi houses consist of three parts: a porch, a main room and a kitchen. The main room is referred to as *indu'bale* (the mother of the house), and is a living as well as sleeping area. The sleeping areas comprise raised platforms which may be defined for different members of the household according to their marital status and gender: unmarried girls, bachelors, parents and parents-in-law. The kitchen area (*depoordn*) is usually built after the family has moved in.

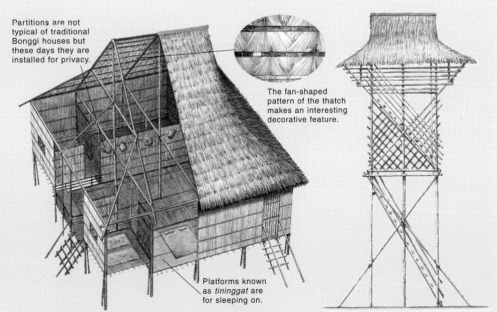

Partitions are not typical of traditional Bonggi houses but these days they are installed for privacy.

The fan-shaped pattern of the thatch makes an interesting decorative feature.

Platforms known as *tininggat* are for sleeping on.

The Bonggi house is usually built on mangrove tree stilts. The flooring is made primarily of timber from palm trees such as the *nibukng* and betel though tree bark is sometimes used. The thatch is laid on the roof to form a pattern, the most distinctive feature of the Bonggi house.

The *londukng*, erected in the fields, serves as a watchtower. It can stand up to 9 metres tall.

Longhouses of Sarawak

The longhouses of Sarawak epitomize the communal lifestyle of ethnic groups such as the Iban, Melanau, Orang Ulu and Bidayuh. Although the Melanau house differs from the others in being tall rather than long, its spatial organization is similar. Several families are accommodated in one large house. Each family has its own private unit but shares communal areas, such as the gallery where social activities take place, and the open deck where crops and laundry are dried.

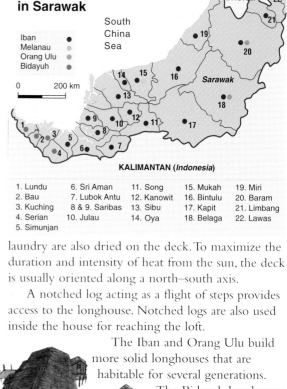

Distribution of longhouse communities in Sarawak

South China Sea

Iban
Melanau
Orang Ulu
Bidayuh

0   200 km

BRUNEI

Sarawak

KALIMANTAN (*Indonesia***)**

1. Lundu	6. Sri Aman	11. Song	15. Mukah	19. Miri
2. Bau	7. Lubok Antu	12. Kanowit	16. Bintulu	20. Baram
3. Kuching	8 & 9. Saribas	13. Sibu	17. Kapit	21. Limbang
4. Serian	10. Julau	14. Oya	18. Belaga	22. Lawas
5. Simunjan				

Longhouses are usually built parallel to a river. The location of rooms is referred to as upriver or downriver.

Notched-log steps provide access to a longhouse. A threatening face is carved at the top of the steps to prevent evil spirits from entering.

An Iban longhouse
In a longhouse, the *bilik* defines the family unit and the *ruai* represents the longhouse community as a whole.

The longhouse community

The longhouse is usually sited by a river for its fresh water and fish. The river is also a major means of transportation. The size of a longhouse may vary from 20 to over 80 apartments. Sometimes, because of site constraints, two parallel longhouses are constructed as the community grows. The average house may accommodate between 200 and 300 people although large longhouses have as many as 700 to 800 people. A longhouse is built of timber raised on wooden stilts which are at least 6 metres above the ground. The family units are arranged linearly along one side of the building and all the units open onto a covered gallery which runs the full length of the house. This is the space where children play, women attend to their chores, guests are entertained and festivals are celebrated. The gallery opens onto an open deck which is the drying area for crops such as rice and pepper; fish and

laundry are also dried on the deck. To maximize the duration and intensity of heat from the sun, the deck is usually oriented along a north–south axis.

A notched log acting as a flight of steps provides access to the longhouse. Notched logs are also used inside the house for reaching the loft.

The Iban and Orang Ulu build more solid longhouses that are habitable for several generations.

The Bidayuh longhouses tend to be built of less durable material because the areas where they live have fewer big trees for lumber. Their construction is mainly of bamboo.

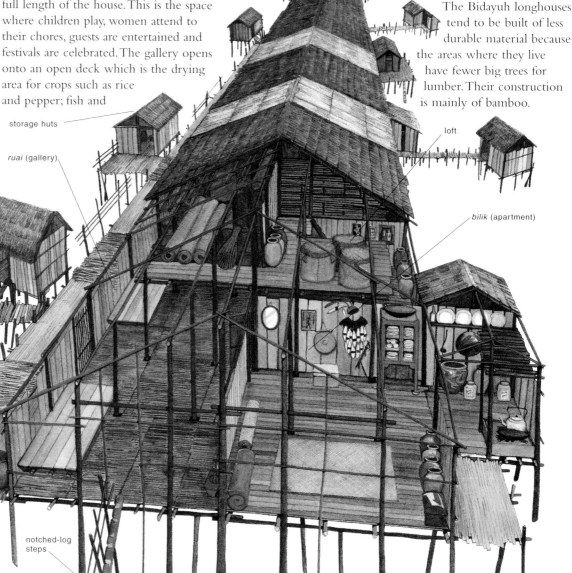

storage huts

ruai (gallery)

loft

bilik (apartment)

tanju (deck)

notched-log steps

Types of longhouses in Sarawak

The Iban longhouse

The Iban form the largest ethnic group in Sarawak. They can be found throughout Sarawak, especially in the lowlands, living in longhouses along the banks of main rivers and their tributaries. The point of entry to a longhouse community is the *penai'*, a bathing place at the river which represents, symbolically, the outer threshold of the community. It is thus through this that visitors enter the community, first bathing at the penai' before being welcomed into the house by their hosts. Each family room (*bilik*) is about 4 metres wide. Above the bilik is a loft for storing family goods. It is also used as a sleeping area for young, unmarried women. The cooking hearth is located near the door to the common gallery (*ruai*), which is where women pound rice during the day. The open deck (*tanju*) is adjacent to the ruai. The walls of the longhouse are made of tree bark and the roof either of thatch or shingles made from ironwood.

The contemporary longhouse is built larger to provide more space for the family. Each *bilik* has its own log steps.

The *tanju* is a sunny spot used mainly for drying crops. Gaps in the floor, made of split palm trunk, allow litter to fall onto the ground below.

The Melanau *rumah tinggi*

The Melanau are coastal people and their traditional dwelling is known as the rumah tinggi (tall house), so-called because it consists of three storeys. The family's valuables, such as brassware, fishing nets and tools, are kept on the top floor. The middle level is occupied by the family. The communal space, where the kitchen area is, occupies the first floor. The house is built on solid timber columns. The walls are made of tree bark and the floor of a double layer of palm trunks which allow for ventilation but are impenetrable to sharp objects. Each rumah tinggi houses about 20–30 family apartments. The fortress-like dimensions of the traditional rumah tinggi were designed to provide safety against attacks by enemies and pirates. As a further precaution, the notched-log steps at the front of the house were drawn up at night. Melanau tall houses are now rare as most Melanau live in individual houses.

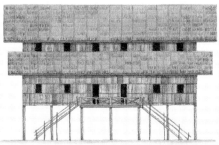

The jungle and the coast provide building materials such as the *nipah* palm used on the roof of a Melanau house.

A corner of the common gallery housed on the second level. The notched steps lead to the storage loft.

The Orang Ulu longhouse

The Kayan and Kenyah are part of a larger ethnic group known as Orang Ulu. They live in the interior highlands and are well known for building impressive longhouses. The Kayan and Kenyah chiefs express their aristocratic status by building larger and grander apartments within the longhouse structure. The chief's veranda is wider to allow his subjects to gather. His apartment walls are also painted with decorative motifs of spirit figures, animals and birds.

The contemporary Orang Ulu longhouse comprises two separate, parallel blocks. The first is a kitchen block which consists of a series of hearths which are linked to the corresponding family block by a covered passage.

The chief's apartment is located in the centre of the longhouse and is distinguished by its raised roof. The open deck is situated at the back, beyond the kitchen.

The chief's apartment in this Orang Ulu longhouse in the Sarawak Cultural Village is decorated with a 'tree of life' mural.

The Bidayuh longhouse

The traditional Bidayuh house is built on stilts using round tree trunks as posts and beams. The roof and end walls of the longhouse are made of thatch. To facilitate ventilation and to allow daylight into the otherwise dark interior, flaps made in the roof are kept open by a rattan rope secured to a post. A similar device is employed for the door.

Family apartments are often connected by internal doorways, especially when families are related.

The headhouse

The most outstanding feature of the Bidayuh longhouse is the circular headhouse, with its conical roof, known as *baruk* or *rumah pangah* (the centre for the community). This is where the village chief and elders discuss local politics and communal issues with the people. It is also where shamans conduct ceremonies and festivals are celebrated. A raised platform around the inside perimeter of the headhouse acts as seating and as a sleeping area for Bidayuh bachelors.

The headhouse is supported by a timber frame tied together with rattan.

In the centre of the headhouse, old skulls from former head-hunting expeditions are hung above the fireplace.

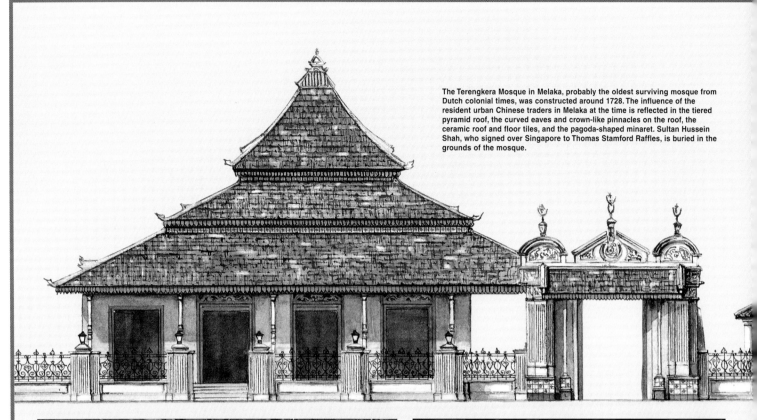

The Terengkera Mosque in Melaka, probably the oldest surviving mosque from Dutch colonial times, was constructed around 1728. The influence of the resident urban Chinese traders in Melaka at the time is reflected in the tiered pyramid roof, the curved eaves and crown-like pinnacles on the roof, the ceramic roof and floor tiles, and the pagoda-shaped minaret. Sultan Hussein Shah, who signed over Singapore to Thomas Stamford Raffles, is buried in the grounds of the mosque.

LEFT: The panelled walls of Istana Tengku Long, Kelantan, display the workmanship of highly skilled Malay woodcarvers. Woodcarving is the principal decorative element in the interior of a traditional Malay palace.

ABOVE TOP: A section of the carved border above the front porch of Istana Sri Menanti in Negeri Sembilan. The carving shows a mythical bird-like creature with a lion's head and a long, feathery tail. The coiled design of the tail, known as *awan larat* (*awan*, a cloud; *larat*, to drag on), is one of the most popular and basic woodcarving designs.

ABOVE CENTRE: Some traditional Malay carvings are formed by the technique known as *tebuk terus* (direct piercing), which produces delicate tracery patterns.

ABOVE: A carving on the interior wall of Istana Balai Besar, Kelantan, displays a form of carving commonly seen on the east coast of Peninsular Malaysia. The design, pierced and cut out from the pane, is made by the technique known as *tebuk timbul* (embossed piercing).

RIGHT: The exquisite decoration on the Istana Kenangan in Perak comprises fine, filigree carvings and patterns on the walls made from woven strips of bamboo.

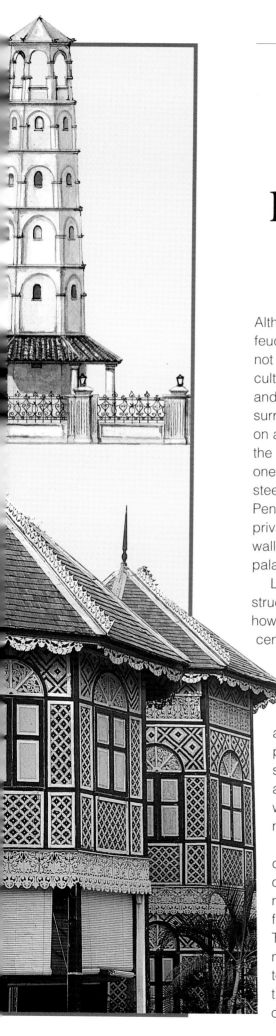

TRADITIONAL ARCHITECTURE OF PALACES, MOSQUES AND TOMBS

Although very few timber palaces over 100 years have survived in Malaysia, in feudal Malay society the palaces of the sultans were of paramount importance, not only as places of residence but as centres of administration, learning and culture. The palaces not only incorporated many of the beliefs of the sultans and reflected their way of life but, using the resources abundant in the surrounding countryside, were also completely attuned to the environment. Built on a larger scale than the traditional Malay house, they nevertheless contained the same basic architectural elements: a post-and-beam structure supporting one or, occasionally, more storeys or a series of connected annexes, and steeply inclining roofs in the style common to the various regions of the Peninsula. Elevated platforms and other internal devices signified public and private domains as well as hierarchy and formality. Elaborate carvings on the wall panels and posts, the work of skilled local craftsmen, distinguished the palaces from the homes of the common people.

Like the palaces, the first mosques in Malaysia were probably timber structures similar to the typical Malay house. Unlike these two residential forms, however, which were largely built on a rectangular plan up until the early 20th century, in the early 18th century, and continuing into the 19th century, mosques in Malaysia came to be built on a square plan with a tiered roof. This mosque style was based on the 15th-century Agung Mosque in Demak, northern Java, the prototype of the Southeast Asian Great Mosque. Following the tradition of timber construction of Malay houses and palaces, the mosque was built raised above the ground as a precaution against the degradations of insects and floods. At about the same time, a unique Melaka-style mosque emerged. Built on a square plan and on the ground, originally of wood but later of masonry, it was characterized by curved eaves, pagoda-like minarets, and stylized Oriental ornamentation.

Although Islam does not encourage the construction of elaborate edifices for remembrance of the dead, the practice of building tombs and mausoleums for royalty and well-known public figures has long been a part of the Malay tradition. The design of most of these tombs—and the larger, more stately mausoleums which may house several tombs—resembles a Malay-style pavilion, roofed in the style of the region where it is erected, and with openings to allow air and moisture to enter.

The tomb of Hang Kasturi, a famous Malay warrior, is in an old Malay burial ground in Melaka, believed to date from the 15th century.

Traditional palaces of the Peninsular west coast

In feudal Malay society, the istana—*the residence or palace of the sultan or raja—was of paramount importance. Not only was it the place where the sultan lived, but it was also the centre of learning, culture and the arts. The populace looked to it for guidance in almost all aspects of their lives, as well as protection from their enemies. In the construction of* istana, *the traditional Malay house post-and-beam method was used but on a grander scale.*

An artist's impression of the palace of Sultan Mansur Shah, Melaka, c. 1455, which was considered the symbol of Melaka's 'Golden Age'. According to the *Malay Annals (Sejarah Melayu)*, 'So fine was the workmanship of this palace that no other royal palace in the world at that time could compare with it.'

Showpieces of Malay craftsmanship

In the early days of the Malay sultanates, many of the Malay rulers and their families lived in timber palaces. These palaces featured beautiful carvings on

Istana Sri Menanti

Istana Sri Menanti in Negeri Sembilan is one of the few remaining timber palaces in Malaysia. It was built between 1902 and 1908 for Tuanku Muhammad Shah, the 7th Ruler or Yang Di-Pertuan Besar of Negeri Sembilan.

Istana Sri Menanti was designed by two local Malay carpenters, Tukang Kahar and Tukang Taib. The head draughtsman at the Public Works Department in Seremban, M. Woodford, was responsible for the detailed drawing, while the contractor in charge of the building was Tham Yoong.

The name Sri Menanti (Glorious Waiting) was given by an ancestor of the Negeri Sembilan royal family on his arrival from Sumatra, when he saw the fields of golden paddy waiting to be harvested.

The layout of the palace

The palace is four storeys high and is raised on timber posts made of *penak* wood, taken from a forest, Bukit Perigi, in Jelebu, about 64 kilometres from Sri Menanti. The first floor consists of reception rooms, and a broad veranda extending the entire length of the palace. At one end of the veranda is a dais from which the Yang Di-Pertuan Besar granted audiences to his subjects. The courtiers would sit on both sides of the veranda and the local chiefs at the far end.

On the second floor are the family bedrooms, including the state bedroom. The only furniture left in this room is a bed raised on a podium of three steps and decorated with richly carved gilt wood and silk drapes. The third floor contains the Yang Di-Pertuan Besar's private apartments, and the fourth, which is in the central tower, used to house the royal archives and the prayer room. These rooms could only be reached by mounting a steep ladder-like staircase in the royal chambers.

The bed in the state bedroom is one of the few original pieces of furniture left in the palace.

Construction with no nails

Altogether, 103 posts were used in the construction of the palace. The four main posts in the central tower, known as *tiang seri*, are 20 metres tall. The entire palace has been constructed without nails. Skilful carpenters used hardwood dowels and rivets instead. The main form of decoration is the carving on the timber posts. Furniture was not an important part of the decor as it was the tradition for members of the royal family, courtiers and guests to sit on the floor.

To show respect to the Yang Di-Pertuan Besar, the courtiers had to move on bended knees along the entire length of the veranda when seeking an audience with him.

The *singah sana* (throne room) where the Yang Di-Pertuan Besar granted audiences to his subjects.

the wall panels and timber posts. The rulers took great pride in the construction of fine palaces and were the patrons of craftsmen who were often housed in their courts.

The first detailed description of a Malay palace, found in the *Malay Annals* (*Sejarah Melayu*), was the istana built for Sultan Mansur Shah in Melaka around 1455: 'There were gilded spires, Chinese glass mirrors, a seven-tiered roof and seventeen bays, and it was tiled with copper and zinc shingles. The whole structure was raised on wooden pillars' (Sheppard, 1972). This palace, like many others, was unfortunately destroyed by fire. As a result, only a few timber palaces over 100 years old have survived in Malaysia.

Istana Kenangan is a 'jewel' of palace design. Its faceted facade sets off beautifully the intricate diamond-shaped patterns on the woven and painted wall panels. Filigree carvings embellish the eaves, fanlights and friezes. The carvings on the friezes are known as *kupu-kupu* (butterflies).

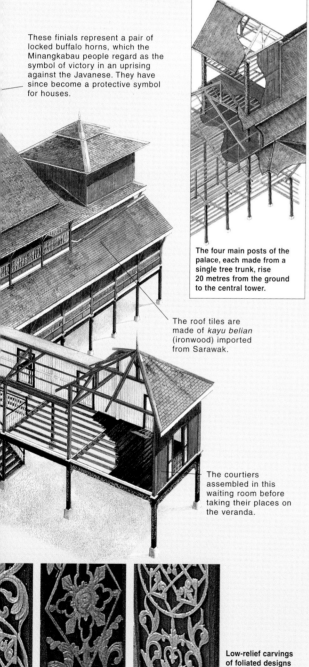

These finials represent a pair of locked buffalo horns, which the Minangkabau people regard as the symbol of victory in an uprising against the Javanese. They have since become a protective symbol for houses.

The four main posts of the palace, each made from a single tree trunk, rise 20 metres from the ground to the central tower.

The roof tiles are made of *kayu belian* (ironwood) imported from Sarawak.

The courtiers assembled in this waiting room before taking their places on the veranda.

Low-relief carvings of foliated designs decorate the timber posts and the front of the veranda. They show the exceptional skills and artistry of Malay craftsmen.

The bamboo palace

Istana Kenangan in Perak's royal town of Kuala Kangsar is the only Malay palace in Malaysia which has bamboo walls. For this reason, it is also known as Istana Tepas (*tepas* being the Malay word for woven strips of bamboo) or Istana Lembah. Istana Tepas was constructed in 1926 during the reign of Sultan Iskandar Shah (1918–38) by Haji Sopian Ahmad and his sons Zainal Abidin and Ismail, leading carpenters from Seberang Perai. It took about a year to complete.

The distinctive features of the istana are the polygonal structures, woven bamboo known as *kelarai* painted in black, white and yellow to highlight the diamond designs, and the carvings on the facade. The palace is made up of a series of polygonal-shaped houses connected by covered walkways. The end tower of the palace has an interesting polygonal roof covering the faceted structure. The diamond-shaped designs of the kelarai, combined with the filigree carvings on the roof ridges, eaves, fanlights and friezes, produce a striking combination of form, pattern, colour and texture. This istana is a showcase for the creative flair and artistic skills of the traditional Malay master builders and craftsmen.

The black timber supports effectively frame the fine carvings and woven patterns on the walls.

Istana Hinggap

Traditional houses in Negeri Sembilan bear a strong resemblance to the Minangkabau houses of Sumatra, Indonesia, because of the migration of Minangkabau settlers to the Peninsula in the 17th century. The ancestors of the Negeri Sembilan royal family came from Pagar Ruyung in Sumatra. The Minangkabau house style is reflected in the Istana Hinggap built at Ampang Tinggi in Kuala Pilah, Negeri Sembilan, around 1865–70, by the Yamtuan Ulin ibni Almarhum Yamtuan Hitam as a gift to his daughter, Tunku Cindai. It was also the temporary resting place for the Yamtuan when he travelled around the states, hence the name Istana Hinggap (*hinggap* means 'to perch'). The plan of the palace is typical of local traditional houses. It consists of a long, covered veranda, which is the public area, and a private area behind the veranda. As in Minangkabau palaces, there are no internal partitions; areas were marked out as occasion demanded. At both ends of the veranda, raised platforms formed daises, one for the Yamtuan and the other for the local chiefs. The inner wall of the palace, called *dinding janda ria*, is peculiar to palaces and is decorated with carved leaf and flower motifs as well as Qur'anic verses.

The Istana Hinggap is well known for its lavish carvings on the walls of the veranda. The palace has now been moved to the cultural complex in Seremban.

A cutaway drawing of a Minangkabau house from the Padang region of Sumatra, Indonesia, showing the typical rectangular plan and curved roof. A modified form of the Minangkabau style was adopted in Istana Hinggap. (After Dumarçay, 1991)

Traditional palaces of the Peninsular east coast

Although the old palaces in Kelantan and Terengganu are no longer occupied, their structures and designs reveal much about the environmental conditions and the diverse cultural traditions of the region. The extreme climate—of heavy rains in the monsoon season followed by a hot and dry period—influenced the construction of the palaces. Social segregation between men and women and the observance of court behaviour in respect to hierarchy dictated the spatial organization. Some of the features also provide evidence of past links with Patani, in southern Thailand, which was once a part of the east coast Malay kingdom.

The Istana Balai Besar in Kota Bharu, Kelantan, was built in 1842 by Sultan Muhammad II. The porch has an interesting polygonal roof. The ends of the roof ridges are shaped like a duck's tail, a feature known locally as *punggung itik*. This is peculiar to the east coast and to Patani in southern Thailand.

Unlike other palaces on the Peninsula, the audience hall was built on the ground for structural reasons. This set a fashion for two other palaces in Kota Bharu—Istana Seri Akar and Istana Jahar—which were also partly built on the ground.

The structure and order of a palace

Like traditional Malay houses, palaces were usually built on tall timber posts for protection from floods and enemies. But the elaborate carvings on the posts distinguished the palaces from the houses of the common people. The palaces usually consisted of a series of annexes with steep roofs whose valley gutters allowed rain to run off. *Singhorra* roof tiles of Thai origin were used in most of the palaces. They were watertight, much more durable than thatch, and fireproof. The high roof and perforated carvings along the wall panels allowed for good air circulation and kept the building cool even during the hot and dry season. Because the palaces were built with tenons and mortises, without the use of steel nails, they could be easily dismantled and reassembled, which facilitated the practice of giving away sections of a palace to married children or moving it in the event of major flooding.

The palaces of the east coast were usually organized into six main areas: the *anjung* (porch), *balai besar* (audience hall), *rumah ibu* (main house), *rumah tengah* (middle house), *rumah dapur* (kitchen area) and *jemuran basah* (veranda).

Hierarchy was expressed throughout the entire palace complex by variations in the floor levels and by raised platforms. Outside the palace, a similar order prevailed. The palace was usually sited in a large compound enclosed by an outer and an inner timber fence which established a barrier of public and private domain, and marked the territories for royalty and commoners.

Unfortunately, except for the Istana Balai Besar in Kota Bharu, Kelantan, none of the large palaces are intact in their original compounds. The Istana Balai Besar is now used only for official functions,

The entrance gate to the compound of Istana Seri Akar was one of the most elaborate found in the region. A *garuda* (mythical bird) formed the 'crown' of the gate. The doors, composed of vertical and horizontal panels, were flanked by stepped posts. Similar elaborate gateways can also be found in palaces and temples in Southeast Asian countries such as Thailand and Cambodia.

A reconstruction of Istana Seri Akar

Formerly known as Istana Tengku Putri, this palace was built by Sultan Muhammad II in 1886 as a wedding gift for his granddaughter, Tengku Mariam Kembing Putri, who was married to Tengku Putih, a Patani prince. It was renamed Istana Seri Akar by Tengku Abdul Kadir, the last owner, who carried the title Seri Akar di Raja. The istana has been abandoned and has fallen into disrepair.

This reconstruction was based on measured drawings produced by the students of the Faculty of Architecture at Universiti Teknologi Malaysia, Johor Bahru.

Perspectives through the thresholds

In traditional Malay architecture, much significance is attached to the threshold. This is demonstrated in the structure and spatial organization of Istana Seri Akar, where different domains were separated and articulated by a series of thresholds.

The first threshold was the main entrance gate and the second a panelled wall-cum-screen between the *balai besar* (audience hall) and the inner domain. The gate was the first of a series of vertical barriers symbolizing hierarchy. It mediated—along a horizontal axis—between a secular, public world outside and a delicate, privileged world inside. The sequence of entrances, from the gate to the door behind the balai, did not form a straight axis but, instead, a 'bent' one, which prevented eyes from peering directly into the complex. The tiled steps to the balai were composed of differing heights and treads. The fourth and last step, at a height of approximately 0.4 metre, compelled a visitor to consciously mount the step to reach the balai, thereby performing both a gesture of respect and indicating that he was of lower rank. The balai was separated from the inner domain by a long wall, the most elaborately decorated element in the entire palace complex.

Tiers signifying status

The door to the private domain was used only by the sultan, Tengku Putri and other members of their immediate family. Ladies of royal rank used the side entrance. The second threshold marked the change in nature of space, status and sacredness. This inner world, a sanctuary for women, was strictly off limits to all outsiders except female and some of the surrounding buildings have been converted into offices. Nearby is the Istana Jahar, which was built in 1885 by Sultan Muhammad III. The most prominent feature of this palace is the Balai Penghadapan, which has a pentagon-shaped balcony supported by columns.

The timber palaces in Terengganu are characteristically taller than the Kelantanese palaces. Because the individual buildings are more compact, they could be supported by the traditional *tiang* (house posts), whereas the complex roof structures of some of the Kelantanese palaces were too heavy and had to be built closer to the ground. The most famous palace was the Istana Maziah, which was the seat of power of the Terengganu sultans in the 19th century. Now only the main house, Istana Tengku Nik, remains intact.

Built by Sultan Zainal Abidin III in 1881, upon ascending the throne, Istana Tengku Nik was formerly part of the Kota Istana Maziah (the Fort Istana Maziah) complex. It has now been moved to the site of the Terengganu Museum at Losong. It comprises only a main house (*rumah ibu*) and a kitchen (*rumah dapur*). The main house, which stands on 16 2-metre posts, has a roof with a two-tier fascia board, while the kitchen has a hipped roof.

Istana Seri Akar, abandoned since 1955 when the last owner died, is no longer standing.

Wood-panelled walls were used on the exterior and interior of Terengganu palaces. The perforated carvings at the top of the panels were not only decorative but admitted light into an otherwise dark interior.

servants and relatives of the royal family. The corridor, on a lower level between the balai and the private domain, was used only by the servants: the necessity of stepping up and down at the boundaries provided an effective way of enforcing the rigid social structure of the time.

The *tapakan*: Prelude to the mother house

The corridor led to the *tapakan*, a raised dining area, where only women of the royal household and their relatives dined at weddings and on other feast days. The royal dining area and the princess's bedchamber formed Tengku Putri's quarters. Her special status was architecturally expressed by the construction of a separate roof over these two rooms. The princess's quarters symbolized the archetypal *rumah ibu* (mother house), the most intimate and sacred part of the palace complex. The canopied bed in the bedchamber, the most prominent object in the room, was the symbolic 'womb' of the mother house. Thus, the palace, built as a wedding gift for Tengku Putri, could be regarded as a fecund symbol of the beginning of a life cycle.

Parts of the palace

1. *Anjung* (porch)
2. *Balai besar* (audience hall)
3. Dais where members of royalty sat
4. Main door
5. Corridor
6. Raised dining area for members of the royal household
7. Tengku Putri's bedchamber
8. Tengku Putri's private washroom
9. Kitchen and servants' quarters
10. Inner fence
11. Outer fence (not completely drawn)
12. Tengku Putri's private garden

Wall panels in the *balai besar* and the bedchamber were decorated with elaborate carvings in foliage designs.

The Southeast Asian Great Mosque

The arrival of Islam in Southeast Asia in the 13th century was heralded by the appearance of a new mosque typology. Although the Southeast Asian Great Mosque that emerged retained the basic elements of its predecessors in the Middle East and the Indian subcontinent, it also differed in significant ways. By adapting to its new habitat, the local mosque became a striking symbol of the adaptability of Islam across cultural boundaries.

A 7th-century stone found at the Bujang Valley, Kedah, shows a multi-tiered design engraved on the stone. This is known as the *gunung-gunung* (mountain) pattern. Similar designs are frequently seen on the roofs of mosques and on Islamic gravestones.

Ancient influences

The many ways in which the Southeast Asian Great Mosque differs from its distant predecessors can be explained by the unique sociocultural and physical conditions of its new environment. Instead of the typical rectangular (or hexagonal) plan and multi-domed structure of the Middle Eastern type, the square plan and tiered roof of the Southeast Asian type were clearly inspired by strong regional and cultural forces.

The first mosques in Malaysia were probably simple timber buildings similar to the typical village house, although none of these structures have survived as evidence of this. It is possible, however, that the evolution of these modest structures into the Southeast Asian Great Mosque could have been influenced by pre-Islamic religious structures in the region. For example, artisans brought to the Malay Peninsula by traders could have built mosques in the temple styles of their homeland. The Chinese cultural origins of the Southeast Asian Great Mosque are also evident from a study of the Agung Mosque in Demak on the northern coast of Java, which is the oldest existing example of this mosque type. Built by a Chinese shipbuilder in the 15th century, it was evidently inspired by the pyramid roofs of Buddhist pagodas which, in turn, came by way of the Buddhist culture in India.

The Agung Mosque, Demak

The square plan Agung Mosque in Demak, northern Java, Indonesia, is usually dated to 1479 CE. It was probably the model for the Kampung Laut Mosque in Kelantan.

1. The mihrab, a wall niche, indicates the direction of Mecca.

2. The *mustaka* (finial), the clay decoration placed at the peak of the multi-tiered roof, is said to be a decorative element derived from pre-Islamic religious buildings.

3. The upper roof is supported by four main pillars called *soko guru*.

4. The *serambi*, an anteroom, was added later. It is used for social occasions associated with the mosque.

Form follows function

Apart from these cultural roots, the unique design of the Southeast Asian mosque type was determined by local building traditions and climatic conditions. The monumental and curvilinear masonry forms which typify Middle Eastern and Indian mosques were not suitable for the traditional post-and-beam construction that predominated in the tropics where timber was abundant.

Post-and-beam construction also allowed for more openings in the walls and eaves for ventilation which, together with the roof overhangs, were more appropriate in dealing with the high humidity and torrential rainfall of Southeast Asia. The use of timber also gave rise to other characteristics, such as the raising of the building on stilts to achieve greater durability against insects and water. In short, the Southeast Asian Great Mosque was a transformation of the Middle Eastern prototype, necessitated by practicality and cultural continuity.

In later centuries, when these timber structures were rebuilt or repaired in masonry, they retained their original form, and today they provide a striking contrast to the domed structures that are directly inspired by Middle Eastern and Indian examples.

Another key departure of the Southeast Asian Great Mosque from its predecessors was the absence of a minaret. Not being a compulsory feature of a mosque, this dominant symbol was significantly absent from mosques built in the early days of Islam in Malaysia. In some cases, it was replaced by the earlier form of calling to prayers which predated Islam—the use of a large, wooden drum. Later, as Islam became the dominant religion, minarets appeared as independent structures, separated from the older main building.

The Kampung Laut Mosque

The oldest surviving wooden mosque in Malaysia is the Masjid Kampung Laut in the State of Kelantan, purportedly built in the first half of the 18th century. It is in the style of the Southeast Asian mosque type, and was probably inspired by the Agung Mosque at Demak. Measuring approximately

Early foreign influences

c. 4000–1000 BCE	200 BCE	400 CE	500 CE	600 CE
Austronesian-speaking seafarers migrated through the archipelago into the Pacific. Houses with pitched roofs, raised on posts, recur and may have originated in southern China.	Peninsular port and inland sites connected by trade routes to the east coast. Long-distance sea trade in bronzeware, beads, pottery and iron tools began with mainland Southeast Asia, India and China.	Early port kingdoms evolved into entrepôts. Conducted trade in rain-forest products with China, India, West Asia and Southeast Asia. Oldest stone inscriptions found in South Kedah and Seberang Perai include Sanskrit Buddhist texts.	Hindu–Buddhist sculptures in stone and bronze found in Bujang Valley, Kinta Valley, and at Santubong. 	Asian maritime trade, centred on the Srivijayan kingdom in southeast Sumatra, prospered at the expense of the overland Silk Route between China, the Middle East and India. Srivijaya also controlled the port kingdoms of the Malay Peninsula.

16 metres square by 16 metres high, this modest timber post-and-beam structure originally comprised three concentric arrangements of columns, each supporting one of three tiered roofs. Later, an additional prayer area along the qiblat wall and a minaret were added.

The original building was undecorated except for the timber panelled enclosure and the roof pinnacle. It is the best preserved example of an authentic Southeast Asian mosque in Malaysia.

The Melaka style

It is probable that some of the earliest mosques on the Malay Peninsula were built in the port of Melaka, the centre for trade and commerce in the 14th–18th centuries. A strong Chinese cultural tradition, brought about by the predominance of resident urban Chinese traders, resulted in a unique Melaka style of the Southeast Asian Great Mosque. This was characterized by stylized Oriental motifs and ornamentation, curved eaves and crown-like pinnacles on the roof similar to Buddhist architectural details. The use of imported materials, such as ceramic roof and floor tiles, was another characteristic.

One of the earliest and best preserved examples of the Melaka style is the Terengkera Mosque, built around 1728 during the Dutch occupation. The Kampung Kling Mosque, built in 1748, is a smaller though more elaborately decorated example.

The Melaka-style mosque is also distinguished by its prominent pagoda-like minarets. These large structures were built in masonry in striking contrast to the timber mosques themselves. Although many people have tried to explain these unusual minarets, they are most likely the result of the Oriental cultural heritage of Melaka combined with the need for a dominant religious symbol to serve as a landmark within a dense urban area.

Decline into provinciality

The Southeast Asian mosque became the predominant style of Malaysian mosques in the Peninsula between the 18th and 19th centuries. In establishing itself within new areas, it would assume some of the characteristics of indigenous architecture. From the end of the 19th century, however, the style was clearly on the decline because of a preference for Middle Eastern and Mogul Indian mosque styles. Nevertheless, the Southeast Asian Great Mosque continues to be a much-cherished symbol in Melaka and also in rural areas throughout the country.

1. The Terengkera Mosque, Melaka (c. 1728). The Chinese-style pagoda-shaped minaret was originally built of timber, but was rebuilt in concrete in 1890.

2. Masjid Lama, Nilai, Negeri Sembilan (1928), is modelled after the Melaka-style mosque.

3. The Melaka State Mosque—Masjid Al' Azim—(1990) is a modern interpretation of the traditional Melaka style.

A pagoda from southern China. The structure is usually circular or octagonal and is built to preserve relics, commemorate unusual acts of devotion, act as an observation tower, or be an omen of good geomantic conditions. Based on the Indian stupa, the form was modified when introduced to China in 200 CE (Kohl, 1984).

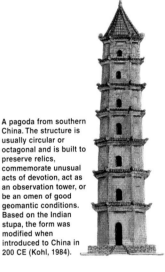

In the mid-1980s, 13 large, modular mosques based on the Southeast Asian mosque style were commissioned in Pahang.

The Kampung Laut Mosque, Kelantan
The timber floor of the mosque is raised about 1 metre above the ground. Four main columns support the uppermost roof, separating it from the double-layered outer roof by timber louvres which admit light and allow ventilation of the central space.

900 CE		1000 CE		1200 CE	1300 CE	1400 CE
First permanent religious shrines built, e.g. Candi Bukit Batu Pahat in the Bujang Valley, Kedah.	950 CE Arab and other Muslim traders began to arrive.	Srivijaya pre-eminent as a centre for Buddhist studies; built temples all over Asia.	1025 CE Cola rulers from southern India attacked Srivijaya and established their colonial capital at Kedah.	Spread of Islam brought about by Indian Muslim and other traders; evidenced by inscribed pillars and gravestones and artefacts such as coins found along the major trade routes; establishment of trading communities.	The Islamic inscriptions on the Terengganu Stone, found at Kuala Berang and dated 1303, are the earliest confirmed evidence of Islam in Malaysia.	Parameswara, a fugitive Palembang prince, established Melaka as a new power base in the Strait, and embraced Islam. The commercial success of Melaka reinforced the spread of Islam throughout the Malay World.

Malay burial structures

Although Islam as followed by the majority of the world's Muslims does not encourage the construction of elaborate structures for remembrance or veneration of the dead, the practice of building tombs and mausoleums for sultans and their close relatives, statesmen and well-known religious and other leaders has long been a part of the traditional Malay interpretation of Islam in Malaysia.

Muslim cemeteries, which are composed of a mixture of paired grave markers, graves demarcated by low walls, and graves sheltered by four-posted 'sheds', exhibit a distinctive landscape along a horizontal north–south axis.

Origins of the tradition

Despite the paucity of written sources and the limitations on archaeological research in the country, it is believed that the Malay tradition of building tombs and mausoleums derived either from religious concepts that came from the Indian subcontinent, especially from entrepôts where Indian influence made its greatest impact, such as the Srivijayan (7th century) and Majapahit (late 13th–14th century) kingdoms, or from organized Arab traders in the mid-10th century or, as late as the 13th century, from Muslim traders from India to whom the spread of Islam in the Malay Archipelago is generally attributed.

Cemeteries and gravestones

The common method of disposing of the dead in Islamic societies is burial in the ground. The majority of Muslims in Malaysia are therefore buried in cemeteries, or *kubur*, usually sited close to villages or within the compounds of mosques. Following a simple burial ceremony, during which the body is placed in a recumbent position in the grave, with the head pointed towards the north but with the face turned towards the west in the direction of Mecca, the grave is filled in with earth. Because all Malay graves are aligned on a horizontal north–south axis, this has resulted in a distinctive cemetery landscape.

The ends of the grave are marked with a pair of temporary 'markers', either of wood or stone or whatever other material is available in the locality, or simply with two small trees or branches. After 44 or 100 days, or even later, two permanent gravestones on which the deceased's name, date of birth and death and some Qur'anic verses are inscribed, are placed at either end of the grave and special prayers are recited.

Sometimes low structures of cement or other materials are built around the grave to demarcate it, and a simple four-posted shed erected to protect it. Resinous trees, commonly *pokok puding* (*Codiaeum variegatum pictum*), may also be planted to provide shade as well as a sweet aroma. Most graves, however, are left exposed to rain and dew because these are believed to be purifying.

Tombs in the Royal Mausoleum in Kelantan range from the simple (above) to the elaborate (below). Some have their own 'roofs' formed of a frame supported by four posts, and decorated with a short, yellow curtain, the colour signifying royalty. The tombstones, of various shapes, are each divided into a symbolic 'head' (*kepala*), 'body' (*badan*) and 'foot' (*kaki*). Yellow head-cloths are tied over the head of the stones when they are erected.

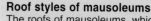

Roof styles of mausoleums

The roofs of mausoleums, which are the dominant architectural feature, do not follow any standard design but adopt the roof styles of houses.

The Royal Mausoleum at Kampung Langgar in Kota Bharu, Kelantan, has a two-tiered *perabong lima* (five-ridge) roof supported by pillars. The simplicity of the open-sided building enhances the serenity of the surrounding cemetery.

The Moorish-style flat roof and arches of the Sultan Mahmud Mausoleum at the Mahmoodiah cemetery in Kota Tinggi, Johor, contribute to a structure which is substantial yet open.

The Royal Mausoleum at Kuala Kangsar, Perak, is built in the style of the adjacent Ubudiah Mosque with a dome and horseshoe arches.

The tomb of Tok Pelam, a well-known religious scholar, at Kampung Ladang, Kuala Terengganu, is shaded by two types of roof: a hipped roof at the front and middle and a two-tiered pyramidal roof at the rear. Lattice work and ventilating blocks alleviate the 'closed' structure of the building.

Tombs

Old graves of notable religious scholars and warriors, such as those of Sheikh Ibrahim in Terengganu (above) and Hang Kasturi in Melaka (below), are often enclosed in a walled compound entered by a sturdy gateway.

Malay tombs, known as either *makam* (from Arabic) or *pusara* (from Sanskrit), are usually associated with royal burial grounds, although other, non-royal but distinguished personalities, such as religious scholars and, more recently, Malaysia's deceased heads of government, may be commemorated with specially erected tombs.

Unlike the simple graves of commoners which are left open to the elements, tombs are usually raised on plinths and encased in slabs of stone (except, sometimes, for a small opening in the centre of the top slab), embellished with Qur'anic verses, and topped with head- and footstones. The paired tombstones are often elaborately carved in a variety of shapes—round, square, rectangular or octagonal—each divided into a symbolic 'head' (*kepala*), 'body' (*badan*) and 'foot' or base (*kaki*).

Tombs may be situated within the compound of a royal burial ground—with or without their own roofs—or housed inside specially erected mausoleums.

Mausoleums

Mausoleums are large, open, pavilion-like structures designed to create a well-defined space to shelter the tombs within rather than as elaborate edifices. They also provide security for the tombs as well as a shelter for well-wishers who come and offer prayers at certain times of the Muslim calendar. They are usually placed in a strategic position within a graveyard adjacent to a mosque, where they perform the role of 'guardian' to the surrounding graves which are on a lower elevation.

Mausoleums are built on a slightly raised plinth, sometimes reached by steps. The roof, which is the most substantial architectural feature, is usually built in the house style of a particular region and is supported by pillars. For example, the Royal Mausoleum at Langgar in Kota Bharu has a two-tiered *perabong lima* (five-ridge) roof reminiscent of Kelantanese house roof styles, whereas the Royal Mausoleum of Johor, located at the Mahmoodiah cemetery, has adopted Moorish-style architecture. A modern interpretation of a Malay mausoleum is the one at the National Mosque in Kuala Lumpur designed for state leaders.

Where walls are a part of the mausoleum, arches or other openings allow air to circulate and moisture to settle as a means of purification and nourishment to the bodies of the deceased.

An architectural expression of 'nothingness' and 'emptiness'

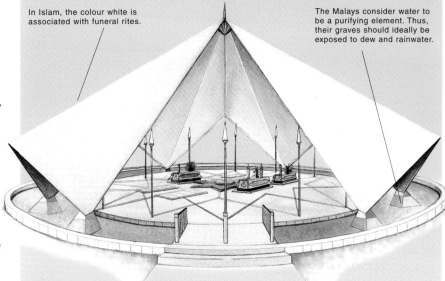

In Islam, the colour white is associated with funeral rites.

The Malays consider water to be a purifying element. Thus, their graves should ideally be exposed to dew and rainwater.

The Makam Pahlawan, or Warriors' Tomb, was built in 1965 within the complex of the National Mosque as a mausoleum for heads of state in Malaysia. It is one of the earliest post-Independence Modernist landmarks in Kuala Lumpur.

'Nothingness' and 'emptiness' are two spatial qualities that have contributed effectively to the solemnity and serenity of the Makam Pahlawan, or Warriors' Tomb, at Masjid Negara, the National Mosque, in Kuala Lumpur. The design, although sophisticated, is of the utmost simplicity and is a fine example of a modern interpretation of an Islamic mausoleum. It employs only two architectural elements: a circular plinth, which provides room for seven graves, covered by a multi-fold umbrella roof. The roof not only provides shelter but dispenses with the need for walls and columns. The triangular openings between the folds, which are large enough to allow a breeze to flow through the structure, also allow an uninterrupted view of the outside. A feeling of being 'in the inside of an outside space' is thus cleverly achieved.

Built in 1965, the architectural style of the Makam Pahlawan, like that of Masjid Negara, is based on a combination of Islamic and Modernist design principles. It is built of reinforced concrete with Italian marble finishing. The whiteness of the concrete roof and the colour, texture and coolness of the marble further enhance the quality of space and light in the interior of the mausoleum.

Kedah's Balai Nobat

The *nobat* is a ceremonial royal band which performs twelve melodies appropriate for joyful and sorrowful occasions, including the marriage and death of a ruler or his royal consort, and for royal processions. The five instruments which comprise the nobat—two drums, a kettledrum, a trumpet and a clarionet—are a treasured part of the royal regalia in the States of Kedah, Perak, Selangor and Terengganu, and are played and cared for by specially appointed court musicians.

In all but Kedah, the royal instruments are kept in a special room within the palace complex known as the *balai nobat*, which is linked to the main procession hall, the *balai rong*. In Alor Setar, Kedah, the nobat is housed in a separate three-storey tower, purportedly for acoustic reasons. Built in 1912–13 in the Western Neoclassical style, the balai nobat comprises three successively smaller octagonal structures supported by squarish pilasters. Blind semicircular arches are positioned between Corinthian columns, while bands of architrave mark each level. A small onion dome is perched at the pinnacle of a steep, octagonal, zinc roof.

ABOVE: The Balai Nobat in Alor Setar, Kedah, is painted yellow, a colour associated with Malay royalty.

LEFT: Nobat players from the court of Terengganu, c. 1920s.

ABOVE: The Teochew Association Temple in Penang is typical of Chinese temples constructed in the traditional style. It is single storey and built on a symmetrical plan. The most prominent feature is the roof, which is decorated with symbolic objects and mythical animals which are regarded as auspicious.

RIGHT TOP: The main doors to the Cheong Fatt Tze Mansion are flanked by side windows with ventilation spaces above.

RIGHT BELOW: A circular opening in the front wall of a temple in Melaka decorated with an elaborately carved *kirin* among clouds.

LEFT: A *kirin* or *kei loon*. This is a mythical half-horse half-dragon which the Chinese believe is a good *feng shui* symbol as it possesses a powerful 'force' that wards off evil.

ABOVE: The statue of Lakshmi, the Mother Goddess, flanked by two elephants, forms part of the *gopuram* (tower at the main entrance) of the Sri Markendeshvarar Temple in Penang. The lotus, which the goddess Lakshmi sits on, is associated with water, fertility and the creation myth in which the god Brahma came forth from a lotus.

FAR RIGHT: The gopuram at the Mahamariamman Temple in Penang is over 7 metres high and features 38 statues of gods and goddesses. In a Hindu temple, the gopuram is considered the threshold between the material world and the spiritual world.

RIGHT: The Hindu symbol 'OM' found in most South Indian temples signifies the trinity of the prinicpal gods: Brahma, the creator of the universe; Vishnu, who preserves it; and Shiva, who destroys it. Hindus intone 'OM' as a means of attaining oneness with a deity.

LEFT: The main hall of the Sri Markendeshvarar Temple leads to the *garbagraham*, the sanctum where the icon of the principal god is kept. Before a devotee approaches the garbagraham, he or she symbolically divests his or her ego by praying on the knees at the sacrificial altar placed in the main hall. The lotus on the ceiling is a common symbol used in temple decoration.

TRADITIONAL ARCHITECTURE OF THE IMMIGRANT COMMUNITIES

The visible face of modern Malaysia is a wonderfully complex tapestry. Strands from every part of both historic and modern-day life—language, dress, customs, religions, food, but more than anything else, the architectural heritage—lead one around the globe, revealing historic connections with other eras, other cultures and other lands. Malaysian architecture can be described as a synthesis of several immigrant architectures. Many of these stylistic or material influences have undergone various degrees of integration with not only the local traditional genres, but also other immigrant practices. The result is a truly Malaysian architecture.

The two major immigrant groups—the Chinese and the Indians—have, however, retained some elements of pure ethnic origin in their architecture, which provides an interesting comparison with the structures that have absorbed alien modifications.

Prominent among these are the temples built by the early settlers, often the first structures they built to both give themselves some link with their homeland, and also possibly to impress the local people. Most of the early community buildings of these immigrants—Indian and Chinese temples and *kongsi* (Chinese clan houses)—were built following traditional specifications and using imported materials. The Khoo Kongsi complex and the Sri Markendeshvarar Temple in Penang are strongly influenced by Chinese and Indian architecture.

In their domestic architecture, the Chinese also retained many of their own traditions. Thus, Chinese houses are firmly rooted to the ground, and follow the concepts of *feng shui* (Chinese geomancy). In some houses, superficial, decorative styles from other cultures have been grafted onto an orthodox form. One of the rare major private buildings in this category is the 19th-century Cheong Fatt Tze Mansion in Penang, one of the few examples built outside China of such an outstanding quality. This house was built following traditional Chinese concepts, but incorporated several Western features, such as wrought iron staircases and stained glass windows.

The influence of Indian architecture on local temples is highly visible. The familiar outline of the Indian temple, both in its simpler village forms in the rubber estates, and in the more structured Hindu temples in the urban areas, seems to have remained unadulterated by long association with Malaysian influences.

With the ever increasing fusion of ethnic styles, it is particularly important that the origins of the various strands woven into the architecture of Malaysia are noted and appreciated, and that the few buildings that are the source of so much of our eclectic architecture are zealously guarded.

A section of the roof from the Kuan Yin Temple in Penang displays colourful *chien nien* (porcelain) ornaments. Chien nien, literally meaning 'cut and paste', is a mosaic technique utilizing broken pieces of glazed porcelain.

Chinese construction and *feng shui*

To people of Chinese origin in Malaysia and elsewhere, feng shui is a combination of mystical beliefs, astrology, folklore and common sense that has a bearing on their daily lives. Evolving some 4,000 years ago in China from the simple observation that people are affected, for good or ill, by their surroundings, feng shui advocates living in harmony with the earth's environment and its energy lines so that there is a proper balance between the forces of nature. Feng shui is now frequently applied in Malaysia to change and harmonize the environment, including the built environment, so that the quality of people's lives will be enhanced.

Feng shui characteristics are clearly visible in the Kek Lok Temple in Penang. The temple is situated halfway up a hill with a commanding view overlooking the sea. A bridge across a meandering stream leads to a pond in front of the main entrance to the temple, which is painted, symbolically, yellow, red, white and green. Each of the five elements of fire, earth, wood, water and metal is ascribed a proper position in the temple building so as to ensure the auspiciousness and totality of the entire structure.

Reference tools of *feng shui*

Philip Cheong, a feng shui practitioner, uses the *lou pan* to note the orientation of a premise and to gauge the feng shui 'atmosphere'.

The *luo pan* is an elaborate reference compass which contains all the clues and symbols indicating good or bad feng shui.

The symbols and meanings on the eight-sided *pa kua*, with its three-tiered combinations of broken and unbroken lines, also offer clues for the practice of feng shui.

The *lo shu* magic square is used to calculate good and bad days for various activities. The grid pattern, which corresponds to the *pa kua's* eight trigrams, centred around a ninth pivotal point, is said to have appeared about 4,000 years ago on the back of a turtle as it emerged from the River Lo. By adding the numbers together in any direction, the result is always 15.

Learned mandarins were the feng shui practitioners at the imperial court in China, where they advised on all building projects. They studied astronomy and astrology and also had a profound knowledge of classical Chinese texts such as the *I Ching* or *Book of Changes* (above), which contained divinations and predictions.

What is *feng shui*?

Feng shui, which literally means 'wind and water', refers to the location and shape of mountains and valleys and the direction of watercourses, which are the direct result of the interaction of wind and water, and to the energy lines which flow from them. The practice of feng shui is concerned with harnessing auspicious energy lines, known as *qi* or 'dragon's breath', and avoiding or combating inauspicious energy lines, popularly called 'killing breath' or 'poison arrows'. The latter are caused by the presence of sharp, pointed objects or structures that channel bad feng shui, such as straight roads, steeply angled roofs or the edges of tall buildings.

Early feng shui practitioners subscribed to either of two schools of thought. These were the Form School, which rationalized good and bad land sites in terms of animal symbolism and the perceived balance of Yin and Yang, and the Compass School, which laid stress on complex calculations using the *I Ching* or *Book of Changes* in conjunction with the compass (*luo pan*), the eight-sided symbol (*pa kua*), and the magic square (*lo shu*). Modern-day practitioners tend to follow a combination of the two.

Regardless of the system followed, feng shui enables practitioners both to diagnose bad feng shui situations and then to find ways of taking precautions against their malevolent effects. The feng shui master, or *sifu*, with his extensive knowledge of the art of feng shui and armed with his compass or magic square and manuals, is thus consulted when a site for a building is being selected,

when the spatial configuration, orientation and landscaping of the building are being planned, and when the furniture is being positioned.

Thus, it is common for high-rise buildings in Malaysia, especially the newer ones in the cities, to incorporate design features that were determined by good feng shui practices. A feng shui master may work with the architect and engineer in the initial stages of a building's design. If an established company is failing, a feng shui expert may be called in to assess the building and suggest alterations to the structure or internal layout to improve the flow of prosperous energy.

Feng shui experts believe Malaysia's capital, Kuala Lumpur, has an abundance of feng shui because of the balance of the five elements: the earth and metal elements, represented by high-rise buildings and roads, are balanced by healthy trees lining the roads; the water element is represented in the many artificial waterfalls and fountains in public parks and in front of buildings; and the fire element is represented by brightly lit streets at night.

Yin and Yang in the environment

The Chinese believe that there are two opposing yet complementary forces, Yin (negative) and Yang (positive), that shape the universe and everything in it. Presented pictorially by the universally recognized symbol of the yolk and white of an egg, when combined Yin and Yang symbolize perfect harmony. The various structures surrounding people—natural or man-made—create varying amounts of Yin or Yang which affect one's *feng shui*. When these are in balance, the *qi* (life force) is auspicious, bringing prosperity and abundance.

A varied, balanced environment which receives plenty of fresh air and light, such as a combination of hills, valleys and waterways, is the the most favourable feng shui environment. When natural contours are lacking, such as in cities, meandering waterways may be imitated by the flow of traffic through busy, preferably curving, thoroughfares, while the silhouettes of buildings may be likened to the shapes of hills. Thus, the built environment in an urban landscape can have as much significance as the natural landscape in a rural setting.

ATTRIBUTES OF YIN AND YANG	
YIN	**YANG**
dark	light
female	male
passive	active
moon	sun
rain	sunshine
earth	heaven
water	mountains
winter	summer
cold	heat
tiger	dragon

Site orientation

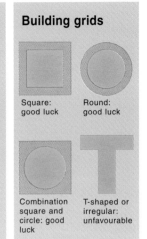

Square: favourable

Triangular: unfavourable

Oval: favourable

Rectangular: favourable

Building grids

Square: good luck

Round: good luck

Combination square and circle: good luck

T-shaped or irregular: unfavourable

Feng shui practitioners believe that people will live in harmony with their environment if the shape and orientation of their house site, as well as the actual shape of the house, follow feng shui principles.

Animal symbolism and landforms

In addition to describing the environment in terms of Yin and Yang, *feng shui* practitioners also explain it in terms of configurations of the landscape visible on the horizon and the position, shape and direction of watercourses suggestive of both real and mythical creatures. These creatures also represent the four points of the compass and are endowed with certain powers or attributes which affect man and his surroundings.

Ideally, a building, be it of Yin or Yang, should be placed halfway up a black tortoise mountain with a commanding view of the south, protected from cool winds and floods, and exposed to plenty of sun. When natural contours are lacking, the Yin–Yang balance can be maintained by carefully altering the natural configuration so as to accumulate *qi*.

Lions, symbols of protection, often stand guard at the main entrances to buildings.

CREATURE	DIRECTION	ELEMENT	SYMBOLISM
black turtle	north	water	winter, mountains, old age
red phoenix	south	fire	summer, growth
green dragon	east	wood	spring, the rising sun, birth
white tiger	west	metal	autumn, harvest, maturity

Feng shui application in the Cheong Fatt Tze Mansion

When Cheong Fatt Tze, a prominent overseas Chinese businessman and mandarin, built his 38-room Chinese courtyard mansion in Leith Street, Georgetown, towards the end of the 19th century, he would have consulted the most enlightened feng shui master of the day.

The main door of the mansion was aligned to face south-southeast, with the hills at the back and the sea in front. The back of the house was raised higher than the front to create a sense of ascendancy. Rainwater falling on the roofs around the central courtyard was collected via two downpipes encased in the west and east walls and allowed to accumulate in the sunken, granite slab-lined courtyard. The water from the west downpipe flowed exactly due east, the direction of the rising sun, while the water from the east downpipe flowed in a southwesterly direction along the top portion of a two-tier drainage channel in the floor, which then turned upon itself causing the water to flow in the reverse direction—northeast.

The water drainage system in the Cheong Fatt Tze Mansion is significant for three reasons: the slow-moving water is allowed to pool temporarily in the middle of the house, facilitating the accumulation of *qi*; the slow accumulation of water is likened to the slow amassing of wealth; the direction of the flow relates to the favourable numbers, 2, 6 and 8, on the *lo shu* magic square, numbers which recur in many other features within the house.

The auspicious drainage system of the Cheong Fatt Tze Mansion is marked on this drawing of the house.

The Cheong Fatt Tze Mansion is painted blue, a colour widely used on buildings in Peninsular Malaysia in the 19th and early 20th centuries. The four red columns on the first floor balcony denote the original owner's high rank.

A section of the internal courtyard built for the auspicious accumulation of rainwater.

Good feng shui is ensured by the use of brightly coloured decorative motifs on the walls.

49

Chinese temples

The Chinese immigrant builders and craftsmen who came to Malaysia built temples according to the architectural traditions of the southern provinces of China, mainly Fujian and Guangdong, where most of the immigrants came from. Initially, the shrines to house their gods or spirit guides were humble thatched structures, but later more elaborate temples, dedicated to deities of Taoist, Buddhist and folk beliefs as well as ancestor worship, were built. The oldest temple in Malaysia, the Cheng Hoon Teng in Melaka, is reputed to have been built in 1645.

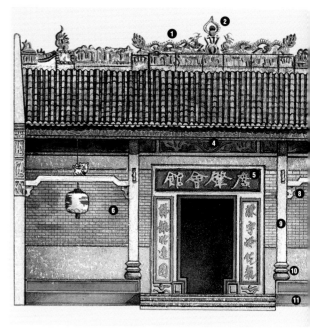

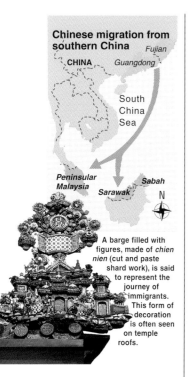

Chinese migration from southern China

CHINA
Fujian
Guangdong

South China Sea

Peninsular Malaysia
Sabah
Sarawak
N

A barge filled with figures, made of *chien nien* (cut and paste shard work), is said to represent the journey of immigrants. This form of decoration is often seen on temple roofs.

Design themes and symbolism

Chinese architectural principles in both domestic and religious buildings are basically the same, with the importance of a particular building determining its extent and grandeur. The architectural style of both types of buildings incorporates the fundamental belief that every aspect of life is closely related to nature. This is expressed symbolically in terms of design and colour. For example, the roofs of temples may resemble the shapes of waves, referred to as cats crawling, and of swallow and fish tails.

The five elements which represent the world, and their corresponding five colours—wood (green), earth (yellow), metal (white), water (black) and fire (red)—are also ascribed a proper position in a temple building to ensure the auspiciousness and totality of the entire structure. Red, in particular, is used extensively in temple decoration as it symbolizes the sun and the male Yang principle, and also suggests joy, prosperity and festivity.

Traditional methods of construction

The Chinese temples built in the 19th century in Malaysia are representative of the more peasant districts of southern China, with forms generally lower and flatter than in the northern temples. The structure of a temple can be divided—from floor to roof—into lower, middle and upper sections.

A lower platform, or base plinth, of stonework constitutes the lower section. The pillars, which carry the weight of the roof via a truss system, form the middle section. The truss system of wooden brackets, which supports the crossbeams and the weight of the roof, comprises the upper section.

A distinctive feature of the Chinese temple is its exposed structural elements which allow air to circulate in halls that are filled with smoke from joss sticks. The massive beams in the temple are often brightly painted and are treated as part of the temple ornamentation. They are also testimony to the carpentry skills of the master builders, whose timber structures are objects of admiration.

Layout conventions

The basic layout of a Chinese temple reveals formal regularity and rigid symmetry. The four local styles—Hokkien, Cantonese, Teochew and Hakka—represent clan or dialect differences. Each, however, adheres to the distinctive symmetrical layout.

Layout of the Cheng Hoon Teng Temple

To monastery
altar | ancestors' altar | rear garden | ancestors' altar | altar | office
"prayer pavilion" | rear courtyard | "prayer pavilion"
altar | altar | altar
side hall | main hall | side hall
ancestors' tablets hall | entrance to main hall | ancestors' tablets hall
stall | prayer pavilion
urn | front courtyard
garden | flag mast | flag mast | well
side entrance | main entrance | side entrance

The layout of a temple, such as the Cheng Hoon Teng Temple in Melaka (above), is basically a series of halls opening onto courtyards aligned along a vertical axis. While some smaller temples consist of only one hall, the more elaborate temples have as many as five interspersed with courtyards. The first hall is usually open-sided and is referred to as the prayer pavilion. This is where worshippers offer prayers before proceeding through an entrance hall to the main hall where the most venerated shrine of the chief deity as well as the temple bell and drum are kept.

The entrance to a courtyard in the Cheng Hoon Teng Temple, Melaka.

The open prayer pavilion, the first place of worship.

50

Features of a temple facade

1. The roof ridge, which may be horizontal or curved, is decorated with auspicious animals, such as dragons, which symbolize strength, justice and power.

2. The pearl in the centre of the ridge, known as the celestial pearl, represents the sun and the Yang force or energy.

3. The gable walls are raised higher than the roof ridge and may be straight, stepped, bow-shaped or wavy.

4. The horizontal wall frieze is either decorated with flower motifs or mythical animals.

5. The name of the temple is usually painted in gold letters on the lintel above the square-headed door.

6. Behind the free-standing porch pillars are the screen walls. These are either solid or pierced with openings carved into round or octagonal shapes formed of cement or ceramic bamboo stalks.

7. Near the top of the porch pillar is a connecting beam known as the lantern beam, on which a lion sits to ward off evil.

8. Decorative brackets carved in floral motifs support the lantern beams.

9. Square pillars embellished with Chinese characters support the roof.

10. The bases of the pillars are made of stone carved into round or square shapes.

11. The pillars in a temple rise from a stone or brick platform, or base plinth, as a protection against damp.

Although the progression of the layout may appear to move along an axis from front to back, the temple in fact extends sideways from the main prayer hall housing the principal deity.

The front pavilion is an open-sided structure which provides protection from the elements when prayers are being offered to the gods. The first hall serves as a reception area, leading to a courtyard or an entrance hall, before the main altar hall is approached. The effect of the elongated structure is to lead the worshipper ever deeper into the sanctuary until the most venerated shrine of the structure is reached. Lesser deities are placed in the side wings or in a hall further behind. Open-sided corridors usually connect the wings which house the administration offices and stores.

Features of a temple

Northern Chinese temples are characterized by wooden pillars, raised on stone bases, which support the roof superstructure. The southern China style, in contrast, features columns made of granite in a number of significant shapes. The main hall has round pillars while square ones are employed in less important corridor areas. The Cantonese, in particular, favour the more rigid square columns. Often a pair of majestic octagonal columns carved with an intricate assemblage of lions, dragons and serpents are used in the main hall, the loftiest in the temple. The Cantonese temple is also distinguished by higher proportions than the other southern Chinese temples. Roof ridges are straight and horizontal and the brickwork is usually plastered and painted. Often the gabled side walls rise above the roof pitch. Another characteristic is the ornate wooden or concrete tie beam, installed between pillars, that acts as intermediate bracing. The approach to the building is generally more rigid and the front prayer pavilion is often eliminated. Ornamentation in the temple usually consists of clay figurines and carvings on brick walls.

The Hokkien temples are closest in form and ornamentation to the Teochew ones, the main difference being that the latter have flatter proportions and less pronounced roof pitches. The Hokkien temple is more ornate, with widely curving roof ridges, although both styles make use of flamboyant porcelain cut and paste shard work known as *chien nien*. The Hokkiens also favour exposed red brickwork while the Teochew prefer plastered walls painted white or limewashed yellow.

The Hakka temples, while bearing a close resemblance to the Hokkien ones, have less ornamentation. The front pavilion of a Hakka temple is often part of the first hall, while the Hokkiens always have a separate but attached structure. The Hakkas, like the Hokkiens, prefer exposed red brickwork.

However, as with other facets of the culturally hybrid lives of the Chinese immigrants in Malaysia, the structural systems and the ornamentation employed by builders have been adapted and modified to suit local construction methods and materials.

Spiritual spaces

The spatial organization of a Chinese temple is not merely functional. It also creates a spiritual ambience through the association of different kinds of space. The semi-enclosed prayer pavilion is the transitional space between the material world and the spiritual; the open-air courtyards provide the nature element and tranquillity; and the enclosed prayer hall, filled with objects of veneration and the scent of incense and lighted joss sticks, imparts an aura of mystique.

This curved roof ridge was built in the style known as 'cat crawling'.

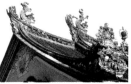
The roof ridge ending in an upward sweep is known as a 'swallow's tail'.

Four typical temple styles

The Cantonese Kuan Yin Temple in Kampar, Perak, has a straight, horizontal roof and prominent lantern beams. The stone lions at the entrance signify justice.

The prominent curved roof of the Cheng Leong Keng Temple in Jelutong, Penang, is typically Hokkien.

Teochew temples have flatter proportions and the roof ridge is not as steep as the Hokkien and Hakka styles. Above is the Teochew Association Temple in Chulia Street, Penang.

The roof and facade of this Hakka temple, the Tua Pek Kong in King Street, Penang, are similar to the Hokkien style but are less elaborate.

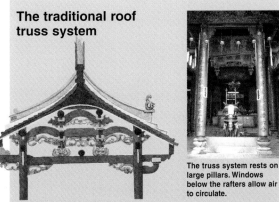

The traditional roof truss system

The truss system rests on large pillars. Windows below the rafters allow air to circulate.

In traditional Chinese buildings, the dominant feature is the roof. It gives shape to a building which otherwise would form a plain square or rectangle. The roof is supported by a truss system resting on pillars on either side of the roof. The entire roof structure, as well as the projecting eaves, is supported by a system of cantilevered units strengthened by brackets, known as *tou-kung*, which are themselves decorative features.

Chinese clan houses

In the early 19th century, many Chinese immigrants came to Malaysia from the provinces of Guangdong and Fujian as indentured labourers or simply to seek their fortune. Arriving on unfamiliar territory, they were drawn to fellow countrymen who shared a common background or who came from the same ancestral village. Out of their need for support grew the clan associations known locally as kongsi, *derived from two Chinese words meaning 'to share' or 'a shared company'.*

Gilt ancestral tablets are placed in kongsi temples for worship by clan members.

A section of King Street in Penang showing a row of kongsi houses. The Toi San Nin Yong Kongsi above is the association of the Sing Ling dialect group from Guangdong Province in China.

A support system

The *kongsi* house served as a dormitory, employment agency, meeting place, bank and social welfare source. The kongsi was also a promoter of education whose members placed great value on academic learning. Achievers in major examinations were honoured by having their names inscribed on wall plaques. Attached to the kongsi house was usually a temple and a prayer hall for housing ancestral tablets.

The two largest groups of Chinese, the Cantonese and Hokkien, established kongsi for different groupings of people: the Cantonese for those from the same districts, the Hokkien for clan or dialect groups. The undisputed leaders of *goh tai seng* (the five major surnames)—the Khoos, Tans, Yeohs, Cheahs and Lims—held control over the southern Chinese community. Each set out to build kongsi houses that would adequately reflect their lineage.

The kongsi enclave in Penang

A visit to the 'kongsi enclave' in King Street, Penang, shows the complex arrangement of buildings along both sides of the street. The kongsi enclave also typifies the complicated and extended relationships between family, clan, dialect and region prevailing in the immigrant settlements of Peninsular Malaysia. It is one of the most important historical-cultural areas in Malaysia.

An elaborate woodcarving (below) decorates the corner of the beam at the entrance to the Loo Pan Hong or Carpenters' Kongsi in Love Lane, Penang.

The Carpenters' Kongsi

Although this kongsi was founded in 1850, its temple was built only in 1865. It is a particularly significant building as it was known as the Mother Kongsi, or Temple of All Building Guilds, in the country. Loo Pan (a contemporary of Confucius, 551–479 BCE), was the patron saint of all building practitioners, from carpenters and builders to engineers and architects. He is credited with the invention of such basic tools as the right angled rule, compass, saw, axe, plumb line, *bak thau* or nib and thread to mark a horizontal line and extendable ladder; also the umbrella. In the 19th century, every Cantonese or Hakka craftsman and builder who came to Malaya would first call at the Loo Pan Hong in Penang before proceeding to seek employment elsewhere. The guild system had master craftsmen and apprentices who laboured for about three years without pay to learn the trade. Initially, craftsmen were located at the back while contractors inhabited the front, but around 1900, they formed a joint temple association, which has remained to this day

The guild building is typically Cantonese, with ornate ceramic figurines on the roofs, open courtyards with roof decorations, brick surface carvings, and a collection of ceremonial objects indicative of the richness of the past.

The decorative curved gables (left) of the Chan Shih Shu Yuen in Jalan Kinabalu, Kuala Lumpur, are visible from the courtyard. *Shek wan* (Guangdong-style pottery) friezes (right) featuring figures from Chinese mythology and popular dramas decorate the walls beside the main entrance.

The Hokkien, Cantonese, Teochew, Hakka and Sing Ling dialect groups erected their association houses, temples and boarding rooms along King Street as early as the 1800s.

The Cantonese Chong San Wooi Koon was one of the earliest to be founded in the 19th century. The well-preserved and impressive Straits Eclectic-style Lee clan house-cum-temple was erected in the 1920s. Both these kongsi paid homage to the memory of Dr Sun Yet-sen (first president of the Republic of China, 1866–1925). The neighbouring kongsi can also trace their roots to the 19th century, the most noteworthy being found in a cluster at the corner of King and Church Streets. They include surname clan associations such as the Ngs, as well as district associations such as the Toi San from Guangdong Province.

The Cantonese and Hakka members worship the Tua Pek Kong (great-grand uncle, symbolically meaning 'protector of the land') in their kongsi. This particular ensemble is especially significant as both the buildings and their surroundings have remained largely unchanged since they were first erected.

Kongsi architecture

The most notable example of traditional clan house architecture in the Straits Settlements can be found in the Leong San Tong Khoo Kongsi in Cannon Square, Penang. In 1852, 102 descendants of Khoo Chian Eng of Hai Teng district, Fujian Province, China, bought a large plot of land in Georgetown, Penang, and established a kongsi. After spending eight years, from 1894, building an elaborate clan temple, it was mysteriously gutted by fire 28 days after completion. It was rumoured that the extravagance of the temple had provoked the anger of the gods. When rebuilt, it was on a lesser scale but the clan nevertheless utilized the finest imported craftsmanship and materials, including a massive spread of gold leaf. Reputed to have cost over 100,000 Straits dollars, it was a masterpiece of Minnan architecture of the late Ch'ing Dynasty (mid-19th to early 20th century).

The Khoo Kongsi complex revolves around the granite-paved Cannon Square, so-called because of a large hole made by a cannon fired by the British during the Penang Riots of 1867. It includes a temple, an administrative building, a traditional Chinese theatre for staging opera, and rows of 19th-century houses that were originally meant only for members of the Leong San Tong (Dragon Mountain Hall). Guarded gateways, passageways and narrow approaches are typical features of the complex.

Other kongsi

Other styles and other groupings throughout Malaysia are no less important in the history of kongsi. In Jalan Kinabalu, Kuala Lumpur, the Chan Kongsi—Chan Shih Shu Yuen—is the site of an ancestral hall and a traditional lineage school. It formed the focus of the tin-mining community when founded in 1908 by Chan Siew Yin. The elaborate rooftop ornamentation in this temple is one of the finest examples of the Guangdong pottery known as *shek wan*.

The Kee Poh Huat Kongsi of Sungai Bakap, Seberang Perai, represents perhaps the only extant clan village in the country. Built by Teochew sugar planter Kee Kai Huat in the 19th century, its walled compound houses the ancestral clan temples and six connected buildings for the male Kees. Unlike other kongsi, the Hokkien Hui Aun Association is housed in a 1930s Art Deco-style building in Magazine Road, Penang. Founded in 1914, its members were trishawmen, mechanics and builders.

Although the kongsi in Penang and elsewhere are far less significant today, they remain an important expression of a traditional social system in a foreign land and are still popular places for worship and clan gatherings.

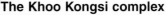

1. The narrow entrance into the Khoo Kongsi complex on Armenian Street.

2. The Khoo Kongsi temple has an Anglo-Indian portico, a feature peculiar to Penang temples.

3. The elaborate gable decoration on the kongsi theatre is a fine example of the intricate porcelain shard work known as *chien nien*.

4. Nineteenth-century row houses form a border around the temple, administrative building and theatre.

The Khoo Kongsi complex

The Khoo Kongsi in Cannon Square is the grandest clan complex in Malaysia and is Penang's greatest historic attraction. The magnificent kongsi temple is constructed on piers so that the three halls of worship are accessible only by climbing two flights of stairs— a feature probably adapted from the Malay kampong house to facilitate ventilation and provide protection. Both temple and theatre roofs typify Fujian styles, with ornate, sweeping curves and elaborate ornamentation of 'cut and paste' porcelain shard work known as *chien nien*. The temple roof, estimated to weigh 25 tonnes, is decorated with porcelain flora and fauna and mythological creatures and figures, including ladies in crinolines.

Indian temple traditions

Although the Indians in Malaysia form a minority ethnic group, they are prolific temple builders. The 17,000 or more Hindu temples and shrines scattered around the country not only range from simple roadside shrines dedicated to folk and tutelary deities to large temples dedicated to agamic gods and goddesses but also reflect the diverse religious practices within the Hindu religion and other subethnic divisions based on caste, area of origin in India and community grouping.

A large number of 'orphan temples'—small, individualized Hindu shrines located near trees by the roadside—can be seen throughout Peninsular Malaysia.

A typical rubber plantation shrine consists of a zinc roof, low walls and a cement floor.

The Ambal Temple at York Close, Penang, was set up by Indian washermen or dhobis. The simple cubical shrine is made more elaborate by the adornments on the roof.

Temple roots

The earliest Hindu temples found in the Malay Peninsula were vestiges of the Indianized settlement in Kedah dating back to the 4th and 5th centuries CE. In the modern era, temple building in Malaysia began with the settlement of a few Hindu Indian traders in Melaka in the 15th century, but it was not until the period of British colonialism (1786–1957) that the process of temple building accelerated.

With the opening up of the country in the 1900s for extensive rubber plantations, thousands of labourers were recruited from India to work in the estates and on the construction of roads and railways. By far the largest number of Hindu temples and shrines, therefore, are still to be found in plantations and in urban enclaves. Moreover, because the majority of the immigrants came from the rural areas of southern India, there was a tendency to build folk deity temples in the plantations and at railway quarters. These temples mostly comprised tin-roofed sheds, which were subsequently enlarged or renovated. The images venerated in these temples were usually ordered specially from India.

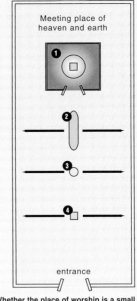

The splendid *gopuram* (entrance tower) of the Sri Kandasamy Temple in Scott Road, Kuala Lumpur, gives the impression of a sculptured mass rather than an architectural form. The structure of such a temple and the installation of the image or icon (*murthi*) would have had to conform to the requirements of agamic texts which contain details of the appropriate location, layout, materials for construction and the correct images to install.

Basic plan of a Hindu temple

Meeting place of heaven and earth

1. *Garbagraham* (sanctum)
   The innermost sanctum where the main image of the chief deity is kept. The square represents earth and the circle heaven.

2. *Vaganam* (vehicle for the deity)
   The vehicle of the chief deity (e.g. Nandhi the bull is the vehicle for Shiva) faces the main sanctum.

3. *Palibeedam* (sacrificial altar)
   This is where food and flowers are placed by the priests and where devotees pray on their knees.

4. *Kodisthampam* (flagstaff)
   Devotees prostrate in front of the flagstaff which points towards the sanctum.

entrance

Whether the place of worship is a small shrine or a large temple it invariably incorporates the following elements: the *kodisthampam* (flagstaff), the *palibeedam* (sacrificial altar), the *vaganam* (vehicle for the god) and the *garbagraham* (sanctum).

The agamic temples, on the other hand, which are related to higher-level Hinduism and use Sanskrit as the ritual language, tended to be located in the urban centres where traders and middle-class Indians settled. The temples built by the various communities nevertheless reflect subtle differences based on their social and professional backgrounds.

The Melaka Chitties and their temples

Since the time of the Melaka sultanate in the 15th century, there has been a small but thriving Indian Hindu community in Melaka called Chitties by the local population because of their involvement in trade. Like their Indian Muslim counterparts, the Melaka Hindus married local Malays and this encouraged them to adopt certain cultural traits of the Malays, such as language, dress and certain food preferences. But unlike them, they clung tenaciously to their Hindu religious worship. Most of them live in the Indian enclave of Kampung Kling in Melaka, where all the important Chitti temples are located. Although agamic in principle, the Chitti temples are plainer than the mainstream South Indian temples.

The entrance to the Chitti Temple in Melaka is marked by a three-tiered tower with a niche in each level for a statue of a god.

The Nattukottai Temple in Penang, built by the Chettiar community, has a magnificent multi-levelled *gopuram*.

Two shophouses in Jalan Dato Keramat, Penang, have been converted into the Patthar temple.

The Chettiar temple

The Chettiars are an Indian community known for their devotion to the Hindu deity Murugan and for their zeal in temple building. Unlike the Indian immigrant workers, the Chettiar community is largely made up of wealthy traders and moneylenders. They are ardent upholders of the agamic tradition and their temples, built in several strategic places in Peninsular Malaysia, are a symbol of authority and arbitration on religious and social matters for the various Chettiar clans. The first Chettiar temples were constructed in Penang and Melaka in the style of the Chettiars' homeland. Only the best teak wood from Chettiar sawmills in Burma was used for the superstructure. Workers were drawn from among their many non-Chettiar servants. One of the best known Chettiar temples in Malaysia is the Nattukottai Temple in Penang, built in the South Indian tradition.

The domes crowning the top of the wall of a Chitti temple in Melaka are not a feature of other Hindu temples in Malaysia.

This image, known as a *vaganam*, the vehicle for the god, also comes in other animal forms.

The Patthar temple

The main concentrations of another small subethnic group, the Patthars or goldsmiths, are in Kuala Lumpur and Penang. Their most prominent temple dedicated to the personal deity of the Patthar caste, Sri Kamatchi Amman, is located in Jalan Dato Keramat, Penang. This ornate temple occupies two shophouse lots which protrude into the street.

Originally built in 1914 as a simple shed, in 1923 two shophouse lots near the place where most Patthars had their business establishments were acquired by the caste elders for the new temple. Since then, the temple has been extended and renovated several times.

The Sri Lankan Tamil temples

The first settlements, or quarters, for the Ceylonese (Sri Lankan) Tamil railway staff, civil servants and others who came to Malaysia were developed close to the railway station in the Brickfields area in Kuala Lumpur, and nearby along Scott Road. These areas later developed and merged into one enclave of Sri Lankan Tamils, which became known as Sinna Yelpanam or Little Jaffna. Here, the first Hindu temple, the famous and highly ornate Sri Kandasamy Temple, was established in 1902 in Scott Road. Since then, several other notable temples have been built throughout the country.

Moving with the times

The increasing sophistication of the Indian community has had an important influence on the construction of temples in Malaysia. Although many new temples have been built in the urban areas, with the present trend of converting plantations into new housing estates, some of the older temples are vulnerable to demolition or relocation.

The North Indian community temples

The North Indian Hindu community in Malaysia is a small but cohesive group consisting of Punjabi, Gujarati, Sindhi, Bengali and other regional groups. The structure of their temples, which are mostly located in urban areas, is radically different from the South Indian temples as are their worship rituals. Externally, the temples are simpler. Internally, the prayer area comprises an uncomplicated hall with the shrines for the images placed at one end. The temple decoration consists mainly of non-figurative carvings in the preferred medium of marble.

A dominant characteristic of the North Indian-style temple is the *sikhara*, a multi-tiered tower composed of semi-domes, such as that on the Kunj Bihari Temple, the country's first North Indian-style temple, built in Penang in 1899. The Lakshmi Narayan Temple in Kampung Kasipillai, Kuala Lumpur, is a striking North Indian-style temple. No expense was spared in building this temple which includes high-quality marble and sculptures imported from India.

The Kunj Bihari Temple in Penang Road features a multi-tiered tower of semi-domes.

The Sikh Punjabi

Unlike the Hindus, the Sikh Punjabi worship in *gurdwara*, which can be housed in any type of building. There is no particular emphasis on religious decorations except that in some gurdwara the main entrance is distinguished by three domes and marked by a Sikh flag.

The Lakshmi Narayan Temple in Kampung Kasipillai is the only North Indian temple in Kuala Lumpur. The domes are painted a deep saffron orange because Hindus consider saffron a sacred colour.

Hindu temples in the South Indian tradition

Temples are called aalayam *or* kovil *in Tamil. The word* aalayam *comes from* anma *which means 'soul' and* layam *which means 'a place where one's anma can find sanctuary'. Similarly,* ko *means 'God' and* vil *or* il *means 'place'; thus,* kovil *means 'God's abode'. As most Malaysian Hindus are of southern Indian descent, the majority of Hindu temples in Malaysia are built according to the South Indian tradition.*

An artisan from southern India working on new figurines in the Sri Kandasamy Temple in Kuala Lumpur. In India, these figures were traditionally carved out of stone, but nowadays it is more usual to build up the figurines with cement plaster on metal frames and then mould and sculpt them to the required shapes. The work is closely supervised by a temple architect known as *sthapati*, a craft guild title that is as old as agamic architecture itself. A sthapati is not only trained as an architect but is also a master sculptor, for in Hindu temples the decoration is an intrinsic element of the design.

The human body and the Hindu temple

The Hindu temple is constructed to resemble the parts of a human lying on his back, with the head pointing towards the west and the feet towards the east.

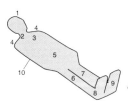

1. *Garbagraham* (head)
2. *Artha mandabam* (neck)
3. *Maha mandabam* (chest)
4. *Thuara palaka* (shoulder)
5. *Sthampa mandabam* (lower abdomen)
6. *Sabha mandabam* (thighs)
7. *Irandavath vaasal* (knees)
8. *Kalyana mandabam* (lower legs)
9. *Gopuram* (feet)
10. *Prakaram and thirumathil* (skin)

A timeless art form

To a Hindu, a temple is more than a place of worship. It is a place specially chosen as the residence of the Supreme Being as the ruler of the universe. The Hindu has chosen three places to worship the Supreme Being: in his heart, in his home, and within a consecrated temple. The temple structure itself is conceived of as the universe, and its principles of construction, form and decoration, as well as the rituals that take place within its walls, are all aimed at achieving the sublime. Architecturally, Hindu temples are an ancient art form born of a great religious tradition. Their design has changed very little over the centuries.

The structure of a temple

The Hindu temple is constructed to resemble the form of a human body lying on its back with the head of the temple positioned towards the west and the feet towards the east. This composition underlies the symbolic functions of a Hindu temple.

The Sri Markendeshvarar in Penang is a fine example of a South Indian-style temple. It is a 'male' temple dedicated to Lord Shiva. Its *garbagraham* or *karuvarai*, the holy of holies, corresponds to the head. This is where the main image of the chief deity, Lord Shiva, is installed. The garbagraham in

this temple is rectangular in form. The design of a garbagraham adheres strictly to the agamic principles of temple construction (the *Agama* are the scriptures that detail all aspects of religious life, including temple building). On top of the garbagraham is a tower or *stoopi* known as the *vimana* which is always elaborately decorated with images or deities.

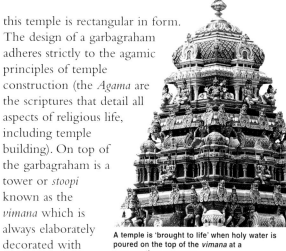

A temple is 'brought to life' when holy water is poured on the top of the *vimana* at a consecration ceremony.

The *artha mandabam* or *muga mandababam*, corresponding to the neck, is the passage between the garbagraham and the *maha mandabam*, the great hall. The priest stands here, facing the garbagraham when he performs the *puja* (prayers).

The *maha mandabam* corresponds to the chest. The shrine for Shakti, the consort of Lord Shiva, is placed at the north-facing side of the maha mandabam which faces south. It is customary to have a separate entrance for a goddess in a 'male' temple. In the Sri Markendeshvarar, the entrance is situated on the southern side.

The *thuara palaka*, or the shoulders, represent the guardians of

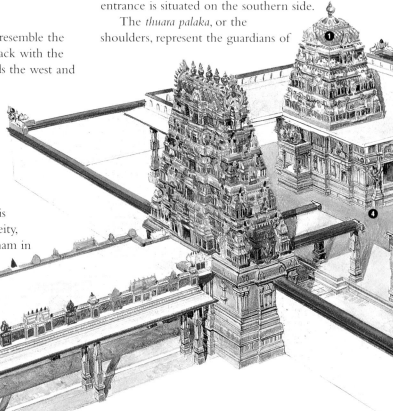

secondary entrance

Each corner of the temple is guarded by a *ghana*.

Sri Markendeshvarar Temple, Penang

This temple in Penang is a fine example of a South Indian-style 'male' temple dedicated to Lord Shiva. Rectangular in plan, its various parts are positioned to symbolize the form of a recumbent human being.

the garbagraham. These guardians assume different names depending on the temples in which they are placed. In a Shiva temple, they are known as Sandan and Prasandan, and in a Vishnu temple as Jayan and Vijayan. The guardians of the Goddess Shakti are known as Soobathra and Subathra.

The *sthampa mandabam* corresponds to the lower abdomen. This is where the *vaganam* (vehicle for the deity), the *palibeedam* (sacrificial altar), and the *kodisthampam* (flagstaff) are placed. The type of vaganam varies according to the deity. In this temple, a statue of a bull, Nandhi, is used as the vaganam. The palibeedam is placed immediately behind the vaganam. Here, devotees symbolically divest their egos, unpious thoughts and arrogance by praying on their knees. As the altar is in the position of the navel, the devotees are supposed to sever their material attachments at the sacrificial altar.

The kodisthampam is usually a timber post encased in copper or silver plate. It symbolizes the soul being freed from evil and ignorance. The base, middle and top of the flagstaff are also representative of the three principal powers of the Hindu pantheon: creation, protection and destruction.

The *sabha mandabam* is the space which corresponds to the thighs. This is where musical and dance performances and lectures

A thuara palaka guards the garbagraham.

are held. Just below the sabha mandabam is the second entrance, the *irandavath vaasal*, which corresponds to the knees.

The *kalyana mandabam* corresponds to the lower legs. Here the decorated statues of the chief deity and other deities used for processions during festivals are stored for safekeeping.

Corresponding to the feet, the *gopuram*, the tower at the main entrance, is the symbol of the cosmos. This is of particular significance since Hindus believe this is where they pray at 'the feet of their deity'. The gopuram is the tallest feature in the temple so that it can be seen from afar.

The outer structure

Prakaram, the 'skin' of the temple, refers to the courtyards and the spaces surrounding the shrines. The principal prakaram is the one surrounding the garbagraham. There are normally three prakaram for an agamic temple. For larger temples there are as many as seven. Devotees are expected to go round the prakaram at least three times before they offer prayers to the chief deity. The *thirumathil*, or external walls, complete the temple complex.

Symbolism in Hindu temple decoration

Gopuram
The gopuram in the Sri Markendeshvarar Temple comprises five tiers of figurines. Each figurine represents the various incarnations of Lord Shiva and characters from legends associated with the period when the temple was built. Sculptures in Hindu temples remind devotees of the physical and the ideal worlds. When devotees enter the temple, they are supposed to divest themselves of concerns with the material world.

Main door
The main door is specially carved out of quality timber, usually teak or sandalwood. The carvings on the panel depict either scenes from legends or religious items. In this particular temple, the carving on the door is of the sacred chariot meant for the gods. The symbol of the sun god can also be seen on the chariot. A *kalasam* (vessel for holy water) decorates the top of the chariot.

Garbagraham

The garbagraham is built on a raised three-step podium to indicate that it is the shrine of the chief deity. It is a free-standing structure inside the temple with its own roof and walls. The entrance is guarded by a pair of *thuara palaka*. On each of their hands a finger points upwards to indicate that God is one. Another finger points downwards to indicate that devotees should surrender their souls at the feet of the deity.

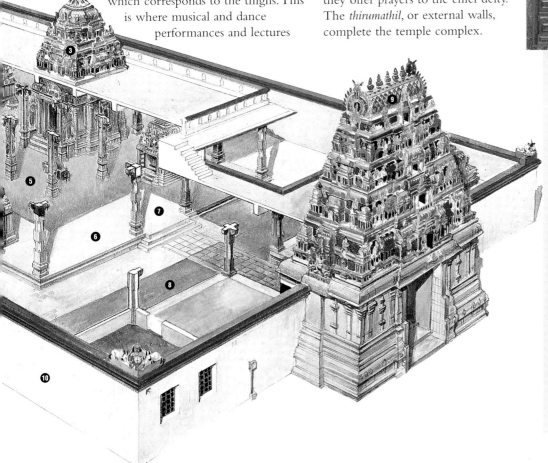

1. Pekan (c. 1900), the capital of Pahang and the seat of the sultanate, was situated by the Kuantan River, which provided transportation into the interior.

2. Beach Street in George Town, Penang (c. 1904), used to run along the waterfront. The southern end of the street was dominated by Chinese wholesalers.

3. Facing Fort Cornwallis in Penang (c. 1907) was the Padang, an open ground used originally for military exercises, and at the other end the City Hall (1903).

4. Following a fire in 1884, most of Kuching—from Main Bazaar to Carpenter Road—was rebuilt in masonry, as shown in this view about 1900.

5. Government House, Sarawak (1860), from Spenser St John's *Life in the Forests of the Far East* (1863).

6. The pavilion-like market in Johor Bahru (c. 1920), located on the waterfront on the north side of the Johor Strait.

7. Melaka (c. 1907), showing the Melaka River running through the town centre and the spires of St Francis Xavier's Church.

EARLY TOWNS

From about the 5th century CE, trade with the Arabs, Chinese and Indians and with other Southeast Asians played an important role in changing the lifestyle of the early inhabitants of the Malay Peninsula. With exposure to outside influences, the early inhabitants became receptive to change, and with growth in economic activities, several coastal villages grew into early towns. These early towns on the Peninsula comprised Melaka and Alor Setar on the west coast, Johor Bahru in the south, and Kota Bharu, Kuala Terengganu and Pekan along the east coast. In these early towns, the local Malays often lived close to the palaces while the foreign merchants coalesced in trading areas on the coast, usually near the mouths of rivers.

The conquest of Melaka by the Portuguese in 1511 started a series of European interventions that were to change the rural nature of the early towns. Clearly aligned streets and, occasionally, town squares, were introduced, and masonry replaced timber in the construction of urban buildings. While the Portuguese used local laterite extensively as building material in Melaka, the Dutch built in brick. At the end of the 19th century, with extensive immigration under the British administration, new towns sprouted throughout the Peninsula, including Taiping, Ipoh, Kuala Lumpur, Seremban and Kuantan, all of which grew in parallel with the growth of economic activities. These new towns were characterized by shophouses along their high streets. It was only after World War II that other building types, such as tall buildings, began to appear.

George Town in Penang, founded in 1786 by Captain Francis Light as a trading post for the East India Company, was the first major British outpost in Peninsular Malaysia. By the 19th century, it had become the largest town in the Peninsula and was served by a comprehensive infrastructure of roads, railways, telephones and telegraphs. Civic and government administrative buildings began to appear, surrounded by shophouses and fringed by the residential buildings of new settlers and traders. The town was a potpourri of different ethnic groups and had the cosmopolitan ambience of a busy entrepôt. George Town today has retained most of its urban fabric and efforts are being made to conserve its early character.

In Sarawak, Kuching was the first settlement to develop into a town. Its early development was inextricably linked with the Brooke Dynasty, which ruled Sarawak from 1841 to 1941. The transformation of Kuching from a bustling trading post under the rule of James Brooke, the first 'White Rajah', into a modern town was largely due to the efforts of Charles Brooke, the second Rajah who succeeded his uncle in 1869. During his 49 years' reign, masonry buildings were introduced, supported by roads, street lighting and a drainage system. By the end of his reign in 1918, Kuching had developed into an organized town with a waterfront bazaar, framed by masonry shophouses, and other civic buildings.

Chetty Street in Penang was dominated by Chetty (Chettiar) moneylenders and other traders from southern India.

The Malay urban tradition

The Malays have traditionally lived in small settlements known as kampongs. Urbanization developed as a result of the gradual transition of a village to an expanded centre of political power focused on a local sultan and a nucleus of trading activities. But apart from a greater concentration of inhabitants, the general appearance of an early Malay town was not very different from a kampong. Most of the structures were built of timber with thatched roofs. The distinguishing features of the town centre were the sultan's timber palace, a mosque and a market.

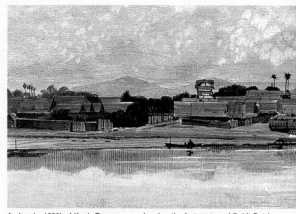

A view (c. 1890) of Kuala Terengganu showing the fort on top of Bukit Putri and the riverine village of timber and thatch houses at the foot.

The royal towns

Kota Bharu and Kuala Terengganu on the east coast of Peninsular Malaysia and Alor Setar and Johor Bahru on the west coast are 'royal towns' representative of the Malay urban tradition. The two main focuses of these early towns were the royal courts and the trading centres of the merchants.

'Malaye Proas', an engraving by Thomas and William Daniell (1810). The development of the east coast towns was shaped principally by trade. The large numbers of natural harbours and inlets attracted both Indian and Chinese traders who were also interested in the wealth of the whole region.

In the centre of the town was the *istana* (palace), usually a complex of several buildings where the sultan lived and from which he ruled. The lifestyle of the sultan influenced and shaped the lives of the common people. He kept a feudal army to protect the populace who, in turn, had to pay rent and tribute taxes. From the rural hinterland, the sultan sought more manpower and territory. The intention was to have a maximum number of dependants to display the strength of the state and, in the event of war, to mobilize the populace to defend its territories. The royal town also supported

From riverine settlement to port town

Although Kuala Terengganu was a well-known trading centre from the 2nd century, it was basically a settlement made up of several villages: Kampung Cina, Kampung Tiong, Kampung Banggol and Kampung Lorong Haji Ismail. The houses were built from wood obtained from the riverside. In 1880, a big fire destroyed a large portion

builders and craftsmen who catered to the needs of the court. But it was trade with countries outside the Malay Archipelago which played the greatest role in converting sparsely populated riverine settlements into thriving port towns. The merchants who came to trade coalesced in various parts of the towns. Out of this complexity, the royal towns created a unity representing the Malay urban form.

East coast towns

The State of Kelantan was closely identified with its capital, Kota Bharu, which was its principal port and the seat of the royal sultanate. Its strategic position

Characteristic features of a Malay town

This plan of Kota Bharu, Kelantan, shows the location of the royal square, the mosque and the market. Boats would carry produce to and from the town.

Early Malay towns usually evolved around the sultan's palace and the mosque because these were the two centres of cultural and religious activities. Traditionally, there were no fixed boundaries in a Malay town, although the distance up to which the prayer calls of the town mosque could be heard sometimes determined the town's limits.

1. The palace gates of the Istana Balai Besar in Kota Bharu, Kelantan. The original gates symbolized the royal status of the town.

2. The Istana Jahar in Kota Bharu, built in 1885 for the Raja Bendahara (State Minister), was where audiences with the common people were held.

3. The Kota Bharu market is a traditional, bustling, one-stop shopping centre where fresh produce, household products and clothing can be bought.

4. The Muhammadiah Mosque, the main mosque in Kota Bharu, continues to be the centre for religious studies.

The Balai Besar (Great Hall) in Alor Setar is an open-sided building featuring a *bumbung Perak* (a hipped roof with gable-like ends), a grand staircase and Art Nouveau wrought iron decoration. Built in 1904, it replaced the 18th-century Balai Besar which was demolished.

Istana Besar in Johor was built by Sultan Abu Bakar in 1866. The palace was furnished with Western furniture and artefacts which the sultan collected on his trips abroad.

Terengganu market scene, Georgette Chen (1907–93). In every Malay town there is usually an open-air market place where fresh produce and other goods are sold.

West coast towns

Located between Sungei Kedah and Sungei Anak Bukit in the paddy-growing region of Kedah, Alor Setar was chosen by Sultan Muhamad Jiwa Zainal Abidin as his seat of government in 1735. It was the eighth and last centre of Kedah's royal adminstration, the capital having moved several times previously because of civil wars and battles with Thailand and Aceh in Sumatra.

Although Alor Setar was said to have no large junks of its own, and hence its shipping was limited to coastal trade, the state did trade with China and Gujarat (northern India) in the 18th century. Not only was Kedah visited by foreign traders but through the influence of Arabs local merchants equipped their ships to convey goods to India and bring back commodities which were in demand along the Strait of Melaka. This had, no doubt, brought prosperity to the state, as the splendid buildings in Alor Setar were testimonies to the wealth of the town. Istana Kota Setar, built in 1763, was sited within a walled compound with a triple-arched gateway. Near the palace was a three-storey Balai Nobat, which contained the instruments of the royal orchestra, or *nobat*, and a two-storey audience hall, the Balai Besar. Both of these buildings were demolished and replaced by newer versions in the early 20th century.

Johor Bahru is the most recent royal capital. Sultan Abu Bakar chose it as his capital in 1866. As late as 1894, the entire population of the state numbered no more than 300,000, the majority of whom were labourers or small-scale farmers. In spite of its economic development, the rate of its urbanization was far less rapid than the towns in the tin-mining states of Selangor and Perak. This was because the modernization of the administrative and economic systems occurred in Johor under the indigenous government which had limited funds. Sultan Abu Bakar was, however, a skilful and shrewd ruler, and he improved the governance of Johor while resisting direct British intervention. Eventually, in 1914, Johor came under British administration and the last of the Malay towns was absorbed by the colonial rulers of the British Empire.

of the settlement. When the settlement was rebuilt, rows of brick shophouses made their appearance in Kampung Cina, on the bank of the Terengganu River. The residential areas, consisting of traditional Malay timber houses, were located close to the royal square, signalling the beginning of the development of modern Kuala Terengganu.

on the coast facing the South China Sea and the Gulf of Thailand made it an ideal trading port, although the town remained uniquely Malay.

The old 'royal square' is located on the eastern side of the Kelantan River where most of the town's prominent buildings can still be found. These include Istana Balai Besar, a pillared audience hall with a Thai-style roof, enclosed by a high, wooden fort wall, which predates the palace built in 1844. The other prominent structure is Istana Jahar, formerly the palace of the Raja Bendahara (State Minister). This palace has a pentagon-shaped porte-cochere with a first-floor balcony from which members of the royal family could watch ceremonies held in front of the palace. Near the royal palaces is Masjid Muhammadiah, built in 1867.

Kuala Terengganu, located at the mouth of the Terengganu River, is one of the oldest ports in Peninsular Malaysia, and one of the two ports marked on Ptolemy's 2nd-century map of the Malay Peninsula. It was also mentioned in 13th-century Chinese mariner's maps.

The town in the 19th century was dominated by a fortress, Kota Bukit Putri, built on a small hill overlooking the estuary of the Terengganu River. Sultan Baginda Omar (1839–76) once resided in the fortress. At the base of Bukit Putri was the royal compound, enclosed by a high, stone wall. It contained Istana Maziah, a palace constructed in 1894 for Sultan Zainal Abidin III. Another landmark, Masjid Abidin, the town's mosque, was originally a wooden structure built during the reign of Sultan Zainal Abidin II (1793–1808) but reconstructed in brick in the late 19th century. The oldest part of the town was centred around the waterfront. Nearby was Chinatown, known as Kampung Cina, which consisted of old, southern Chinese-style shophouses with distinctive curved roof ridges, arched windows, carved signboards and decorative tiles.

Kuala Terengganu's Chinatown, strategically located near the river, is the oldest enclave of Chinese shophouses in the town.

The colonial legacy in Melaka

Melaka is unique in being the only town in Malaysia to have been ruled by three Western colonial powers. Already a wealthy port and an important centre of trade by the early 16th century, it attracted Westerners who came to the East to set up trading posts. In 1511, a fleet led by Alphonso d'Alburquerque, the Portuguese Viceroy of India, conquered Melaka, thus establishing a long period of colonial rule which began with the Portuguese, followed by the Dutch, then the British, that lasted for almost 450 years. The most tangible legacy of the colonial period are a number of buildings which exhibit the architectural styles of the colonists.

Built in 1521, St Paul's Church, now a ruin, was originally known as Our Lady of the Annunciation. The Portuguese used local laterite which was suitable for building solid, massive walls which could withstand attacks from enemies.

The Santiago Gate (Porta de Santiago) is all that remains of the great Portuguese fort A Famosa. Also known as the Land Gate because it opened onto the suburb of Ylier (Bandar Hilir), it was modified by the Dutch in 1670 to include an S-shaped passage to prevent direct gunfire.

The Portuguese in Melaka

After their conquest of Melaka in 1511, the Portuguese consolidated their position by building a fortress at the foot of St Paul's hill, near the mouth of the Melaka River, which they called A Famosa ('The Famous'). Bordered by swamps, the river and the sea, it enjoyed a natural strategic position. It was marked by a huge, square tower 36 metres high, built of laterite, the red clay found near Melaka. Soon afterwards, a massive wall with many bastions was constructed around the hill to fortify the whole town. After each attack by Johor and Aceh, and later by the Dutch, the fort was strengthened, eventually becoming so strong that it lasted until 1641 when the Portuguese surrendered to the Dutch.

The building activities of the Portuguese converted Melaka into a Christian town characterized by many masonry buildings, among them five churches, several chapels, a monastery, two hospitals and two palaces. The local laterite was used extensively as building material. It was also during this period that Melaka developed some form of town planning and drainage of the surrounding area. Streets were laid out in an orderly fashion and houses were built in designated areas along the coast, on the banks of the Melaka River and along the Ayer Leleh, a stream which flowed south of the town. Around the town of Melaka three suburbs developed, the largest being Upeh, or Tranqueira, the Portuguese word for 'rampart', on the northwest side of the fortress. Upeh consisted of a market, the two parishes of St Thomas (Kampung Kling where the Indians lived) and St Stephen (Kampung China where the Chinese lived), surrounded by the Melaka River, the sea and the 1.6-kilometre-long rampart. A bridge at the mouth of the Melaka River connected Upeh with the fortress. The other two suburbs, each with a parish church, were Sabac and Ylier (Bandar Hilir). The timber houses in Sabac, northeast of the fortress, were built on stilts over the river and were inhabited by fishermen. Ylier extended from the stream Ayer Leleh to Ujong Pasir.

Cosmopolitan Melaka

Melaka under the Portuguese continued to be a thriving trading centre because of its strategic position. The town was divided into two parts. The Portuguese governor and administrators lived within the fort while the general population lived opposite, on the other side of the river. There was a cosmopolitan mixture of local Malays and immigrants—Chinese, Indians, Burmese and Javanese—who settled in various quarters of the town. The Malays lived in Kampung Bendahara, named after the Bendahara, one of the chief administrative officials of the state. The foreign merchants' quarter was known as Tranqueira or Upeh. The Java bazaar, or central market, was situated at the mouth of the river. Here, every variety of rice and edible grain was sold by the Javanese merchants.

Melaka and its suburbs as it existed under the Portuguese in 1613, based on the maps and texts of Eredia.

The Portuguese fortress A Famosa ('The Famous') was located at the foot of St Paul's hill, upon which the palace of the Melakan Sultanate was originally sited. A 2.4-metre-thick stone wall encircled the entire hill. On the seaward side, a four-storey tower guarded the fort, while on the landward side, nine bastions were built at stategic points. According to Manoel Godinho de Eredia, a 16th-century writer, the fortress contained the castle, governor's palace, bishop's palace, town hall, five churches and two hospitals.

1. Fortress (A Famosa)
2. Cathedral of Our Lady of the Annunciation
3. Town Hall
4. Prison
5. Pauper Hospital
6. Royal Hospital
7. Bishop's Palace

The Dutch era

The Dutch seized Melaka after a five-month seige in 1641. By then the city was in ruins with almost every building damaged by the bombardments. The Dutch, however, rebuilt the damaged fortifications and cleared the ruined buildings. Churches and monasteries were converted into hospitals and arsenals, and two more bastions were added (named Mauritius and Middelburgh) at the river mouth, with walls between 6 and 7 metres high. A drawbridge was built to connect the civilian quarter to the other side of the river.

The Dutch occupation of Melaka extended the range of building types in the town. Where the Portuguese had concentrated on the construction of fortifications and churches, the Dutch built comfortable brick houses and a large administrative building, the Stadthuys, to house the Dutch governor and the town's civil administration. The architectural style of the Stadthuys is similar to colonial Dutch buildings in South Africa.

The Dutch architectural style is still highly visible in Melaka. Decorative influences can be seen in the trimmings and ornamental details of the facades and window copings of many of the buildings in Heeren Street (Jalan Tun Tan Cheng Lock) and Jonker Street in Melaka, as well as in other parts of the Peninsula (see 'The Chinese shophouse' and 'The Melakan townhouse').

ABOVE: This lithograph from Auguste-Nicholas Valliant's *Voyage Autour du Monde* (1852) shows the Town Square in Melaka, with Christ Church in the centre and the Stadthuys (town hall) on the right. The church, which took 12 years to build, was completed in 1753. Its timber beams, each cut from a single tree, are still intact. The gable designs are characteristic of the Dutch style at that time.

LEFT: The central courtyard in the Stadthuys. Constructed in 1641, the Stadthuys was the residence of the Dutch governor and also the administrative centre. The building features thick masonry walls, sash windows and doors framed in heavy hardwood.

This view of Melaka by an anonymous English artist (c. 1870) shows how much Melaka had expanded from a small settlement to a burgeoning town by the time the British occupied it in 1824. At the base of the hill is a house with Dutch gables. Across the river are Chinese houses backing onto the sea.

British Melaka

A turn in political events in Europe spearheaded the British presence in Melaka. In the Napoleonic Wars, the armies of revolutionary France overran Holland in 1795. The Dutch, fearing their overseas settlements might also be taken over by the French, requested the British to provide protection to all their trading posts. Although the British were expected to occupy Melaka temporarily, their arrival was an important turning point in Malaysian history. In 1824, with the signing of the Anglo-Dutch Treaty, the British exchanged their trading post in Bencoolen (Sumatra) for Melaka and consequently Melaka came under British colonial jurisdiction. By the end of the 19th century, the British were involved as a colonial power throughout the Peninsula to protect tin mining and other interests.

Sadly for Melaka, the British Governor, William Farquhar, was ordered to demolish the fort that the Dutch had rebuilt after capturing it from the Portuguese. But over the next 162 years of British rule, its administrators did bring about improvements in land and sea transportation. An iron jetty at the harbour was built for steamers in the 1880s to replace the old wooden one. By 1900 the Public Works Department had constructed about 320 kilometres of roads in and around Melaka. They had also installed a telephone and telegraph communications system. Public buildings, with their emphasis on symmetrical planning, harmonious proportions and the use of classical motifs, reached their height during the period of British rule.

The heavy timber door set into the archway at the entrance to Christ Church epitomizes the solid construction of the Dutch style. The fanlight above the door is a feature widely adopted in Melakan shops and houses.

Built in 1906, the Chee Mansion on Jalan Tun Tan Cheng Lock exhibits Dutch decorative styles on its facade.

The Melaka Club, now the Proclamation of Independence Memorial, was a stronghold of the colonial community. Architecturally, the building is an eclectic mix of the bungalow form, Islamic domes and European columns and pilasters.

Early George Town, Penang

The earliest British influence on Malaysian architecture can be traced to the buildings of George Town, a trading post of the East India Company, established in 1786. Starting with the construction of Fort Cornwallis at the tip of the northeastern cape of Penang Island, the colonial town spread west and south towards the central range, eventually becoming home to what is today Malaysia's largest collection of 19th- and early 20th-century buildings and of its best examples of Anglo-Indian, Chinese and Indian Muslim architecture.

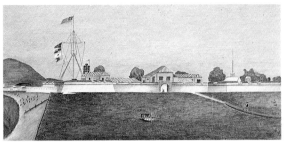

This 1853 watercolour of Fort Cornwallis by a Madras Artillery gunner, marks the spot near where Captain Francis Light first landed in 1786. The present stone fortifications were constructed (like most public works at the time) by Indian convict labour in 1810. It is a good example of military fortification of the period, although it was obviously not designed to oppose a serious attack.

Penang's Clock Tower, 60 feet tall, was erected in 1897 to mark the Diamond Jubilee (60 years) of Queen Victoria's reign.

Building George Town

After Captain Francis Light took possession of the British settlement of Penang in 1786, he assumed responsibility for mapping out the nucleus of George Town, the island's new capital, named after the reigning British monarch, King George III.

Light laid out the site of George Town by clearing Penaga Point, a flat, triangle-shaped piece of land on the northeast of the island, separated from the mainland by a 3-kilometre-wide strait. The town centre was immediately occupied by the various ethnic groups whom Light had invited to help build George Town. The Eurasians of Phuket and Kedah set up their presbytery and church along Bishop Street and Church Street. The Chinese from Kedah and Melaka lived and traded from their shophouses in China Street. The Indian Muslims from Kedah, as well as those who followed the East India Company to George Town, quickly expanded Chulia Street westwards with their bungalows, mosques and saints' tombs, strongly modelled on the traditional South Indian style. A common market was set up by the water's edge at the end of Market Street.

Pitt Street was reserved for religious purposes; eventually, the Anglican church, St George's Church, the Chinese Goddess of Mercy Temple, the Hindu Mahamariamman Temple and the Kapitan Kling Mosque all came to be built along this axis. Within this densely built-up grid, timber and *atap* were uniformly replaced by brick and terracotta after the last major fire in 1826.

The streets of George Town

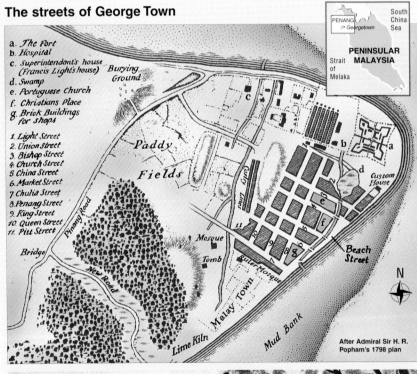

a. *The Fort*
b. *Hospital*
c. *Superintendent's house (Francis Light's house)*
d. *Swamp*
e. *Portuguese Church*
f. *Christians Place*
g. *Brick Buildings for shops*

1. *Light Street*
2. *Union Street*
3. *Bishop Street*
4. *Church Street*
5. *China Street*
6. *Market Street*
7. *Chulia Street*
8. *Penang Street*
9. *King Street*
10. *Queen Street*
11. *Pitt Street*

After Admiral Sir H. R. Popham's 1798 plan

Early George Town, located at a point called Tanjung Penaigre (Penaga Point), consisted of a rectangular grid of crisscrossing streets bordered by Light Street along the north beach, dotted with the buildings of the East India Company officers and merchants; Beach Street along the eastern harbour front, lined with government offices, shops and godowns; and two smaller roads, Chulia Street to the south and Pitt Street to the west.

These postcards of early George Town illustrate the prosperity and beauty of this main northern entrepôt.

1. Bishop Street, c. 1910, showing the modest, first-generation brick shophouses in the commercial part of the town.
2. The handsome Customs Building near the waterfront, with its prominent clock tower, was originally the Malayan Railway Building—'the only railway station without a rail'— completed in 1907 to service passengers who wanted to travel to the mainland.
3. The Penang Sports Club, set in an extensive garden, was an exclusive club for the colonial élite.
4. City Hall, on the western side of the Esplanade, completed in 1903, is an example of turn of the century Victorian-style public architecture.

The arrival of Asian immigrants

The commercial town was soon taken over by immigrants from southern China who arrived in increasing numbers from the mid-19th century. With typical industry, they rapidly developed streets of shophouses interspersed with *kongsi* (clan houses) and temples. The latter were mostly erected by itinerant craftsmen, some of whom later settled in George Town and joined the Carpenters' Guild in Love Lane. Taxes levied on every 20 feet of frontage determined the layout of these pioneer shophouses, which up to the early 19th century were mostly low, plain buildings placed back-to-back, and limewashed in indigo, with wells dug in their courtyards. The facades of the handful of merchant shophouses of that period were decorated with ceramic shards along the ridges and cornices.

To the south lay the 'Malay Town', subsequently carved into Armenian Street and Acheen Street. The Muslim communities here and elsewhere dwelt in dense kampongs in half-brick half-timber bungalows clustered around their *waqaf* (trust) lands. As the early port thrived mainly on the Sumatran trade, the Acehnese formed a colony and were joined by their trading partners, the Hokkien Straits Chinese, in the mid-19th century. In a climate of secret society feuds, the Straits Chinese clans, expanding through family migration, built fortified neighbourhoods around their clan temples, of which the most famous is the Khoo Kongsi (see 'Chinese clan houses').

Penang's public facilities were greatly improved in the 1830s. The British, relying for the first hundred years on public works staffed with convict labour from India, built handsome government buildings which were typically scaled-down versions of their imperial monuments in India. The Malabari builders whom they employed were retained into the 20th century to work on Muslim structures, and to work for Chinese contractors servicing government contracts.

Moving to the suburbs

As the town spread haphazardly beyond the initial grid towards Prangin Canal and the Bound Ditch (now Transfer Road) in the early 19th century, the Europeans, Eurasians and Armenians retreated in waves to the suburbs, where the Malayan bungalow continued to evolve (see 'Origins of the Malayan bungalow'). Tree-lined avenues led to the clubs, country houses and plantations, and to the Waterfall and Penang Hill, popular places for recreation. The Penang Free School, a fine example of colonial architecture, was chief among the English-medium educational institutions to play a role in westernizing the tastes of the local populace.

In the last quarter of the 19th century, the more refined residential row houses, with their ornate facades and carved wooden interior screens, started

Two of the earliest places of worship in Penang were the Acheen Street Mosque (left) and St George's Church (right). Founded in 1808 by a prominent Arab trader from Aceh, Tengku Syed Hussain Al-Aidid, the Acheen Street Mosque is noted for its unusual octagonal minaret. St George's Church, built in 1818, was the first Anglican church in the region. The facade, featuring a pediment supported by four pairs of columns, is reminiscent of a Greek temple. In front stands a colonnaded rotunda in the Classical style, erected as a memorial to Francis Light.

to appear in neighbourhoods like Armenian Street, Malay Street, Love Lane and Muntri Street.

Penang's fortunes soared when the port became the main outlet for the produce of the northern Malay states in the 1870s. Inspired by Singapore, George Town constructed a modern front along Beach Street and the newly reclaimed Weld Quay, and implemented new standards of architecture for public buildings, banks and shipping offices. The Town Hall (1880) and City Hall (1903), standing abreast by the Esplanade, symbolized this new civic pride and consciousness.

The Chinese towkays, prospering from tin and rubber and the franchised sales of opium and liquor, built extravagant villas on large plots of land along Leith Street, Northam Road, Anson Road and Macalister Road. In the mid-1920s, the new wealth and the increasing number of immigrant Chinese women led to the creation of middle-class terraced family houses north of Magazine Road and west of Penang Road.

Modern influences became more pronounced with the appearance of professional architects at the turn of the century. Government quarters and social housing designed by colonial architects introduced modern plumbing and electricity. The country's oldest Municipal Commission, formed in 1856, largely succeeded in establishing British standards of town planning and hygiene. On its centenary on 1 January 1957, George Town was declared a city by royal charter.

George Town's small Chinese population in the early 1880s lived in row houses such as the one (top) built on swampy land in Carnavon Street, originally known as Lower Pitt Street. An early Malay community lived around Acheen Street in the area marked as the 'Malay Town' on Admiral Sir Popham's plan. These half-brick half-timber compound houses (above) were built by Arab and Sumatran traders who settled in Penang.

The indigo-washed stucco plasterwork seen on the facades of many of Penang's old buildings, such as the arabesque decoration on the facade of the Noordin family tomb (above) in Chulia Street, was the work of Muslim craftsmen from India.

The Eastern & Oriental Hotel, opened in 1885, belongs to the grand 19th-century tradition of hotels catering for European visitors travelling in style to the East. It boasted the 'longest sea front of any hotel', and ranked among the finest hotels east of the Suez.

Early Kuching

Kuching's early development was inextricably linked with the Brooke Dynasty, which ruled Sarawak from 1841 to 1941. James Brooke was ceded territories in Sarawak (then part of the Brunei Sultanate) and given the title 'Rajah' by Sultan Omar Ali of Brunei in 1841 after he successfully helped to suppress a rebellion by the local inhabitants. Soon afterwards, the first 'White Rajah' made Kuching his headquarters and established it as a trading post.

Charles Brooke, the second White Rajah (1868–1917), changed Kuching from a village into a town of fine buildings.

The growth of Kuching

At the time of James Brooke's arrival, Kuching was a small settlement confined by the Sarawak River in the north, Sungai Gartak, Kampong Datu and Kampong Jawa in the west, and Sungai Kuching in the east. On both sides of the Sarawak River Malay kampongs spread out in haphazard fashion. The buildings in the town, where the Chinese and Indians congregated, were mainly built of wood with *atap* (thatched) roofs. The only public amenities were the small hospital and the Reading Room in a corner of the Anglican Mission grounds. James Brooke's immediate concern was not so much with town building as with restoring peace in order to promote the export of local products, such as antimony and spices.

It was not until Charles Brooke, the second Rajah, who succeeded his uncle in 1868 and ruled Kuching for 49 years until his death in 1917, that Kuching changed from a ramshackle little place into a town which was clean and had street lights, good roads and fine buildings. After a disastrous fire in 1884, Charles issued orders to have all shophouses rebuilt in brick with roofs made from *belian* (ironwood) tiles instead of the highly inflammable atap. Roads were resurfaced and a proper drainage system installed.

The majestic Astana, home of the 'White Rajahs', is now the residence of the Governor of Sarawak.

Fort Margherita, named after Rajah Charles's wife, Margaret, was based on late English Renaissance castles.

The Court House complex is constructed around a courtyard and surrounded by green spaces. The wide, colonnaded verandas are evocative of buildings in Tuscany.

One of the first grand buildings to be constructed was the Astana, the Rajah's residence, on the north side of the river overlooking the town. Built in 1870, it was a romantic representation of an English country home with whitewashed walls and wood-framed glass windows. Broad, arcaded verandas were incorporated into the design to accommodate the hot, humid weather. A tower was added later, probably about the same time that Fort Margherita was built.

The public buildings constructed during this period included the new Court House which, in addition to a large courtroom, housed the Resident's office, treasury and audit office, surveyor's office, post office and shipping office. The other notable buildings were a hospital, the jail and Fort Margherita, which was built in the style of an English castle favoured by Margaret Brooke. The architectural styles adopted for the other public buildings were typical of 19th-century Neoclassical European buildings with their imposing pediments, columns and grand facades denoting rank, dignity and prestige. Other important additions to the town were the Gothic-style schools and churches built by the Anglican and Roman Catholic missionaries.

At the same time, prosperous Chinese traders built brick shophouses along the Main Bazaar and Gambier Road facing the river. The facades of the shophouses, as elsewhere in the country, ranged from those typical of traditional Chinese houses to a hybrid architectural style combining Western Neoclassical ornaments and arched windows on the front facade and Chinese clay tiles on the roof. Everything within the house remained Chinese.

The transformation of Kuching

The period between 1890 and 1917 witnessed the greatest transformation in Kuching. More buildings were erected and good roads, leading from the town to various kampongs, were constructed. The two most spectacular buildings put up in Kuching during these years were the Sarawak Museum, which was completed in 1891, and the Pavilion, which became the Medical Headquarters, in 1909. The rebuilding of old shophouses continued; those along Court House Road and India Street had been nearly all replaced by the mid-1890s. At the east end of the town, an area prone to flooding, an embankment, using belian piles, was built along the river in front of the Main Bazaar. Later on, in 1902, another retaining wall was constructed along the river front, from Pankalan Batu to the end of Gambier Road. This, with its flights of stone steps, took 11 years to complete. Public transport in early Kuching was confined to bullock carts and rickshaws until 1912 when the first public bus service was set up. In the same year, Rajah Charles also introduced the first phase of the railway service which extended 16 kilometres into the interior to transport freight and passengers.

The last of the White Rajahs

Charles Vyner Brooke, the second son of Charles Brooke, succeeded to the title of Rajah of Sarawak in 1917. His reign during the interwar years was not impressive in terms of town building although he carried on his father's tradition of public works development. By 1939, Kuching's population had grown from about 1,000 in 1841 to 34,500 but the Japanese Occupation from 1941 to 1946 retarded the growth of the town. Although Charles Vyner Brooke had decided as early as 1941 to end Brooke rule and establish a Constitution, it was not until 1946, after liberation, that Sarawak was ceded to Britain as a Crown Colony, bringing to an end the Brooke Dynasty. The 100-year rule of the Brooke Raj bequeathed a distinctive civic architectural heritage

Early views of Kuching

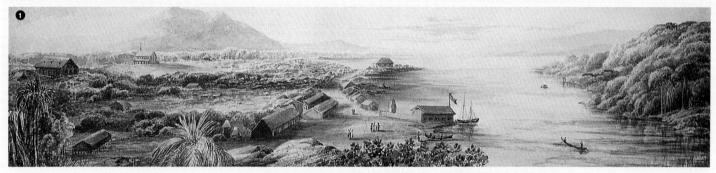

1. 'A View of Kuching' (1852) by an anonymous painter shows a dirt road, now named Gambier Road and Main Bazaar Road, running parallel to the Sarawak River. Wooden shophouses line the left side of the road.

2. 'Mr Brooke's First Residence', from Spenser St John's *Life in the Forests of the Far East* (1863), shows a group of timber structures with thatched roofs located on the east bank of the Sarawak River.

3. The Main Bazaar on the waterfront, comprising a row of shophouses, is still the commercial hub of Kuching. In the early days, goods were conveniently transported by boats on the Sarawak River.

4. The Tua Pek Kong Temple (c. 1876), located originally on one bank of what was a former tidal stream, the Sungai Kuching (Cat River), was probably used as a shrine as early as 1843.

to Kuching, one which reflected the British origin of the Brookes. They brought with them a colonial style characterized by classical proportions and scale, pillars and white stucco walls.

The local Malay aristocracy and Chinese merchants were soon attracted to this new colonial style. Abandoning their kampong houses and Chinese shophouses, they built airy, whitewashed villas incorporating European decorative features. The result was an idiosyncratic blend of East and West. These villas were usually double-storey, but like the Malay house generally incorporated a single-storey kitchen and a servants' block at the rear.

Perhaps the biggest influence on traditional local architecture was the introduction of new building materials. Atap and ironwood shingles were replaced by clay tiles and reinforced concrete, making traditional timber structures obsolete.

The Sarawak Museum, built to house Charles Brooke's collection of ethnographic specimens, is believed to have been modelled on a French provincial town hall.

The Medical Headquarters, also known as the Pavilion (1909), was the first building to use reinforced concrete.

The two-storey whitewashed villa emerged as the favoured style of the merchant class.

Opencast mining, such as at this mine at Kampar in the early 1900s, was extremely labour-intensive, employing large gangs of coolies imported from China who lived in shared quarters (*kongsi*) on the perimeter of the mine.

The vast European rubber plantations employed teams of Indian labourers who cleared the land, planted seedlings and tapped the trees. The estate manager's bungalow was in complete contrast to the 'coolie lines' where the workers lived.

It took only 80 years—from 1859 to 1939—for Kuala Lumpur to develop from a small trading post into the largest town in the Peninsula, complete with shophouses, such as these in Petaling Street in about the 1920s.

OPENING UP THE LAND

Until about 1880, Peninsular Malaysia, Sabah and Sarawak were covered by dense rainforest interspersed with small settlements along the coastline and rivers and intermittent clearances of slash-and-burn agriculture. Although the faces of Sabah and Sarawak were to change very little until the exploitation of timber began in the 1970s, from the middle of the 19th century two factors were responsible for swift and dramatic changes to the landscape of the Peninsula: tin mining and the rise of large-scale estate agriculture. Although tin had been mined manually by Malays for centuries, it was the discovery in Perak, in 1848 and from 1870 onwards, of major tin deposits that propelled Straits Chinese entrepreneurs and, later, European capitalists to invest in new techniques. By the turn of the century, Malaysia was the world's largest tin producer.

The British colonial administrators were quick to spot the benefits of building an infrastructure of roads and railways linking mining areas to the west coast of the Peninsula. Recognizing, too, that tin was a non-renewable resource and keen on long-term investment, they experimented with various agricultural crops, eventually establishing vast plantations, especially of rubber, in the early 20th century for commercial exploitation. The infrastructure established for the tin industry also benefited the rubber industry. Close on the heels of economic growth came demographic change—large-scale migration of Chinese coolies into the tin districts and recruitment of Tamil labourers into the plantations—and geographical concentration, especially in the tin-mining areas.

Opening up the land contributed greatly to the building boom of the late 19th and early 20th centuries and involved the construction of railway stations, utilitarian housing for plantation workers, bungalows for expatriate estate managers and other colonial officers, places of worship, shophouses, and imposing colonial-style administration buildings. The towns in Perak and Selangor, including Kuala Lumpur, which served the tin mines and growing rural communities, grew from ramshackle settlements of wood and thatched-roof houses into neat, colonial towns featuring a central *padang* (a large field) set amidst imposing administrative buildings, residences for the chief officers of the government, a market, rows of one- or two-storey shophouses, and separate areas of simpler housing for the local population.

In pursuit of rest and recreation—and a refuge from the perceived health hazards of the lowlands—the British colonial administrators also turned their attention to Malaysia's highland areas, establishing small, isolated hill stations on Penang Island and, principally, at Maxwell's Hill, Fraser's Hill and Cameron Highlands along the ridges and flanks of the rugged Main Range.

LEFT: The Padang Rengas Pass in the early 1900s.

RIGHT: Some of the best examples of early 20th-century Malaysian bungalows are the tin mine and estate houses of expatriate managers. The styles of these bungalows were modelled on Anglo-Indian bungalows because many of the planters and builders had come from India.

Tin mines and plantations

British colonial administrators, who were drawn in the wake of mining booms into the affairs of Perak and Selangor, had realized that greater prosperity in the country could be achieved by improving its infrastructure. Thus, in 1886, Frank Swettenham, later Resident-General of the Federated Malay States, declared that it was 'Britain's duty to open up the country by great works: roads, railways, telegraphs, wharves'.

Large-scale tin-mining activities were introduced by Chinese immigrants in the mid-19th century after a major tin deposit was discovered in Larut, Perak.

Building railways and roads

In the early days of the tin-mining industry, which was concentrated on the west coast of the Malay Peninsula, the only roads were those from the tin mines to navigable rivers where the tin was then transported to the coast. Between 1885 and 1895, however, railway lines were constructed to link tin mines in an east–west direction directly to a coastal port. The first such railway, from Taiping to Port Weld (now Kuala Sepetang), was opened in 1885, and the second, from Kuala Lumpur to Klang, in 1886. Only later, towards the end of the century, did the focus shift towards building railways and roads to link the urban centres along the west coast. Indeed, the earliest railway line east of the Main Range was not constructed until 1912–17.

The pattern of road development, to a large extent, matched that of the railways: an initial emphasis on developing in an east–west direction later gave way to the development of main roads linking the west coast from north to south. The first road over the Main Range was that from Kuala Kubu to Raub and Kuala Lipis. It was constructed in response to keen anticipation of a mining boom in that part of west Pahang in the late 1880s. The boom, however, failed to materialize. The second road followed the Gombak Valley to Genting Sempah and down to Bentong. Again, the road was built in direct response to mining initiatives, in this case, the granting of enormous mining leases in Bentong to Loke Yew, a Chinese entrepreneur.

The development of plantations

The colonial administrators also recognized only too clearly that mining was a non-renewable resource, and that it was desirable to place the economy on a better long-term footing. Agriculture appeared to be the answer. The beginning of the 19th century had witnessed modest attempts to plant spices in Penang, and later Singapore. These gave way to the planting of gambier in Johor, and, more successfully, sugar in and near Province Wellesley (Seberang Perai). The failure of coffee in Ceylon (Sri Lanka) due to disease drove many planters from there to seek better conditions in Malaya. Although coffee became the preferred crop by the last quarter of the century, as a commercial crop it did not take off due to the shortage of labour and because of pests.

Agriculture in the country would have faced ruin had it not been for the introduction some years earlier of seeds of rubber (*Hevea braziliensis*) from Brazil. Experimental plantings established and nurtured by such pioneers as Sir Hugh Low in Kuala Kangsar and Henry Ridley of the Botanic Garden in Singapore ensured that many of the all but bankrupt coffee planters were able to turn to rubber.

The result was a dramatic rubber boom in the first decade of the 20th century. This affected the landscape far more profoundly than tin mining, because estate production is by its nature extensive. The existing infrastructure in the country, with its concentration on the west coast of the Peninsula, focused the development of the industry primarily in that area, while the advent of the motor car in the West ensured an almost unlimited market with rapidly rising world prices. This fuelled the agricultural development of the country.

In contrast to the scars left by mining, the rubber industry replaced the forest after felling and burning with

Taiping Station, built in 1885, was the country's first railway station. The railway joined Port Weld 12 kilometres away.

By 1886, railways and roads had been constructed to link main towns in the tin-mining areas to coastal ports.

Structures seen in tin mines

LEFT: This timber structure, known as a *palong*, is found in tin mines that employ the gravel pump method. Gravel containing tin ore, washed out by powerful jets of water, is collected in a sump at the base of the palong and then pumped up a long, sloping sluice box where the ore is separated from the gravel.

RIGHT: Built on a natural or man-made lake, the tin dredge resembles a floating factory. It has a flat bottom, sides and a roof, and carries a chain of heavy buckets. These can scoop out huge volumes of tin-bearing soil in a day and transport it to the cleaning plant in the upper part of the dredge. The first tin dredge was introduced to Malaysia by Malayan Tin Dredging Ltd in the Kinta Valley tin mine in 1913.

Tin-mining sites in Selangor and Perak in the 1880s.

A rubber estate in the early 20th century shows workers carrying latex in buckets. In the foreground, a worker and a manager collect rubber seeds.

serried rows of rubber trees, which in the early years took no account of the contours of the land. Only later were terracing, contour planting and covers encouraged. Later, too, came oil palm (*Elaeis guineensis*), first planted on a major scale in the 1960s, thus contributing an element of variation in an otherwise uniform landscape. With such vast clearances in the early years of the century, enormous numbers of workers were required, far more than the country itself was capable of providing. As a result, large numbers of Tamils from southern India were recruited. Traces of this influx remain in the comparatively high proportion of Indians in rural areas on the west coast and in the often colourful temples which they erected, both on the estates and in nearby towns.

The building boom

In architectural terms, the opening up of the land contributed greatly to the building boom of the late 19th and early 20th centuries. The building of railway lines called for the construction of railway stations. These were originally simple constructions, such as the Taiping Railway Station and the first Kuala Lumpur station, which had an *atap* (thatched) roof. But as the economy improved, greater importance was placed on the construction of public buildings. By far the most famous of the railway stations is that of Kuala Lumpur (its third), completed in 1911, and based on designs by A. B. Hubback (see 'The British "Raj" style'). The Singapore Railway Station, though not within Malaysia, is Malaysian Government owned and is also significant architecturally.

In the plantations, the workers required housing. The results were utilitarian and rather squalid. In the later years, the demand for better housing for staff came from an increasingly assertive Labour Department. Such considerations did not, however, apply to the managers' bungalows. The first half of the 20th century saw the rapid establishment of such dwellings throughout estate areas. The expatriate managers who, together with their families, were obliged to inhabit such houses on tours of duty lasting 5–7 years, came to regard them as home. They often put enormous care into their siting, design and construction, while their wives took pride in the furnishings and gardens. These houses provided the only comfort in a tough environment.

Houses for planters and miners

The planter's bungalow was the first thing to be built after the jungle had been cleared for a rubber plantation.

This Malay kampong-style building housed the Negeri Sembilan Miners' Association, which was officially opened in 1904 by the British Resident.

Common features of tin mine and estate managers' bungalows were *atap* (thatched) roofs, now invariably replaced with tiles, and construction in timber on masonry posts. This encouraged air circulation in days when there was no air conditioning. It also provided some security from snakes and wild animals. More recently, the area under the main house has tended to be bricked in to provide additional living or storage space.

A home in a plantation

The most famous of estate houses is undoubtedly Socfin's 'Maison des Palmes'. Built in the early 20th century by Henri Fauconnier, a planter and the celebrated author of *Malaisie* (published in English as *The Soul of Malaya*), the house was destroyed during World War II, but was rebuilt by the company after the war to the exact design of the original. Two rows of stately palm trees line the driveway to the house, which is surrounded by a beautiful garden. The most striking feature is the magnificent Minangkabau thatched roof whose wide overhang covers the windows. Green striped *chiks* (bamboo blinds) provide additional shade. The timber walls are varnished to a deep red, the colour of the soil.

Henri Fauconnier and his brother Charles in the living-room of 'Maison des Palmes' in 1922.

The 'Maison des Palmes', set in a beautiful undulating garden, was built in a clearing on the fringe of virgin jungle, as was typical at the time. Fresh water came from a nearby river and oil lamps were used for lighting.

MALAISIE
HENRI FAUCONNIER

PRIX GONCOURT

The present 'Maison des Palmes' is used as a weekend retreat by the senior staff of Socfin.

In the Socfin Estate, the workers are accommodated in neat, single-storey houses, a far cry from the tiny huts of the early days.

LEFT: *Malaisie*, a highly acclaimed novel about life on a rubber estate, was published in 1930, followed by an English edition, *The Soul of Malaya*, in 1931.

Taiping and other early tin-mining towns

Taiping in Perak is a typical example of a town created in response to the development of the tin-mining industry in the latter half of the 19th century. It was designated the administrative centre of the state in preference to the royal residence of Kuala Kangsar because it was more accessible, and also because the climate was less malarial. Other towns, such as Ipoh, Batu Gajah, Kuala Lipis and Bentong, developed slightly later to service the tin mines and growing rural communities which expanded as a result of the growth of coffee and rubber estates.

Catholic mission schools were established by Catholic nuns and brothers in most of the colonial towns. The Taiping Convent was built in 1899.

Mining towns in Perak and Pahang

Perak
• Taiping
• Ipoh
• Kuala Lipis
Batu Gajah
• Bentong
Strait of Melaka
Pahang
0   160 km

Until the discovery of tin in a rich seam that ran down the west coast, most settlements were located on the coast. Profits from tin, and later rubber, enabled the colonial administration to build an infrastructure of roads and railways linking the early mining towns of the interior.

Taiping: The town that tin built

Taiping, or Kamunting as it was formerly known, originated in the middle of the 19th century as the site of feverish tin-mining activites by immigrant Chinese who were financed and controlled by wealthy Chinese merchants in Penang. Rivalry between the different secret societies, together with the succession crisis which arose from the death of Sultan Ali, persuaded the British Government to reverse its policy of non-intervention in local affairs. The result was the Pangkor Engagement of 1874, which instituted British rule known as residential government. A commission appointed by the governor, Sir Andrew Clarke, which included the young Frank Swettenham (who later became the governor), resolved the boundaries of the tin concessions amongst the warring factions in the area. As a result of the settlements between the feuding Chinese tin miners, the name Taiping, meaning 'Everlasting Peace' in Chinese, was

adopted. Taiping benefited greatly from the subsequent peace. In 1884, Hugh Low, Perak's long-serving Resident, left orders with Frank Swettenham to press ahead with the construction of buildings appropriate for the senior officers of the Protected Malay States.

Many of the public buildings which still stand in present-day Taiping were constructed between 1884 and 1886. They include a large market, residences for the chief officers of the government to replace the ramshackle wood and *atap* (thatch) houses which they had used previously, the Taiping Museum, and the draining of an old area of tin mines, which was later to be converted into the Taiping Lake Gardens. This later conversion was masterminded by

---

The *padang* and other characteristic features of colonial towns

One of the most notable features of British colonial towns was the *padang*, a large field set against a backdrop of imposing administrative buildings. When used for parades on formal occasions, it was a public symbol of British 'officialdom', and when used as a cricket field by the British community, with its clubhouse and an Anglican church close by, it was reminiscent of an English village green.

Colonial-style buildings

Most of the administrative buildings and colonial houses were constructed by the Public Works Department. Its architects were mostly expatriates who had worked in India. The dominant style of architecture was the Anglo-Indian Neoclassical which evolved in India in the 18th century.

The 'local' part of town

For the locals, their centre of town was the market square, which consisted of the market and rows of one- or two-storey shophouses which were used for business as well as residential purposes.

The *padang*, a feature of every town laid out by the British administrators, was used for official parades and for games.

A street of early 20th-century shophouses in Papan, a mining town in the Kinta Valley.

The City Hall in Ipoh, with its Greek-style pediment and columned porticos, is typical of public buildings erected by the British.

This bungalow in Taiping is typical of houses built by the Public Works Department for British colonial staff.

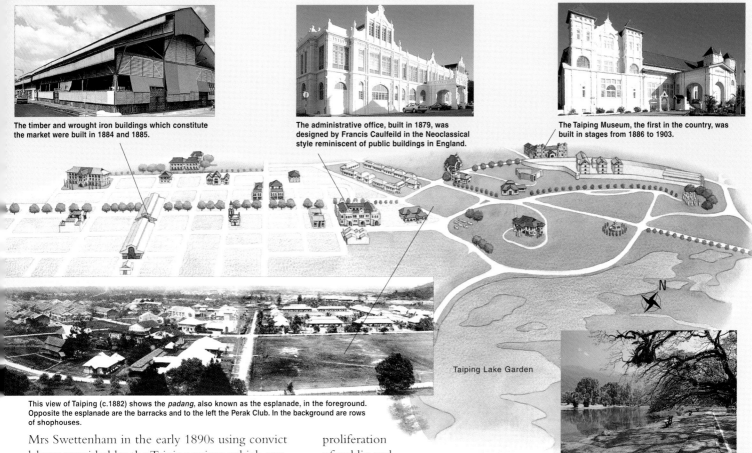

The timber and wrought iron buildings which constitute the market were built in 1884 and 1885.

The administrative office, built in 1879, was designed by Francis Caulfeild in the Neoclassical style reminiscent of public buildings in England.

The Taiping Museum, the first in the country, was built in stages from 1886 to 1903.

Taiping Lake Garden

This view of Taiping (c.1882) shows the *padang*, also known as the esplanade, in the foreground. Opposite the esplanade are the barracks and to the left the Perak Club. In the background are rows of shophouses.

In the late 19th century, an area of disused tin mines was converted into the beautiful Taiping Lake Gardens.

Mrs Swettenham in the early 1890s using convict labour provided by the Taiping prison which was established in 1879.

Beyond the town, on the hills to the east, a number of holiday bungalows were built to enable the administrators to escape from the heat on the plains. This area was known as Maxwell's Hill (Bukit Larut) after William Edward Maxwell who became the British Resident for Selangor.

Other mining towns

By the late 19th century, many mining towns were established on the west coast of Peninsular Malaysia. Towns such as Ipoh, Batu Gajah, Bentong and Kuala Lipis flourished when the tin rush took off with the rise of the tin-canning industry in the West. With Malaya's economic success considerable revenues were added to the British Empire's resources so that an increasing amount of funds could be allocated to developing the infrastructure in these new towns. This led to an upsurge in road construction and a proliferation of public and commercial buildings. In 1917, Ipoh assumed the look of an important town with the building of the magnificent railway station. Two other imposing buildings, the Supreme Court and the Town Hall, followed. In Batu Gajah, the cluster of colonial buildings found on Changkat, the low hill rising from the town centre, is testimony to the town's colonial history. The red brick rest house in Kuala Lipis is reminiscent of an Anglo-Indian bungalow, a style which the British adopted in building residential houses. Besides colonial buildings, rows of Chinese shophouses appeared in every town centre.

Many of the architectural features of these early towns have succumbed to redevelopment in recent years. Their original outlines, however, are still evident to the careful observer.

Present-day Taiping showing 19th-century landmarks
After Taiping was destroyed by fire in 1880, the town was rebuilt to a new plan. The main streets were widened and the former village of *atap* (thatch) huts and narrow lanes was replaced by blocks of brick buildings traversed by well laid out streets. By 1882 Taiping had been transformed from an unruly settlement into a tidy, modern town.

Batu Gajah in Perak, a district headquarters in the late 19th century, has several fine colonial-style offices.

The district courthouse in Batu Gajah was built in 1892. Its Palladian facade features plaster bas-reliefs accentuated in black.

The Kuala Lipis Rest House, like several in the country, provided accommodation for colonial officials going 'outstation' (a term used by the colonials when they left for a remote area) in the days when there were no hotels.

Early Kuala Lumpur

In the course of 80 years, from 1859 to 1939, Kuala Lumpur grew from a small trading post in the remote interior into the largest town in the Malay Peninsula, with a population of more than 120,000. The centre of the town, on the east bank of the Klang River, had roads running outwards, like the spokes of a wheel, to nearby mining areas, a pattern that persisted and caused much congestion as the town grew. From a collection of shanties, Kuala Lumpur changed into a town of shophouses, bungalows and untidy and insanitary areas of working-class settlement sprinkled with a few prestigious government buildings.

1884: A view of Kuala Lumpur showing the thatched (*atap*) houses of the Chinese and Malay quarters sited in the 'native town' on the east bank of the Klang River. The boundary between the Malay quarter and the Chinese settlement was a rough track, nowadays Jalan Tun Perak.

Built in 1908–9, the Jamek Mosque stands on a promontory between the Klang and Gombak rivers. Boats making the four-day transit to and from Klang used to load and offload their cargoes at this point.

A face-lift for Kuala Lumpur

To service the tin mines in the surrounding areas, boats plied the Klang River as far upstream as its junction with the Gombak River where the Jamek Mosque now stands. From the east bank, where the boats loaded and unloaded cargoes, tracks ran through the jungle to the mines. Jalan Pudu, Jalan Ampang, Jalan Petaling and other roads preserve the names of those outlying villages. High Street, now Jalan Tun H. S. Lee, was the site of the original village.

The character, as well as the importance, of the town changed in 1880 when the administrative capital of Selangor was moved from Klang to Kuala Lumpur. New government offices and bungalows, of a very simple type, were built on the high ground to the west of the river as a European quarter. On the east bank, the shops and huts were replaced during the 1880s by buildings of brick with tiled roofs separated by wider streets to reduce fire and health risks. In 1890, a Sanitary Board (town council) was established to maintain roads, regulate new building, and provide nightsoil services and street lighting. Along each side of the main streets the land was divided into building plots on which shophouses were built, with 'sanitary lanes' at the back. Offensive trades, such as abattoirs, tin smelters and brick kilns, were moved away from the town centre. The original, pot-holed earth roads were surfaced with laterite gravel.

1890: The 'official quarter'—home of the government offices—was sited on the west of the Klang River, and at a distance from it, on the rising ground roughly at the back of the Padang (now Merdeka Square) where present-day Jalan Sultan Hishamuddin runs. The Residency was built on yet higher ground to the north (where the Prime Minister's Office Complex now stands).

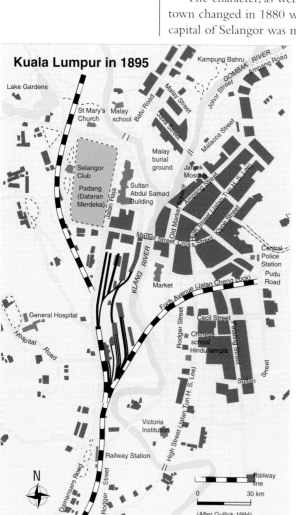

Kuala Lumpur in 1895

(After Gullick, 1994)

Kuala Lumpur began as a small village on the east bank of the Klang River. The village grew around the space known as Old Market Square and along High Street.

1900s: Two-storey brick shophouses replaced atap sheds after a fire in 1881 destroyed most of the houses in the narrow streets of congested Chinatown. To make the best use of limited space, the individual plots had a narrow street frontage but greater depth. Pedestrians used the covered pavements in front.

1920s: Old Market Square, now Leboh Pasar Besar, was one of the more orderly areas in Kuala Lumpur although it was only after the death of Yap Ah Loy, the Kapitan China, in 1885, that the square was cleared of the stalls for which petty traders paid rent to him, and the roads were improved.

Although there had been mosques and temples, and later churches and schools, from the early years, until they were replaced in the late 19th century they were modest structures of brick, tile and timber. Among the new buildings the most striking

'Carcosa', completed in 1898, was the residence of Frank Swettenham, Resident-General of the Federated Malay States.

Simple lines were introduced in the design of the Hotel Majestic, at present the National Art Gallery, built in 1932.

Built in the late 1890s, after the completion of the Sultan Abdul Samad Building, the design of the new Sanitary Board conformed to the 'Raj' style used for public buildings.

were St Mary's Church (now Cathedral), built in 1895, the Selangor Club, built in a Mock Tudor style (1890), and the Bangunan Sultan Abdul Samad (1897) on the Padang, now known as Dataran Merdeka. Charles Norman, who had served his apprenticeship in Devon, England, designed the first two buildings and had a hand in the third. The wooden buildings of the first secondary school, the Victoria Institution (1893), were in the town centre, but the school moved to its present buildings in 1929, after the great flood of 1926.

Green spaces
The Lake Gardens, now known as Taman Tasek Perdana, were first laid out in 1889 as an open space and botanic garden, and are the finest legacy of this period to the modern city. On the other side of the town, a racecourse and, later, a golf course were valuable open spaces as the town grew around them. Even at this time, the Lake Gardens were earmarked as the major public precinct, with official residences such as 'Carcosa' (1898) and 'King's House' (Istana Tetamu, 1913), built to accommodate the governor during his visits from Singapore. On the other side of town, Chinese millionaires built pretentious mansions along such roads as Jalan Ampang.

Development between the wars
In the 20 years between the wars (1919–39), there was less exuberance in building styles, as slumps between the booms undermined confidence and public and private finance. A project for a new hospital had to be cancelled due to lack of funds. Architectural styles now tended to follow Western fashion. The Hotel Majestic (1932), opposite the Railway Station, was originally designed as a block of luxury flats (a novel form of dwelling in Kuala Lumpur at that time), but with little prospect of letting flats at high rents during the recession, it was adapted during construction to a 51-bedroom hotel, the largest in the town. Office buildings and shops were also built in functional style. For example, the Anglo-Oriental building (1936) has a reinforced concrete structure, masonry walls and geometric Art Deco plaster exterior (see 'Art Deco').

Until 1920, municipal control of building had generally been limited to approval of plans of individual buildings from the standpoint of safety and hygiene. The Federated Malay States town planning department, established in 1921, gave priority to the difficult task of redeveloping Kuala Lumpur on more rational lines. A broad Victory Avenue (Jalan Raja) provided a processional way towards the Padang. This, and one of the first housing estates, on Jalan Imbi, were designed by Henry Lanchester, a distinguished town planner brought in to help the local agency find its feet. The existing built-up area was divided into 28 'schemes', each with a long-term pattern in view.

A perennial problem was the tendency of the Klang River to flood the lower, central part of the town after abnormal rains. Thus, the river course through the town was straightened in the early 1890s and again, more extensively, after the 1926 flood. Tarmac surfacing of the streets eliminated the nuisance of red dust thrown up from the former laterite roads. The more general use of cars, first seen in the town in 1902, added to the traffic problems. However, the scourge of malaria was much reduced by an elaborate network of monsoon drains over a wide area to check the breeding of mosquitoes.

The railway line, built in 1886, from Klang to Kuala Lumpur, was then extended through the town to destinations further away. At one time a line skirted the west side of the Padang and another spur passed along Foch Avenue (Jalan Cheng Lock), which is still unusually wide, to the town railway station. Some lines crossed busy streets, creating hazardous unmanned level crossings for slow-moving traffic, such as bullock carts, pony traps, rickshaws and hand carts. There was growing congestion in the streets; one particular black spot was the exit from the station goodsyard into Market Street. The railway lines were eventually rerouted or put into tunnels.

By 1939 Kuala Lumpur was neither an old nor a modern town but an untidy mixture of the two.

Kampung Bahru
With the rapid development of Kuala Lumpur in the 1890s, there was some concern that the Malay community, apart from the police, was being crowded out of a town in which the original Malay quarter, north of Java Street (Jalan Tun Perak), was identified by Malay Street, Johor Street and Malacca Street. In 1902, a modestly successful scheme for a 'Malay agricultural settlement', known as Kampung Bahru, was

The Suleiman Club, now the Wanita Umno Building, is one of the oldest buildings in Kampung Bahru.

established on an area of about 90 hectares further to the north of the town, between Batu Road (Jalan Tuanku Abdul Rahman) and Ampang Road. In addition to providing living space for Malays working in the town, it was hoped that Malay industries would flourish in a village environment. This was an early experiment in town planning, and although the settlement did not succeed as a centre for cottage industry, it flourished as a Malay residential quarter.

Hill stations

Malaysia's four principal hill stations—Penang Hill, Maxwell's Hill (Bukit Larut), Fraser's Hill and Cameron Highlands—owed their origin and early development to the British colonialists who sought an escape from the hot, humid and unhealthy conditions of the lowlands. Known as 'change-of-air stations' or 'sanatoria', each was small and isolated and mainly comprised a collection of bungalows perched on ridges or strung along the flanks of hills, whose architecture was influenced by the romantic ideals permeating the middle class in Britain in the late 19th and early 20th centuries.

The hill stations of Malaysia

THAILAND
Perlis
Kedah
Penang Hill (761)
Pulau Pinang
Bukit Larut (Maxwell's Hill) (1152)
Kelantan
Terengganu
South China Sea
Gunung Kledang (808)
Perak
Cameron Highlands (1640)
N
Fraser's Hill (1305)
Pahang
Strait of Melaka
Selangor
Bukit Kutu (923)
Gunung Angsi (825)
Negeri Sembilan
Melaka
Johor

■ Land above 305 metres
▲ Hill station

0   100   200 km

(After Aiken, 1994)

Although bungalows were erected on Gunung Kledang in Perak, on Bukit Kutu in Selangor, and on Gunung Angsi in Negeri Sembilan in the 1890s and early 1900s, none of these diminutive outposts attracted the growth of the hill stations on the island of Penang or along the rugged spinal range of Peninsular Malaysia.

This bungalow and its outbuildings on Maxwell's Hill is surrounded by typically neat, English-style gardens and tree-lined paths.

A timber-framed bungalow built of local limestone blocks was the favourite architectural style in Fraser's Hill.

76

Origins of the hill stations

Penang Hill, the oldest of the hill stations, was established by the English East India Company on the island of Penang in the late 18th century. Occupying part of a narrow, steep-sided, undulating ridge whose highest elevation is 761 metres above sea level, the present-day hill station is primarily a collection of bungalows at staggered elevations, together with a hotel, police station, post office, tea kiosk, mosque and other minor buildings. Among the handsome villas and picturesque bungalows that originally studded 'The Hill' was 'Bel Retiro', the governor's bungalow located on Flagstaff Hill, which consisted of two thatch-covered bungalows connected by a covered plank passage, the Convalescent Bungalow, the Crag Hotel, and a number of spacious private residences, all reached by foot, on horseback or by sedan chair before the funicular railway, which descends from near the top of Strawberry Hill to the lowlands close to Ayer Itam, was completed in 1923.

Maxwell's Hill, the earliest hill station on mainland Peninsular Malaysia, was situated on the Larut Hills of Perak, overlooking the mining and administrative centre of Taiping. Named after the British Resident for Selangor, William Edward Maxwell, the hill station never comprised more than a dozen bungalows. The first to be built, in 1884, was 'The Cottage', for the Resident of Perak, followed by three bungalows for the use of Perak government officers: 'The Tea Gardens' (1887), 'Maxwell's Hill' (1887) and 'The Hut' (1889). Despite experiments with flower and food production (including tea), the hill station failed to develop because of the lack of flat land and the difficulty of access. Today, only six government bungalows and rest houses remain on Maxwell's Hill, built mainly of timber and brick.

ABOVE: This detail of an 1818 aquatint by William Daniell of the view from the Convalescent Bungalow on Penang Hill, illustrates how most hill station bungalows were positioned to enjoy an extensive view of the surroundings and cool, bracing air.

RIGHT: An 1860s sketch by an unknown artist of 'a journey up the hill'.

Fraser's Hill was named after Louis James Fraser, an adventurer who ran a transport service by mule between Kuala Kubu and Raub in the 1890s. Bukit Fraser (as the hill was originally, and is still, called), where he built a bungalow, was linked by a rough 8–10 kilometre path to the Gap, near the highest point on the cross-mountain road between Selangor and Pahang. A rest house at the Gap served as a health resort. Following a topographical survey of the hill station site in 1918, work began on an access road from the Gap (completed in 1922), building sites were cleared of jungle, the first bungalows started to go up, and work began on the golf course. By 1930, the hill station covered an area of about 140 hectares and had 50 kilometres of well-kept jungle paths. Although it boasted 63 bungalows, the hill station's constricted site could not accommodate further growth, and the focus of interest thus shifted to the Cameron Highlands.

Cameron Highlands was named after a government surveyor, William Cameron, who discovered the plateau in 1885 whilst on a map-making expedition on the Perak–Pahang border. Based on his report, the British Resident of Perak, Sir Hugh Low, proposed, in 1887, that a health, farming and gardening resort be built for the British expatriate community. It was only in the 1920s, however, that the area's potential for development received attention. A metalled road from Tapah was completed, some of the larger tea plantations were established, and numerous bungalows were built on the area's ridges and spurs.

The ubiquitous hill station bungalow

Malaysia's hill stations were essentially modest collections of bungalows, which served not only as private residences but also as rest houses, hotels, clubs and government offices. Many were given names reminiscent of England or of fondly remembered trees, flowers or fruit. The earliest bungalows were low, oblong or square buildings set on slightly raised plinths, with mud or woven mat walls, a pyramidal thatch-covered roof, a veranda on one or more sides and a porte-cochere. To the rear of the building was a kitchen, servants' quarters and a storage area. Some eventually acquired an overlay of fashionable architectural details, while others were replaced by more substantial structures, some two storeys high. Timber formed the structural framework while local limestone blocks or concrete came to be used for the walls and lower floors and corrugated iron or tiles for the roofs.

The bungalows were usually set well away from their neighbours in a neat, English-style garden filled with temperate flowers, surrounded by a wall, hedge or bank. Nearly all the bungalows were designed by amateur architects, most of whom were military engineers or employees of the Public Works Department. They depended on the labours of Indian immigrant labourers with little access to machinery.

The two main influences on Malaysia's hill station architecture were the preferences of the middle-class British for detached bungalows set in compounds, which provided both privacy and space, and the revival, in the late 19th and early 20th centuries, of English architectural styles of the past, particularly the Tudor style.

Recent developments
'Ye Olde Smokehouse', in both the Cameron Highlands and Fraser's Hill, and 'The Lakehouse' in the Cameron Highlands were to greatly influence the architectural expression of later buildings in the two main hill resorts. Apart from the Merlin Hotel in the Cameron Highlands, built in the 1970s, most of the other resort hotels were built during the

The revival of English vernacular styles
Parallel to the discovery and development of Malaysia's hill stations, art and architecture in Britain underwent a romantic period in reaction to industrialization and mass production, which was to spread throughout the British Empire. Spearheaded by William Morris (1884–96), the most vocal critic of the effect of capitalism on architecture and the co-founder of the Arts and Crafts Movement, new vernacular styles emerged inspired by the crafts of medieval England and architectural styles of the past. These included the revivalist Queen Anne style, popularized by Richard Norman Shaw (1831–1912), original vernacular styles developed by Charles Francis Voysey (1857–1941) and Edwin Lutyens (1869–1944), and the Tudor style, characterized by half-timber frame houses, which came to be known as Mock Tudor.

A 15th-century timber-framed house whose walls were made of mud, manure and straw.

The 'Red House' that Morris and his architect friend, Philip Webb, built in 1859, prompted the spread of a new vernacular movement. The asymmetrical plan of the house reflected a preference for informality.

construction boom of the 1980s and 1990s, particularly in the Cameron Highlands where there was a greater area for building and more flat land, and where there was a greater transient population. Although the buildings generally sought to emulate the Tudor style, the higher density, speed and scale of construction, and the priority given to commercial interests, resulted in a large number of high-rise buildings which are not only incompatible with the vernacular scale that existed previously, and which was so suited to the hilly terrain, but which are intrusive on the environment and are built in sham copies of the Tudor style.

Mock Tudor: Favoured hill station style

The exterior timber frames in 'Ye Olde Smokehouse' in Cameron Highlands are a decorative rather than a structural element used to imitate the real Tudor style, hence earning the term Mock Tudor.

Stanley Foster used concrete, instead of local limestone blocks, to fill the wall areas between the timber frames of 'The Lakehouse' at Cameron Highlands.

In response to the revivalist romantic movement in Britain, the Tudor style was widely adopted for Malaysia's hill station bungalows and guest houses and has come to characterize the architecture of more recent resort hotels and shophouses.

Planter William Warin's eight-room boarding house at Cameron Highlands—'Ye Olde Smokehouse'—built in the 1930s, was the first to follow the Tudor style. Strategically placed at the junction of the roads to Tanah Rata, the main town in the highlands, and Brinchang, it was named after the smokehouses used for curing sheets of rubber. Later, Colonel Stanley Foster built a boarding house outside Ringlet, at the commencement of the road to Tanah Rata, also in the Tudor style. Straddling the side of a hill overlooking a lake, it is known as 'The Lakehouse'. The Gap Resthouse in Fraser's Hill, at the foot of the one-way road to the peak, is also built as an English-style tavern. Most other buildings in Cameron Highlands and Fraser's Hill, including the shops along the main street in Fraser's Hill and the resort hotels built during the construction boom of the 1980s and 1990s, have also sought to emulate the Tudor style.

The public square at Fraser's Hill resort is also modelled after an English village green. The road leading to the resort culminates at a public square no bigger than a village green. Surrounding the square are Tudor-style buildings. Anchored in the middle is a stone clock tower (right) marked by a circle.

Some houses in the hill resorts have fireplaces, hence the tall chimney seen in the Gap Resthouse at Fraser's Hill.

Fraser's Hill resort is spread over seven hills. The road leading to the resort culminates at a public square.

The Silver Park Condominuim in Fraser's Hill is representative of hotels built in the hill resorts in the 1980s and 1990s.

Gleaming copper domes, an airy chatri atop the dome of the clock tower, arched colonnades, minaret-like finials and crenellated parapets characterize the Mogul style of the Sultan Abdul Samad Building, Malaysia's most photographed edifice. Built between 1894 and 1897 to house the offices of the newly established Federated Malay States (FMS) Government as well as those of the Selangor State Government, it set the style for the rest of the public buildings around the Padang (later renamed Dataran Merdeka or Independence Square), the civic heart of the city. Today the building houses the Judicial Department and the High Court.

In the background is one of Malaysia's most elegant interpretations of an Islamic style, the 35-storey-high Dayabumi Complex, built in the 1980s. Lattice grilles, extruded from a 12-point star-shaped plan, veil the building and provide delicate shading.

IN SEARCH OF A 'MALAYAN' STYLE

Architectural 'style' is the collective artistic and decorative expression of a period or school of architecture, such as Western Classical, Gothic or Mock Tudor, applied to a building type. Before Independence in 1957, it was accepted that there was no single recognizable style of 'Malayan' architecture. However, some major architectural styles were discernible among the great diversity of the country's buildings: the vernacular style of the Malay timber house; the traditions of temple and domestic building brought by the immigrant peoples from their different homelands; and the Western Classical idiom imposed by the British colonial power, notwithstanding the British 'Raj' or Mogul style which enjoyed a brief but enduring popularity. There was no single line of development. The various styles were built from the memories of immigrant builders and adopted from pattern books. Over time, and without conscious effort, each style came to influence others so that an eclectic mix often appeared in a single building. This style came to be known as Straits Eclectic. The most constant influences on all these architectural styles were the harsh tropical climate and the building materials available locally.

Although the Dutch bequeathed a distinctive architectural style, seen in the high pediments of the Stadthuys and Christ Church in Melaka, it was the British who left the greatest architectural legacy. The widespread use of the Western Neoclassical style, characterized by rows of stately classical columns supporting pediments, imposed an indelible urban character on all major towns of the country where it was applied with varying degrees of correctness to administrative and commercial buildings, churches, schools, palaces, mosques and shophouses. The exception was in Kuala Lumpur, the capital of the Federated Malay States, where the Mogul style was chosen for the new government offices—the Sultan Abdul Samad Building—as being more appropriate to an Islamic country. The Mogul style spread further afield, especially to mosques and other Islamic buildings throughout the Peninsula.

The beginnings of a Malayan style of architecture were most apparent in the dwellings of the various communities, where the successful blending and assimilation of different influences from the various cultural traditions reflected the people's adaptability and their innate artistic expression. The early houses of the British, derived from the Anglo-Indian bungalow, shared features with the houses of the Malays and other indigenous peoples, and to this house form other features and decorative elements were added by the urban Indians, Sumatrans and Chinese. The eclecticism of the Malayan style, however, was most highly developed in the country's ubiquitous terraced shophouses and townhouses whose facades reflected a variety of local and foreign architectural styles.

A Dutch-style grid of windows is found in conjunction with mouldings and swags on the facade of this shophouse in Melaka.

In the late 19th-century Cheong Fatt Tze Mansion in Penang, stained glass windows featuring floral designs are flanked by wooden shutters.

The fanlight above this sturdy panelled door on a townhouse in Kuching, Sarawak, is covered with a grille in a traditional Iban design.

Ornamental glazed tiles imported from Europe were a favourite decorative device on the steps of Malay houses and mosques in Melaka.

Exposure to colonial architecture encouraged Chinese builders to adopt a variety of Neoclassical features on the facades of townhouses, resulting in an eclectic local vernacular.

Public buildings in the Western Classical style

Classicism in architecture refers to ancient Greek and Roman designs used in temples, theatres and other civic buildings. In Europe, the movement generally referred to as Neoclassicism began in the 1750s as a reaction against the excessive decorative styles of the 17th and early 18th centuries. Many of the public buildings in Malaysia, commissioned in the late 19th and early 20th centuries by the British colonialists, emulated the Neoclassical style prevalent in England at that time.

Built in 1931, the portico of the Main Post Office in Kuching, Sarawak was based on Classical Greek temple design

The Villa Saraceno, Lombardy, Italy (c. 1545–8), is an early example of Andrea Palladio's architectural style. It consists of a simple linear block with a triple-arched entry loggia crowned by a pediment. The division of the building into three distinct horizontal parts—a raised basement, the *piano nobile* (main storey) and an upper storey—is the hallmark of a classic Palladio design.

The Palladian movement

The dominant influence in English architecture from the 16th to the 19th century was the Neoclassical movement known as Palladianism. It was named after Andrea Palladio (1508–80), a Venetian architect who revived and developed classical architecture, especially the Roman ideals of symmetrical planning and harmonic proportions. His principles were formulated in his book *Quattro libri dell'architettura*, published in 1570. The facade of a Palladian building was usually divided into three distinct horizontal parts: a raised basement, the *piano nobile* (principal storey) given prominence by its ornamentation and large openings, and an upper storey with small square openings. The verticality of the central part of the facade was emphasized by the presence of a central door and special ornamentation, such as a triangular pediment or a Venetian window. Many 18th-century English and American architects built houses and public buildings modelled on Palladio's principles.

Cross-boundary classicism

Neolassicism was brought to Malaya by the British via India, their other colony. The imposing scale and the formal appearance of this architectural style was considered eminently suited to signify dignity, rank and prestige. However, closer observation of these Western-style buildings in Malaysia reveals that certain measures have been taken to suit the buildings to the tropical environment and climate.

An important British architect whose work greatly influenced the colonial architecture in British Malaya was George Drumgold Coleman, a professionally trained architect who worked in Calcutta from 1815 to 1820. Coleman worked for the Singapaore Government from 1830 to 1841 and was responsible for many of the early public buildings in Singapore. What distinguished Coleman as an innovative architect was that he interpreted designs for building in the tropics in original and more practical ways than most of his contemporaries. He transposed Western Classical traditions and combined them with principles he observed from his studies of the Malay house. The result was a style of colonial building whose design was much more suited to its Southeast Asian setting and climate and which contributed considerably to the development of the 'Anglo-Straits' architectural style. Although Coleman did not work in Peninsular Malaysia, his designs influenced a whole generation of later buildings. In Malaysia, where most of the colonial public buildings were not constructed until the late 19th and early 20th centuries, British architects successfully designed buildings which combined classical dignity with modifications for the tropics by using devices such as high ceilings, verandas, expansive windows and louvred panels.

Tropical innovations on imported styles

The architect for the Ipoh Railway Station was Arthur Benison Hubback. He had worked in India and had considerable experience in building for the tropics. In the design for the Ipoh Railway Station, he characteristically adopted a modified Western Classical style but made concessions to the tropical climate by introducing deep, continuous, arcaded loggias on the ground floor, which provided shade and shelter, and broad verandas that run the length of the building on the upper floors to ensure adequate ventilation.

Railway stations in the main towns in Peninsular Malaysia were the status symbols of modernization in the early 20th century. Hence, extravagant designs incorporating columns, pilasters, domes and arches were used to create majestic structures, such as the Ipoh Railway Station, Perak (1917).

The interior of the Ipoh Railway Station was built with high ceilings. Rooms opened directly onto broad verandas shaded by *chiks* (bamboo blinds). The first-floor veranda, converted into a comfortable, open, airy coffee lounge, conveys an unmistakable tropical ambience.

Characteristics of Western Classicism in Malaysian buildings

The origin of Classicism

The art of building in stone developed in ancient civilizations for the construction of temples and theatres, which were also used as shrines. The Greeks saw the temple as the dwelling place of a god. Hence, the design of such buildings was to convey a sense of majesty and awe. The various classical revivals were attempts to return to the glories of the ancient Greek and Roman civillizations. The architectural styles of Western Classicism came to Malaysia by way of British architects and also through copy books, such as James Gibbs' *Book of Architecture*, and the English translation of *Vitruvius Britannicus*, which builders referred to for classical designs of doorways, windows, facades and other standard parts of a building.

The ruins of a 5th-century BCE Doric temple at Selinute in Sicily showing a colonnaded structure and the facade with the characteristic pediment.

The system of orders

In Classical architecture, proper porportions are the basis of a good design. These are achieved by using a system known as 'orders'. It was first devised by the ancient Greeks, adapted by the Romans, and revived with the Renaissance in the 15th century. The term 'order' refers to a grouped number of parts in three designs: Doric, Ionic and Corinthian. Each order consists of an upright column or support, which in most instances has a base at the foot and a capital at the head upon which rests a horizontal lintel. The lintel, known as the entablature, is divided into three parts: the lowest is the architrave, the centre the frieze and the top the cornice. Each order possesses specific relative proportions between the parts. The size of the building does not affect these proportions which remain constant, and the differing scale does not impair the perfection of such proportions.

The State Assembly Building in Georgetown, Penang, was built in the early 19th century in the Anglo-Indian classical style. The dignity of this simple, single-storey building is enhanced by the pure geometrical forms of the triangular pediment and cylindrical columns of the portico. The building originally served as the Magistrate's Court.

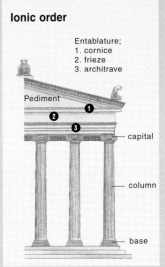

Ionic order

Entablature;
1. cornice
2. frieze
3. architrave

Pediment

capital

column

base

Symmetry—balance and rhythm

Symmetry is one of the most notable characteristics of Classicism. Designs for buildings are based on a rectangular block which features a central section, usually a porch, balanced on either side by wings of similar dimension and size. Symmetry can also be further enhanced by the use of matching pediments, bay windows, gables, columns and pilasters.

The influence of the Classical revival is most evident in the treatment of the facade of the City Hall, Georgetown, Penang (1903). The central porte-cochere is balanced equally on each side by identical wings composed of four bays and articulated by attached columns, making the facade a pleasing symmetrical composition. This style was widely adopted by the Public Works Department and similarities can be seen in the Penang and Ipoh town halls and the Negeri Sembilan State Secretariat Building.

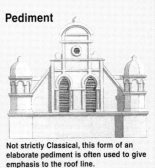

Pediment

Not strictly Classical, this form of an elaborate pediment is often used to give emphasis to the roof line.

Harmonic proportions and elegant lines

Renaissance architects discovered that the calculation of ratios for harmonic scales in music could also be applied to architecture. Leon Battista Alberti (1404–72) used this discovery to combine various parts of a building into a proportionate and pleasing composition. Andrea Palladio's tripartite division of a building also evolved from ideas of harmonic proportions based on musical theories.

FAR RIGHT: The Hong Kong and Shanghai Bank, Ipoh, Perak (c. 1920s), shows the classical tripartite divisions of the base, *piano nobile* (main storey) and the attic floor. Each is given a different treatment: the base is arcaded, the piano nobile is defined by a series of bays and the attic level is emphasized by the double band of cornices enclosing the row of panel windows. Seen as a block, it presents a harmonious whole.

RIGHT: In contrast to the rest of the building, the scooped out loggia and Giant Orders topped by a galleried cupola at the main entrance gives the building a rounded dimension.

Bay

A bay is a vertical compartment of a building, such as the space between one column or pier and the next. Bays are usually repeated and may project beyond the wall alignment.

The British 'Raj' style

The British 'Raj' style first evolved in India in the 1870s as a combination of the principles of Gothic architecture, with its arches and strong vertical lines, and the decorative features of buildings of Muslim India and the Middle East. The intention was to combine an impressive and attractive exterior with cool and airy interiors in which to live and work. The first such building in Malaysia was the Bangunan Sultan Abdul Samad in Kuala Lumpur, completed in 1897.

The semi-dome and the horseshoe arches in the law courts (the former Municipality Building) in Jalan Raja give this bay window an Oriental look.

Kuala Lumpur's first grand building

After 100 years, the gleaming copper domes, 40-metre clock tower and stately arched colonnades of the Bangunan Sultan Abdul Samad, stretching majestically along Jalan Raja in Kuala Lumpur, and overlooking a green expanse, still form one of the most impressive landmarks in Kuala Lumpur. This forerunner of the capital's 'Raj'-style buildings would have been built as a Neoclassical town hall but for the timely intervention of C. E. Spooner, State Engineer in the Public Works Department, who had the drive and imagination to commission the Bangunan Sultan Abdul Samad at a time when a building on this grand scale had never been seen in Kuala Lumpur and when the town itself consisted mainly of small shophouses. Spooner told the architect, Charles Norman, to redesign the building—'I then decided on the Mahometan style'—to reflect the Islamic mores

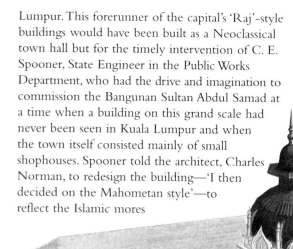

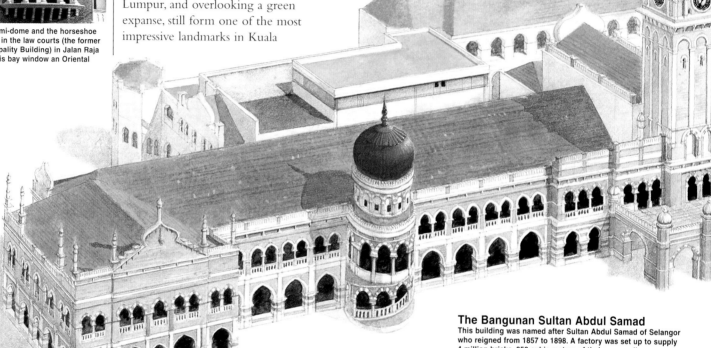

The Bangunan Sultan Abdul Samad
This building was named after Sultan Abdul Samad of Selangor who reigned from 1857 to 1898. A factory was set up to supply 4 million bricks, 850 cubic metres of timber, as well as cement, lime, copper, steel and iron. The building cost Straits $152,000.

Chararacteristics of the 'Raj' style

The term British 'Raj' originated from the colonial era in India. The style combines the grand proportions and classical symmetry of European historic buildings with the decorative Indo-Islamic features of the Mogul courts. Some of the most beautiful buildings in India were constructed during the reign of the Mogul emperors (1526–1857). The Mogul style introduced the dome, large arch and minaret and structures such as monumental tombs.

The bulbous dome, a characteristic of Indo-Islamic buildings, is believed to be a style adopted from Persia and Syria in the 7th century.

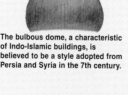

The Classical pediment is given an Islamic treatment by breaking up the triangle with a leaf-shaped ogee arch at the top.

The twinned arch is used effectively as a variation of the pointed arch in the Bangunan Sultan Abdul Samad.

This keyhole arch on the clock tower breaks up the mass of solid brickwork and also emphasizes the vertical lines.

This ogee arch, which decorates the clock tower, consists of four arcs which produce the outer and inner concave and convex curves.

The pointed horseshoe arch is usually used as the basic motif in Islamic buildings.

Rows of rounded horseshoe arches feature on the upper levels of the Kuala Lumpur Railway Station.

Multifoil arches adorn the chatris of the Railway Station, creating an impression of space and light.

of the country. Although Norman's name was inscribed on the foundation stone, only the ground plan was his work. The detailed design in the 'Mahometan style' preferred by Spooner was the work of R. A. J. Bidwell, who had the flair and originality to create the design, and who later became a leading architect in Singapore. Both men, however, brought in their knowledge, styles and ideas from northern India.

The Bangunan Sultan Abdul Samad is a perfect backdrop to the Padang in this early 1900s view of Kuala Lumpur.

The building is two storeys high, constructed of red brick with a tiled roof. Its roof parapet is decorated with crenellations terminating at both ends with a stepped pediment topped by an ogee arch. The symmetrical facade is punctuated by two towers with spiral staircases on either side of the central clock tower, which is square in plan and topped by a chatri. All three towers have Middle Eastern–inspired, onion-shaped domes with copper coverings. The 3.5 metre-wide verandas surrounding the buildings on both floors are airy colonnades of pointed arches. Accentuated by borders of white plaster, the arches produce a pleasing series of rhythmic curves. The larger arches on the ground floor are neatly counterpointed by the upper rows of twin arches.

Other elegant landmarks

The Sultan Abdul Samad building set a new trend in civic buildings. The style was reproduced in the Municipality Building, the old Town Hall, the General Post Office and the office of the Public Works Department. (All these buildings now house the law courts except for the Public Works Department which houses a textile museum.) Seen together across the open space of the Dataran Merdeka (Independence Square), there is no other collection of buildings in the country that is more imposing nor architecturally as harmonious.

The style reached its climax in the Kuala Lumpur Railway Station which was completed in 1911. This building was designed by A. B. Hubback, who was Spooner's aide in the later stages of work on the Bangunan Sultan Abdul Samad. He had arrived in Kuala Lumpur just after the debate concerning an appropriate style for public buildings in the town.

To continue with the Islamic theme of the other public buildings along Jalan Raja, Hubback adopted features from northern Indian Mogul architecture. In addition, he introduced clever devices, such as faceted bays, which produce a sense of movement and flow. This 'movement' is further enhanced by two tiers of horseshoe arches. The most dominant features are the towers, capped by domed, Mogul-inspired chatris, which give the building its imposing silhouette.

At ground level, the Railway Station was planned as a simple linear set of halls with a deep, continuous, covered loggia in front providing shade and shelter for passengers. The train platforms inside the building were laid out parallel to the loggia. The rooms of the Station Hotel (only one of three hotels in the capital at the time) were housed on the mezzanine and first floors of the building.

The architecture of the Railway Administration Building complements the Railway Station located directly across the street although its completion was delayed until after World War II.

Architectural icons

Although the 'Raj' style was successful in creating elegant, highly visible public buildings, it lasted for only a few years, from the 1890s to the early 20th century. The introduction of the 'Raj' style did, however, set an important precedent, for apart from being used for many later buildings in the country, this style has stood the test of time and is still very much admired.

The Kuala Lumpur Railway Station, one of the most notable landmarks in the city, was the third to be built. The present building, completed in 1911, was designed by A. B. Hubback to cope with demands of the increased railway traffic. It was described by a traveller in the 1930s as 'of the late marzipan period'. Like all major railway stations, it incorporated a hotel.

Indian and Mogul influences on mosques

As a result of the active promotion by the British administrators of trade between their colonies, India and the Malay Peninsula, most states had a growing Indian population, many of whom were affluent Indian Muslim traders. Their presence, coupled with the deployment of British architects from India, had a profound effect on mosque architecture in 19th-century Malaysia. Both groups introduced the building of mosques in masonry.

Built in 1802, the Kapitan Kling Mosque in Georgetown, Penang, is representative of the Indian Muslim style. The beautifully proportioned arches of the *iwan* (main entrance), the onion-shaped domes and the arched verandas reflect Mogul influences.

The minaret, although a common feature on many mosques, is not obligatory. It is used by the muezzin to call Muslims to prayers. In many early Malaysian mosques, a large wooden drum was struck instead. Minarets were an imported feature from India. The above shows the minaret on Masjid India, the India Mosque, in Kuala Lumpur.

The Indian Muslim communities

Although Arabs and Indian Muslims had traded in the Malay Peninsula since the 11th century (bringing Islam with them), there is surprisingly little built evidence today of the influence of this more developed foreign culture. Masonry, the primary construction material used in India, was little known beyond the forts and garrison towns of the European colonialists. The local traditions of mosque architecture were entirely timber, based on post-and-beam methods of construction. Aside from the geometrical symmetry of their plans, the early mosques were similar in character to the Malay vernacular buildings.

By the early 19th century, however, the beginning of British trading dominance brought with it a surge of Indian Muslims to the bustling trade centres of Penang, Ipoh and Kuala Lumpur (Melaka by this time had already declined in importance). Intent upon retaining their cultural identity, these wealthy Indian communities embarked upon a programme of constructing large religious compounds in the hearts of Malaysian towns where they found solace within their own community. These building complexes, which were dominated by the mosque, were built in brick in the Mogul style so prevalent in India.

The most notable of these is the Kapitan Kling Mosque, located in the centre of Georgetown on the island of Penang. It is situated in a large complex which includes a *madrasah* (religious school) and administrative facilities. Built by a wealthy local Indian leader in 1801–3, it exhibits all the characteristics of the Mogul style, such as an axially symmetrical plan, a prominent minaret and dentiform archways. The onion shape of the main dome, the numerous sub-domes and the imposing entrance archway or *iwan* are also characteristics of the Mogul style of mosque architecture.

As transplanted Indian Muslim communities sprang up and prospered in the other trading cities, so too did their socioreligious centres. The Kinta Mosque in Ipoh, and the India Mosque in Kuala Lumpur, built in the early 20th century, are more recent examples of this unique cultural adaptation.

The British legacy

Despite the resources of the Indian trading communities, their mosques were dwarfed by the immensity of those built by the British for their Malay subjects. The British were the only colonial

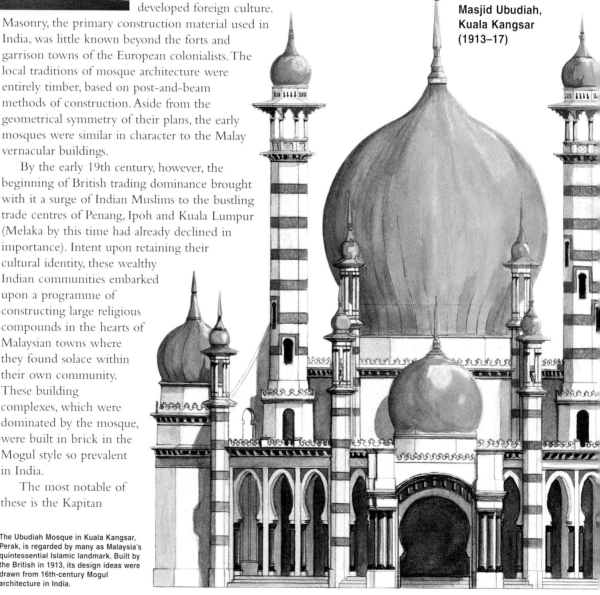

Masjid Ubudiah, Kuala Kangsar (1913–17)

The Ubudiah Mosque in Kuala Kangsar, Perak, is regarded by many as Malaysia's quintessential Islamic landmark. Built by the British in 1913, its design ideas were drawn from 16th-century Mogul architecture in India.

The British-built Jamek Mosque in Kuala Lumpur displays a wide range of stylistic elements. It combines the distinctive red and white masonry bands seen on the Great Mosque of Cordoba in Spain with Mogul-style onion domes and minarets.

The Syed Alwi Mosque in Kangar, Perlis, was built by the British in the tradition of a simple prayer hall. Smaller in scale and less flamboyant than the Ubudiah Mosque, it is nevertheless distinctive in its simplicity.

The black domes of the Zahir Mosque in Alor Setar, Kedah, contrast dramatically with the exquisite lace-like details of the parapet, minarets and arches. The arcaded veranda creates an intermediate zone between the exterior and interior spaces.

power to succeed in governing beyond the trading cities to the entire country. Despite wresting political power from the sultans and rajas, the British conceded the continuing cultural-religious leadership by these rulers. As a symbol of their commitment to this relationship, the British administrators built numerous grand mosques in the expressive style of Middle Eastern, Mogul, Moorish and Western Neoclassical traditions (see 'Western and modernist influences on mosques'). Constructed in a mixture of concrete, brick and plaster, they completely overshadowed their local timber counterparts.

A detail of one of the pavilion-like chatris which top the minarets of the Ubudiah Mosque—a distinguishing feature of Mogul-style architecture.

Unlike the Indian Muslims, the British did not feel the need to adhere to an accurate cultural heritage in their architecture. Moreover, traditional Malay culture at that time did not have the architectural vocabulary with which to assemble an imperial scale of buildings. Thus, the British architects felt free to fashion their own unique interpretations, vaguely modelled after the Mogul mosques they had discovered in India.

Probably the most awe-inspiring of these royal mosques is the Ubudiah Mosque, built by the British administration in the royal town of Kuala Kangsar, Perak, in 1913–17.

The shape and arrangement of the domes and numerous minarets, together with the dentiform arches, are clearly Mogul in origin. However, the distinctive exterior banding of Italian marble is Moorish in design..

Eventually, all nine royal towns were presented with mosques built by the British. Some of the more noteworthy are the Zahir Mosque in Alor Setar, Kedah (1912), the Syed Alwi Mosque in Kangar, Perlis (1933) and the Sultan Abu Bakar Mosque in Johor Bahru (1892). In all these grand projects, historical accuracy was overshadowed by the need to achieve monumentality, with striking cross-cultural results.

In addition to royal mosques, which were usually built in the vicinity of palaces, the British also built mosques for the Malay civil servants within their administrative centres. Although built on a lesser scale, they are similar in inspiration to their royal counterparts. The most important is the Jamek Mosque in Kuala Lumpur, built in 1909 at the site of the founding of the city. Aside from the distinct Mogul form of the dome, the mosque is similar to Moorish mosques with grids of collonaded arches, detailed with bands of brick, plaster and marble.

Local interpretations

Towards the end of the 19th century, geopolitical forces in Malaysia gave rise to a growing Islamic orthodoxy among the people, requiring greater and more authentic expression of Islamic symbolism by embracing architectural styles of the Middle East and Mogul India. Even the modest rural timber mosques, built in the style of the Southeast Asian mosque, were replaced by local interpretations of grand masonry structures.

The open and bare interior of the Zahir Mosque effectivley sets off the elegant decoration on the ceiling and the walls, and the Islamic calligraphy above the arches.

The dentiform arch of the Moti Masjid in Delhi is typical of Mogul mosques in India. Marble was popularized as a building material by the Moguls.

The Mogul tradition

The Mogul architectural tradition came to India by way of the Muslim Mogul emperors who originated in West Asia and ruled India for over 300 years, from 1526 to 1857. Emperor Akbar, who ruled from 1556 to 1605, built the palace city of Fatehpur Sikri (1571–85), setting a new standard for the grandeur of such structures. The complex, comprising mosques, palaces and audience halls, was designed in a combination of Persian-Islamic and Indian styles.

Emperor Shah Jahan, who reigned from 1628 to 1657, was an enthusiastic patron of architecture. He commissioned the famous Taj Mahal, the Jami Masjid, the largest mosque in India, and several buildings in the Red Fort in Delhi, including the Moti Masjid or Pearl Mosque. The architectural style perfected by Shah Jahan became synonymous with Islamic buildings and was widely imitated by the architects of later Mogul emperors and minor rulers in northern and central India.

Western and Modernist influences on mosques

There is no indication that the Portuguese or Dutch rulers of Melaka influenced the architecture of the Malaysian mosque. However, from the late 19th century, the British administrators of Malaya encouraged the building of mosques incorporating Western features, thereby introducing Western architectural styles into an already complex lineage of influences from India, China, Java and the Middle East. This lineage was further extended by the advent of Modernism in the early 20th century.

An aerial view of Masjid Negara.

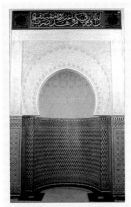

The direction of Mecca

The mihrab, a niche indicating the direction of Mecca, is in the main prayer hall in Masjid Negara. It is decorated with finely carved geometric patterns and Islamic calligraphy known as *khat*.

Western-style mosques

The Western designs of 19th-century mosques in Malaysia arose partially from the desire of certain sultans and the court aristocracy to emulate imperial British culture. As a result, mosques built during this period were modelled after Georgian architecture, popular in England from the 18th to the 19th century. They were grand structures, symmetrical in shape, and decorated with classical motifs such as capitalized columns, keyed arches and pediments. Because they were 'royal' mosques, the temptation to achieve the 'palatial' effect of buildings in British courts was often greater than the need for functionality or the desire to preserve local architectural traditions.

A second mosque style popular during the same period was the Indian or Mogul mosque, another import of the British administrators, as well as of the growing Indian Muslim community in Malaysia during the late 19th and early 20th centuries (see 'Indian and Mogul influences on mosques').

Prominent examples

Two important examples of Western-style mosques are the Sultan Abu Bakar Mosque of Johor Bahru, built in 1892, and the Jamek Mosque of Muar, built in 1925. In both, the central hall is flanked by spaces lined with columns not unlike the arrangement of cathedral naves and side aisles in Western church architecture.

In the case of the Masjid Jamek of Muar, in particular, there is considerable use of stylistic features to achieve a Neoclassical effect. The minaret is in the form of a turret, while the ablution space resembles a circular Roman temple. The various building parts are rather inelegantly joined and overdecorated with Classical ornamentation, such as columns, balustrades, French windows and keyed arches.

Western Neoclassicism, however, enjoyed only a brief popularity in early mosque architecture in Malaysia. With the rise of orthodox Islamic thinking in the early 20th century, the more authentic styles of Mogul India and the Middle East eventually overtook Western Neoclassicism. Mosque architecture increasingly combined Mogul and Moorish traditions, resulting in some distinctive mosque buildings.

Western Modernism

Modernism's relatively late influence on mosque architecture in Malaysia is exemplified by the design of the Sultan Sulaiman Mosque of Kelang, Selangor, built in 1932. Like other royal mosques built at the time by the British, the Sultan Sulaiman Mosque was modelled principally on a Mogul mosque, with a central dome space surrounded by smaller domed verandas. The shape of the dome, however, is a departure from the onion shape of the Mogul type, and is similar to the flatter Western forms.

Other early attempts at Modernism in mosque architecture in the Malay Peninsula echoed similar experiments occurring in Europe at the time. Heavy

Late 19th-century and 20th-century mosque styles

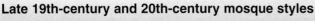

Sultan Abu Bakar Mosque, Johor Bahru (1892). Although Western in style, this mosque clearly expresses the symmetry of the traditional mosque.

Jamek Mosque, Muar, Johor (1925). Sited by the Muar River, a notable feature of this mosque is the unusual minaret, reminiscent of a lighthouse. This British-designed mosque also features Doric columns.

Sultan Sulaiman Mosque, Kelang, Selangor (1932). The main dome is capped by an elegant wrought iron glazed cupola surrounded by filigree finials.

Jamek Mosque, Mersing, Johor (1952). A reflection of its time, this mosque is based on less ornate modernistic lines.

Masjid Negara, Kuala Lumpur (1965)

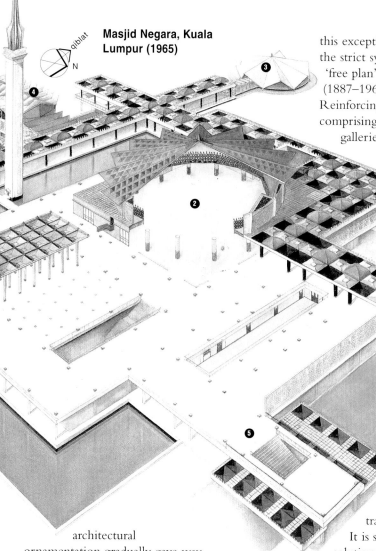

this exceptional building was the first to depart from the strict symmetry of earlier mosques, resulting in a 'free plan' akin to that advocated by Le Corbusier (1887–1965), the renowned French architect. Reinforcing this interpretation, the building, comprising two levels, rests on *pilote* columns. The galleries surrounding the main prayer hall are treated like wide-open verandas.

Geometrically patterned grillwork forms the walls.

Adhering to the early Modernist principle of 'form follows function', the internal space is organized along the principal functions of a mosque. The first floor, where the main prayer hall is situated, is devoted exclusively to the performance of prayers and rituals. The lower floor houses the public facilities, such as the administration office for the collection of *zakat* (tithes), a clinic, and classrooms for religious instruction. Probably the most radical departure from mosque traditions, however, is the 'umbrella' roof. It is simultaneously a creative construction solution (a 360 degree folded plate structure) and an ingenious combination of the two main traditions in Malaysian mosque architecture: the dome inspired by imported Middle Eastern and Mogul architecture and the roof inspired by the pyramidal forms of more indigenous origin.

Because of the success of the design of Masjid Negara, and coinciding with an international trend, structural expressionism (the attachment of symbolic meanings to the structure of a building) became the predominant inspiration for early post-Independence mosques in Malaysia. The Negeri Sembilan State Mosque (1967) and the Penang State Mosque (1980) are two of the best examples of the use of structure as the main design feature.

architectural ornamentation gradually gave way to stylized detailing. The complex arrangement of massing, which typified the early Mogul and Western Neoclassical designs, was overtaken by simple geometric forms. Using the Mogul mosque as a prototype, these early Modernist experiments are exemplified by the Jamek Mosque of Kluang, Johor, and the Jamek Mosque of Mersing, Johor, both built in the 1950s.

Post-Independence Modernism

Probably the most significant event in the history of early Modernism in Malaysian architecture was the construction of Masjid Negara, the National Mosque, in Kuala Lumpur in 1965. In its design,

1. The main entrance to the mosque faces the direction of the qiblat.
2. The main prayer hall is on the upper level of the mosque. Women pray behind the lattice screen on the mezzanine floor.
3. A covered passageway leads from the mosque to the mausoleum. Its faceted roof echoes the design of the main roof of the mosque.
4. A separate wing of the mosque houses several classrooms for religious instruction.
5. The ablution area is situated below ground level. As a main mosque area is considered holy, the ablution area is never situated within it.

Negeri Sembilan State Mosque (1967). This is based on the plan form of a nine-sided polygon, symbolizing the number of districts in the state.

Penang State Mosque (1980). The curved main beams were inspired by Oscar Niemeyer's sculptured design in Brasilia, Brazil.

Sultan Salahuddin Abdul Aziz Shah Mosque, Shah Alam, Selangor (1988). Its dome is the largest of any religious structure in the world.

Sarawak State Mosque, Petra Jaya (1990). Its monumental box-like design is reminiscent of a North African mosque. The plain form also typifies the minimalist architectural approach.

The story of schools

Before the introduction of formal education in Malaysia, children of the various ethnic groups went to vernacular schools housed mainly in modest timber structures. The building of large, prestigious schools began in the mid-19th century with the founding of English-medium schools by the British colonial government and the Christian missionaries. After Malaysia gained Independence in 1957, new schools were built in functional, standardized designs to reduce costs and to reflect the government's policy of forging national unity through education.

St John's Institution in Kuala Lumpur, founded by the Roman Catholic Mission as a school for boys, was started in 1904 and moved into the present building in 1907. Apart from some extensions, the school building—the most substantial school building of its time—stands as it was when first opened.

An early 20th-century thatched roof Malay vernacular school in Sepri, Rembau, Negeri Sembilan.

This national-type school, opened in 1931 in Merlimau, Melaka, is raised on posts and features a two-tiered tiled roof.

Known as the 'floating school', this Chinese school was built on piles above the sea in Kukup, Johor.

A Tamil school at the Glenealy Estate in Perak. This picture was taken in 1993.

Vernacular schools

Most vernacular schools were orignally set up in the 19th century by the main ethnic groups—the Malays, Chinese and Indians—to cater to the educational needs of their children. The children were taught in their mother tongue. In the Malay schools, religious instruction was the norm.

The first schools

The first schools to be built in Peninsular Malaysia were vernacular schools built in the house styles of the various communities. Most Malay schools were religious schools housed in kampong-style wood and thatch structures in rural areas. The Chinese built schools in both rural and urban areas. Modest in scale, the village schools were usually built of timber with tiled roofs while the town schools were constructed of brick. Some were housed in *kongsi* (clan houses). The Indian schools, located mainly in rubber estates, were basic wooden structures.

Colonial and mission schools

Until the formation of the Education Department in the late 19th century, very little effort was made by the colonial administration to set up schools for the children in the colony. In 1890, the first Government English School was established by the Revd Frederick Haines, a Church of England vicar. Following pressure from the Malay members of the colonial administration to employ more Malays in government service, especially from the Malay aristocracy, a Raja School was established in 1892 at the edge of the Padang (giving rise to the name 'Jalan Raja'), which in 1893 was absorbed into the Government English School. Renamed the Victoria Institution, the school moved into new buildings in 1894 funded from money left over from Queen Victoria's Jubilee Fund. In 1905, the colonial government also opened a residential college in Kuala Kangsar, Perak—the Malay College— to educate boys from royal and noble families for government service.

In addition to the government's initiatives, the conviction of the Christian missionaries that education was the best way to inculcate Christian values also played an important role in the founding of several English-medium schools throughout the country from the late 19th to the early 20th century. The first English-medium school in Penang, the Penang Free School—it was free in the sense that children of all races and creeds were admitted—was founded in 1816 by the Revd R. S. Hutchings. Although the school started in a house in Love Lane, it was only in 1896 that construction began on a proper school building in Farquhar Street.

The success of the Penang Free School led to the founding of more mission schools. In the mid-19th century, the Catholic La Salle brothers arrived in Peninsular Malaya to set up a chain of schools for boys, while the Catholic nuns of the Order of Infant Jesus opened similar schools for girls. Other missionaries of various denominations followed suit and opened several notable schools, such as the Anglo Chinese schools in Penang and Ipoh, the Methodist Boys' School, Bukit Bintang Girls' School and St John's Institution in Kuala Lumpur, and St Thomas' Anglican Boys' School in Kuching.

Architectural styles

While the history of the construction of these early schools is scanty, a hybrid of architectural styles, including Romanesque, Neoclassical and Neogothic, indicate that the designs of the schools were very much influenced by those built in the West.

Standard elevation for national-type schools

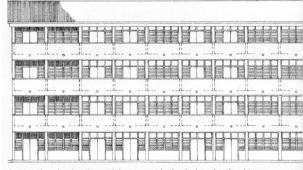

An elevation showing the modular concept in the design of national-type schools in Malaysia. Each classroom comprises three bays with two doors. The size of a new school can thus be extended lengthwise according to the projected student population.

The Penang Free School in Georgetown, Penang, which now houses the Penang State Museum, was the first school to be accommodated in a large, late 19th-century Western Classical-style building. The scale and style of the building enhanced the prestige of the school and set the standard for other English-medium schools. The school originally consisted of a two-storey structure which was later extended with blocks of a more solid masonry construction with arched openings along the corridors, typical of many of the school buildings built during that period. The Malay College in Kuala Kangsar was also built in the Western Classical tradition. The original structure that formed the centrepiece is a pedimented two-storey building adorned with friezes and Ionic columns with voluted capitals resting on plinths in the best Neoclassical tradition of the colonial era. The pioneer missionary school for girls, the Convent of the Holy Infant Jesus in Light Street, Penang, founded in 1852, combined Neogothic and Anglo-Indian architecture, an eclecticism that was influenced by the cultural exchange introduced by British colonialism.

The garden landscape

A common characteristic of these schools is their garden landscape, acknowledged at the time as an essential component of a good learning environment. Often the layout of a school was carefully planned according to the general topography. The Malay College in Kuala Kangsar, set in acres of playing fields, and the Convent of the Holy Infant Jesus in Light Street, Penang, with its cloistered gardens, were examples of architecture that mediated between the concerns of the building and its function and the surroundings. The serene, monastic setting of the Convent gardens, for example, contrasted with the austerity of the nunnery and the splendour of the Gothic chapel.

Nation building through education

In contrast to the selective education policy of the colonial administration, the period after Independence may be described as an era of rapid

The present Victoria Institution opened in 1929. Its place as one of the leading English-medium schools in the colonial era is reflected in its imposing structure and position on Petaling Hill in the capital.

The stately facade of the Malay College (1905) in Kuala Kangsar represents the best Neoclassical tradition of the colonial era.

St Michael's Institution in Ipoh, Perak, started in an old Malay house in 1912 and entered its present building in 1923, which was designed by a French Catholic missionary in the late Gothic style.

Rows of shuttered windows, arcaded verandas and balustrades overlooking internal courtyards (below) lend dignity to the Light Street Convent in Penang.

quantitative expansion in education. To meet the ever increasing demand for more schools, both primary and secondary schools were designed and implemented by expatriate and foreign-trained local architects in the Public Works Department (PWD), later renamed the Jabatan Kerja Raya (JKR). These plans were formulated so that schools could be built economically and quickly anywhere in the country. Although they were easy to build and solved the problem of cost and numbers, their utilitarian nature spawned buildings that were entirely devoid of character and identity.

Designs for the future

Moving into the next millennium, there are, however, signs indicating a shift from the paradigm of quantitative expansion to qualitative improvement. A network of 'smart schools', which will utilize advanced technology as teaching and learning tools, will be established to spearhead education reforms in order to prepare the next generation for the Age of Information Technology. To allow students and teachers access to television, computers, CD-ROMs, laser discs and cable television, a change in the physical design of schools will be necessary. Instead of the traditional classrooms, there will be more flexible use of space to incorporate work stations-cum-laboratories-cum-self-study areas in a single classroom.

Early modern primary and secondary schools in Malaysia were built quickly and economically using standard Jabatan Kerja Raya, or Public Works Department, plans, which specified the sizes of buildings and the materials to be used in construction. The size of a particular school was determined by the projected number of students attending the school and the number of students per classroom. The schools, which are regimentally laid out in parallel blocks, are usually 2–3 storeys in height. A veranda on one side of each storey, aided by ceiling fans in the classrooms, facilitates ventilation. Stairs at either end allow access to the various levels.

A typical three-storey JKR school. The blocks, placed parallel to each other and joined by walkways, are set back across a broad playing field.

The Minister of Education, Dato' Sri Mohd Najib bin Tun Hj Abdul Razak (on the right), inspecting a model of the new 'smart school' buildings for Sekolah Menengah Perempuan Seri Puteri, Kuala Lumpur, on 27 May 1997. The buildings are designed so that information technology can be harnessed smartly for the benefit of the students.

The Chinese shophouse

The commercial centre of every Malaysian town before World War II was characterized by one or more main streets lined with shophouses, usually two storeys high, with the lower floor used for trading and the upper floor for residential purposes. The emergence of this urban building type can be traced to the influx of Chinese immigrants from the densely populated southern coastal provinces of China in the 19th century until World War II. They brought with them both knowledge and methods of house construction which they then adapted to the Malaysian urban shophouse. By the early 20th century, this urban form was to spread to every major town in the country.

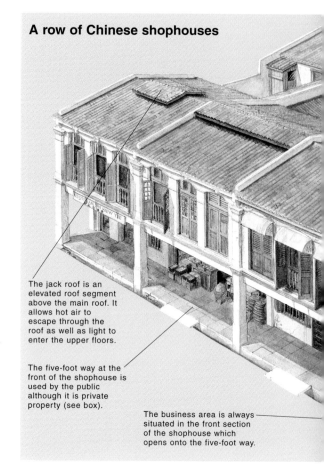

The jack roof is an elevated roof segment above the main roof. It allows hot air to escape through the roof as well as light to enter the upper floors.

The five-foot way at the front of the shophouse is used by the public although it is private property (see box).

The business area is always situated in the front section of the shophouse which opens onto the five-foot way.

A row of early timber shophouses on a street in Penang. The windows and shop frontages are very much narrower than the later versions.

Features of early shophouses

The early masonry shophouses built in the 19th century were usually around 6–7 metres wide and 30 metres deep, sometimes extending to 60 metres. They were always built in rows with uniform facades and a continuous, covered five-foot way in front (see box). The walls, built of bricks, were plastered and the roofs tiled. Other typical features included a jack roof—a smaller roof raised above the main roof to allow accumulated hot air in the house to escape—and low, rickety, shuttered windows on the front of the first floor. The shop front on the ground floor had no wall. Goods were displayed along the full width facing the five-foot way, leaving a narrow central aisle. To close the shop, the front was boarded up with fitted timber panels and secured with horizontal bars.

Inside the shophouse there was a central courtyard, which was later reduced to an airwell when space became more precious. Courtyards were typical of residences all over China, especially in the less densely populated areas of the north, where they were central to the layout of houses often surrounded by high walls. In southern China, the courtyards were surrounded by built-up spaces.

Western facades on Chinese forms

The decorative styles which typified the facades of Malaysian shophouses constructed up to the 1920s were built from memory or based on copy books of styles found in parts of southern China, where European revivalist influence played a major role. The nouveau riche in both the emerging Malaysian towns and the treaty ports of southern China

A century of shophouse styles

Transitional (c. 1890s)
Shophouses built of brick with tiled roofs replaced the timber and thatch hut.

Neoclassical (c. 1920s)
A Grecian pediment, columns and moulded plaster swags decorated the facade.

Neoclassical (c. 1920s)
This style included a parapet on the top of the building and ornate window frames.

Dutch Patrician (c.1930s)
A Dutch-inspired gable was adopted for the front facade of this shophouse.

Art Deco (1930s)
Geometrical shapes and simplified lines were a departure from the 1920s style. The ground floor and windows are not original.

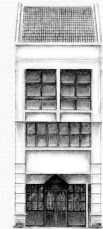

Modern (1990s)
Coming full circle, the 1990s utilitarian shophouse is devoid of any decoration.

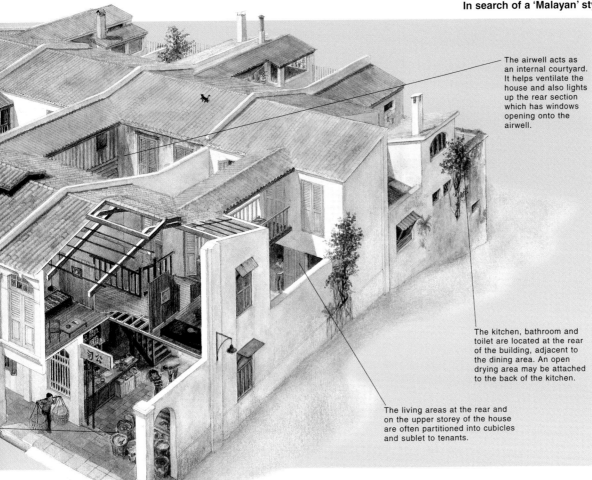

The airwell acts as an internal courtyard. It helps ventilate the house and also lights up the rear section which has windows opening onto the airwell.

The kitchen, bathroom and toilet are located at the rear of the building, adjacent to the dining area. An open drying area may be attached to the back of the kitchen.

The living areas at the rear and on the upper storey of the house are often partitioned into cubicles and sublet to tenants.

Window decoration
Influenced by the facades of colonial buildings, Chinese builders adopted European forms to decorate the facades of shophouses. Windows were framed by Classical-style columns with foliated capitals, while the fanlights above the shutters were often decorated with Malay-inspired carved grilles or Venetian glass.

The five-foot way
In a ruling which was first imposed by Sir Stamford Raffles in Singapore in 1822, the British colonial administration specified that all shophouses had to include a minimum five-foot-wide veranda on the ground floor. This requirement was to make the Malaysian (and Singaporean) shophouse unique. The five-foot way addressed the extremities of the tropical sun and rain and created pedestrian linkages at ground level. Because these shaded areas were conducive to browsing and trading, shopkeepers used them to their advantage by displaying their products at the front of the shop, sometimes spilling the display onto the five-foot way itself.

(among them Canton, Amoy, Foochow-Fu, Ningpo and Shanghai which had come under British jurisdiction in 1842) were attracted to stylistic interpretations of European architecture.

The decorative styles which emerged on the facades of Malaysian shophouses thus varied from Neogothic, Baroque and Classical to Palladian. Stucco designs of flowers and birds decorate the walls below the windows, while wreaths, festoons and swags decorate the walls. The windows appear in various shapes: some comprise square-topped openings with arched fanlights, others full-length windows with balustrades, while yet others have square or segmented vents above. In accordance with the Neoclassical Palladian style of the period, the facades of these shophouses were always symmetrical in their arrangement since the row of houses was usually designed as a block or entity.

The construction of shophouses reached its peak in the 1920s during the rubber boom but slowed down during the 1930s depression up until World War II. During the postwar period, particularly from the 1960s onwards, the form of shophouses was to continue along similar lines, but with the advent of International Modernism, and the move away from excessive ornamentation, the facades of shophouses were no longer embellished in revivalist styles but were left completely unadorned. With rising land values, the shophouses became taller, sometimes reaching four storeys.

A new lease of life

In the 1960s and 1970s, shophouses again became the common building idiom, especially in the central areas of new towns and in housing estates. In the 1980s, however, the new-found affluence of urban Malaysians sparked a booming car population and a consequent demand for car parks. Shophouses were replaced by high-rise buildings, complete with parking bays and surrounded by roads, which often became 'islands', isolated from adjacent buildings.

The 1980s also marked the appearance of powerful corporations seeking expressions through their buildings, and these were provided by the construction of high-rises. In the late 1980s and 1990s, the merits of these isolated buildings as urban forms, unsupported by a structured urban framework, began to be questioned.

These doubts were paralleled by a surge of interest in conservation and the environment. The shophouses were seen by the conservationists as representing the typical Malaysian urban form, one that was particularly well suited to the climatic conditions of the country. Conversely, the high-rise was viewed as an anonymous international form common to every city in the world. There was concern that Malaysian towns were losing their unique character. Shophouses, which have provided Malaysian streets with a continuous framework and, occasionally, the frames around town squares, were preferred to isolated high-rises. Hence, the shophouse is seen again, in modern guise, in housing estates and new towns built after the 1980s.

The Melakan townhouse

A derivative of the shophouse, the elongated Melakan townhouse, built on a narrow plot in a row facing the street, was the prototype house of the urban Chinese from the 17th century. The evolution of the townhouse in Malaysia epitomizes the diverse assimilation of cross-cultural traditions in building methods, construction materials and ornamentation. This was brought about by centuries of vibrant trade between the Chinese and Malays and European colonialists.

The back portion of the Melakan house was formerly built on piles over the sea or river to allow goods to be loaded and unloaded and also access to water transportation. This is no longer possible because of land reclamation from the sea.

Traditional features

Apart from some mid-19th century examples in Penang, the Melakan townhouse of the latter half of the 17th century represents the earliest townhouse still seen in Malaysia. Among the features peculiar to it is a central pair of timber panelled doors at the front of the house. On either side of the doors are square windows with bars and shutters. Above the windows are curvilinear-shaped ventilation spaces. Set in front of the main doors is a pair of intricately carved half-doors (*pintu pagar*). These half-doors, a feature adopted from the Malay house, provide the household with a semblance of privacy during the day when the main doors are left open for light and ventilation.

The house, laid out along a longitudinal axis, opens pleasantly onto a number of sections. A recessed porch with adjacent side archways leads into a reception hall. Considered a public area, it is separated from the private portion of the house by a decorative carved screen. The private parts of the house are connected by covered passages and interior courtyards (the smaller versions are referred to as airwells). The courtyards admit air and light into the long and narrow house which is otherwise

Western influences are seen on the facade of a Melakan townhouse in the pilasters and columns covered with plaster motifs, the decorated frieze indicating the division between the two floors, and the imported glazed tiles.

This side view indicates the length of a typical Melakan townhouse. Two or three internal courtyards break up the house into various sections.

completely secluded from the outside world. The house usually includes a sitting room, an ancestral room, dining-rooms, a kitchen and bathrooms. The kitchen and bathrooms are always at the rear of the house where the well is situated. In some houses there is a trap door at the back which allowed the residents to board boats at high tide.

An ornate timber staircase with balusters leads to the private family quarters at the upper level, which are characterized by timber floors and high ceilings. The most important room is the bridal chamber.

Ornamentation

Decorative elements in townhouses were very much influenced by the colonial presence in Melaka (see 'The colonial legacy in Melaka') and the Europeans who lived in the Chinese treaty ports (see 'The Chinese shophouse'). By the late 19th century, after a period of adaptive transition, the immigrant craftsmen and builders had introduced elements of opulent ornamentation in the Palladian and Baroque treatment of facades. Features such as Neoclassical pediments, pillars and stucco decorations over windows, combined with the local tradition of timber craftsmanship, are typical of the townhouses in Heeren Street (Jalan Tun Tan Cheng Lock). Heeren Street, once known as the Dutch village

Features of townhouse facades

Ventilation openings with carved decoration can be seen above the ground floor windows.

The half-doors in front of the main doors are known as *pintu pagar*, or 'fence door' in Malay.

Prosperous house owners favoured ornate decoration.

Imported glazed tiles are commonly used on the walls of the facade and around the courtyards.

Floral plasterwork is often seen on pilasters and columns.

Geometrically patterned tiles provide a contrast to the glazed tile end pieces of roofs.

because of the Dutch merchants who used to live there, was later occupied by affluent Straits Chinese merchants. The title deeds of some of the older houses are indeed Dutch although it is unlikely that any of the original Dutch houses still exist in Heeren Street. It is possible that some of the houses were demolished by the Chinese who then built their houses on the sites, retaining some Dutch features, such as red laterite floor tiles and cornices.

In the interior, rooms have high ceilings and are furnished with finely crafted Chinese blackwood furniture inlaid with marble and mother-of-pearl, and decorated with expensive ornaments. The most important piece of furniture is the ancestral altar, which is gilded and elaborately carved.

Construction trends

By the late 19th century, the townhouse had become a major building type as more and more Chinese prospered. But the opulent style of these early townhouses has since yielded to new styles and tastes, characterized by the use of modern materials and simplified designs, as seen in modern townhouses that cater to those living in high-density housing estates. In the past, the Melakan townhouse represented the success of the wealthy Chinese merchants, whereas the contemporary townhouse is now more of an egalitarian form adopted by developers to create medium- and low-cost housing for the majority.

The formal sitting room contains the ancestral altar. The room would typically be furnished with imported Chinese blackwood chairs with matching tables placed along the walls on either side of the room.

This sitting room looks out onto the internal courtyard which is often treated as an indoor garden. Courtyards ventilate and admit light into the enclosed areas.

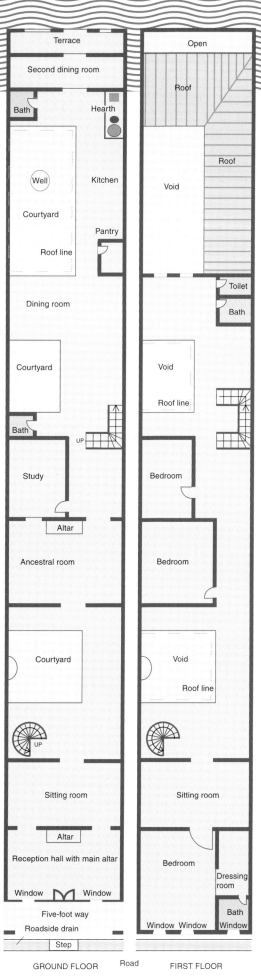

GROUND FLOOR

Terrace
Second dining room
Bath · Hearth
Well · Kitchen
Courtyard
Roof line
Pantry
Dining room
Courtyard
Bath
Study
UP
Altar
Ancestral room
Courtyard
UP
Sitting room
Altar
Reception hall with main altar
Window · Window
Five-foot way
Roadside drain
Step

Road

FIRST FLOOR

Open
Roof
Void
Roof
Toilet
Bath
Void
Roof line
Bedroom
Bedroom
Void
Roof line
Sitting room
Bedroom
Dressing room
Window · Window · Bath · Window

The floor plan of a Melakan townhouse
Most Melakan townhouses have a narrow frontage of about 10 metres but they stretch back to about 68 metres.
(Not drawn to scale)

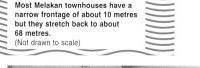

The kitchen is usually spacious. A wood fire was formerly used in the cooking range which required a large hood to expel the smoke.

In addition to the main internal staircase, some houses have wrought iron spiral staircases at the rear of the house.

The doors and windows on the landing of the first floor are arranged symmetrically and parallel the entrance on the ground floor.

The bridal bedroom is the most elaborately furnished of the upstairs bedrooms.

93

Origins of the Malayan bungalow

Although the word 'bungalow' originates from the modest Bengal house—a timber structure with a thatched roof and a veranda built on the ground—the bungalow in Malaysia refers to a much more substantial detached house. As in a Malay village, the Malayan bungalow and its cluster of ancillary buildings were set in a large 'compound' (a word derived from the Malay 'kampong').

An early tropical bungalow in Penang, built by the Chinese miller Amee, incorporated local features, such as timber posts to raise the house above the ground, a thatched roof and covered steps. However, in its roof shape and symmetrical form, it departed radically from the traditional Malay house.

Francis Light's 'Suffolk House' in Ayer Itam Road, Penang, is an example of a grand garden house built in a mixed style of English and Indian architecture. The original house had a flat roof of Indian floor tiles bordered by a low parapet. In the late 19th century, the main roof was replaced by a hipped pantile roof, which was better suited to the climate. The symmetrical design is typical of a late Georgian house.

A later version of a grand house is this whitewashed colonial-style bungalow in Ipoh, Perak. Its symmetrical facade, with a central porch and black timber finish on the front gables, was a style popular with British architects in Peninsular Malaysia from about 1910 to 1940. The original shuttered windows have been altered for air conditioning.

Eighteenth-century bungalows

By assimilating various building traditions from the East and the West, the early settlers in Penang constructed houses which reflected their adaptability to the new environment. The typical Malayan bungalow emerged as a large, airy, detached, two-storey house constructed of timber or brick, covered by a hipped pantile roof with a porte-cochere, the latter built so that horse carriages could stop for passengers to enter or alight at the main entrance. The main building was usually connected to the kitchen and servants' quarters by means of a covered walkway, the whole forming an I-shaped plan.

Around all sides of the house was a series of full-length windows with moulded reveals, timber shutters and balustraded rails. In the late Victorian era (the 1890s), cast iron window rails, etched glass fanlights and stucco arabesque decoration on the facade were incorporated.

An early usage of the word bungalow is found in Francis Light's will of 1793, in which he left his 'Garden house' and 'bungaloe in George Town' to his common-law wife, Martina Rozells. The garden

An Anglo-Indian bungalow, the *College-General* retreat at Mariophile, Tanjung Bungah, Penang.

The Anglo-Indian house style

The Anglo-Indian house style, which developed in British colonial India from the 17th century, was the offspring of a marriage between European and Asian building traditions. The colonial architects built European-style houses with distinctive symmetrical facades (a style prevalent during the reigns of the English kings, George I, II and III (1714–1820)), but adopted local features such as deep verandas, high ceilings and full-length windows with balustrades to keep the house cool. When Francis Light established Penang as an outpost of the East India Company in 1786, colonial administrators, British merchants and planters transported this house style from India. As Penang flourished, traders from South India, China and Sumatra arrived, each adding their own characteristic styles to the bungalow.

house, as it was understood in the 18th century, was a country house with a garden estate planted with tropical produce such as pepper, cloves, nutmeg and coffee. It was a grand house, set apart from other structures, to be admired from all sides. After several more such showpieces were put up in the early 19th century, the type became locally extinct as the estates became fragmented. Light's 'Suffolk House' is the only surviving garden house in the country. In contrast, the bungalow flourished on the outskirts of Malaysia's towns throughout the 19th century.

The Anglo-Indian bungalow

The first Anglo-Indian bungalows in George Town were built by European settlers, followed quickly by Indian Muslim merchants. While the pioneer timber houses have since been demolished and replaced, some of the early brick houses, because of their sturdy construction, are still in use. Thatched roofs were subsequently replaced with terracotta pantile roofs.

The best known survivors of the Anglo-Indian bungalow are Light's bungalow (c. 1790) and the *College-General* retreat at Mariophile, which was built in the early 1800s. These early buildings tend to have walk-in porches, rather than carriage porches. The porte-cochere, which became popular during the early Victorian period (the 1840s), was often added to existing buildings, as it was to Light's bungalow and 'Suffolk House'.

Local hybrid styles

Taking after its Anglo-Indian antecedent, the early bungalow in George Town had all the simplicity and symmetry of a provincial late Georgian (1820s) house. The facade was plain and symmetrical. The front door opened onto a narrow hall running down the centre of the building with rooms on both sides. Those built in the first half of the 19th century can be identified by a porch supported by imposing columns. Double-storey brick bungalows of this style, often limewashed yellow, can be found along Chulia Street, Hutton Lane and Penang Road. By the 1830s, a variation of the above had developed using timber construction with full-length windows to facilitate ventilation. Instead of a set-in porch, shelter from the sun was provided by an awning across the width of the house just above the door.

James Low, in his book *The British Settlement of Penang* (1836), remarked that 'a substantial bungalow, from 60–70 feet long by 35–40 feet broad—the under storey of brick and mortar, the upper constructed with the best kinds of wood, with a tiled roof, and the whole interior and exterior of the upper storey painted—might be built perhaps for some twelve hundred Spanish dollars.' Detached bungalows of this type, locally called 'compound houses', can still be seen along Chulia Street, Argyll Road, Burmah Road and in the compound of the Acheen Street Mosque.

While the above bungalows remained solidly on the ground, by the mid-19th century, the Jawi Peranakan (people of mixed Indian and Malay descent) began to produce a hybrid of the compound house and the Malay house which had timber floors raised on brick piers. In contrast to the Georgian symmetry of the Anglo-Indian house, the homes of the Jawi Peranakan community featured an *anjung*, or porch, set off to one side inspired by the *serambi* (veranda) construction of the traditional Malay house. Examples of such houses can be found in Kedah Road and Transfer Road in Penang.

Lifestyles and house styles

Trends, however, were very much set by the suburban lifestyle of the Europeans. The bungalow evolved in the days of the horse carriage. One would ride through the gateway, with its massive gate posts and perhaps a wrought iron gate, along a circular driveway skirting the front lawn, and right up to the porte-cochere. From here a side road would lead to the stables or the mews at the back.

The true 'colonial bungalow' was taken to new heights by European settlers such as government

This bungalow in Ladang Changkat Kinding, an estate near Ipoh in Perak, was built by a British lowland tea planter in 1934. The black timber frames used for decorative purposes came to be popularly known as the 'black and white style'.

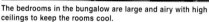

The bedrooms in the bungalow are large and airy with high ceilings to keep the rooms cool.

The dark, wooden staircase and the fireplace on the right are reminiscent of old English houses.

officials, merchants and planters. Set in extensive gardens, these houses tended to be dignified and plain, with deep verandas protected by bamboo *chiks* (blinds), and constructed using the best timber from the Malaysian forests. As soon as modern plumbing was introduced, large bathrooms were installed. In showy contrast, the Chinese and Eurasian élite, indulging in late Victorian fancies up until the 1920s, produced the embellished Straits Eclectic villas (see 'Villas and mansions').

Syed Alatas Mansion

This house belonged to an Arab trader, Syed Mohammad Alatas, leader of the Acehnese community in Penang. The layout of the ground floor, which is repeated on the first floor, comprises a central corridor and rooms on both sides partitioned by brick walls.

1. The eaves are fringed with dentilated fascia boards.

2. Stucco arabesque decoration adorns the facade.

3. Fanlights allow sunlight into the interior of a room even when the shutters are closed.

4. Moulded architraves along the internal walls suggest mid-Victorian influence.

5. The timber board ceiling is decorated with gilded roses.

An Indo-Malay or Jawi Peranakan compound house on Kedah Road, Penang. The ground floor is built of bricks and the upper floor of timber. The house has full-length windows with louvred and panelled shutters for ventilation. The tiled steps are a feature adopted from the Melaka kampong house.

Villas and mansions

The late 19th- and early 20th-century private residences of the wealthy Chinese are among the most spectacular buildings in Malaysian cities. They are eye-catching for their sheer ostentation and for the ways in which they combined European classical forms and styles with traditional Chinese house plans and motifs. Results varied from the elegant to the whimsical. These architectural hybrids are also known as 'compradore mansions', for just as their capitalist towkay owners prospered as agents between foreign power and capital on the one hand, and small-time Chinese entrepreneurs on the other, so too did the monuments they built reflect their double allegiance to the East and the West.

'Homestead', on Jalan Sultan Ahmad Shah (Northam Road), Penang, is a wide, E-shaped building. Western-style features, such as the pediment and symmetrical facade, were incorporated to give the mansion a European look.

This mansion in Penang was formerly the home of Tye Kee Yoon. It was designed by Chew Eng Eam (c. 1930), one of the first Western-trained architects to use geometrical patterns as a decorative device.

Set in a landscaped garden, the Nam Hoe villa in Melaka, with a balustraded balcony above a colonnaded porch, emulates the style of a European villa.

The Straits Eclectic style

This term refers to the mix of Chinese, Malay Indian and European architectural styles found in 19th- and early 20th-century houses in Penang, Melaka and Singapore, which were then collectively known as the Straits Settlements. The Straits Eclectic style eventually spread from the Settlements to other towns in Malaysia.

Mansions of the towkays

The towkay mansion was a status symbol *par excellence*, for behind almost every architectural extravangance was a rags-to-riches story of how a penniless coolie became a towkay. The main means of securing wealth was usually through clinching government concessions in various businesses, ranging from mining to opium. Miners and planters made their wealth in Perak only to spend it on lavish homes in metropolitan Penang.

Who was responsible for these Straits Eclectic creations? At first, Chinese builders must have simply incorporated elements from existing colonial bungalows and traditional Chinese buildings. By the early 20th century, however, European architects from Singapore-based firms such as Stark & McNeill and Swan & McLaren were preparing syncretic designs at the bidding of their towkay clients. In the 1920s and 1930s, Western-trained Chinese architects such as Chew Eng Eam and B. H. Ung enjoyed the generous patronage of many a Penang Straits Chinese. Attuned to local tastes, Chew was known for incorporating Chinese forms, such as the moongate, into his Art Deco houses.

The roots of the towkay mansion lay in the West. It was the detached bungalow, essentially Anglo-Indian, and the decorative qualities of late Victorian architecture in England which inspired and gave licence to the flourishing of ornamental houses in the British Straits Settlements. The Straits Chinese found ornate cast iron, Italianate stucco detailing and floral tiles so appealing that they took these architectural expressions further than their Victorian counterparts, and also sustained them longer, up to the early 1930s.

The introduction to the chapter on Penang in Wright and Cartwright's *Twentieth Century Impressions of British Malaya* (1908), describes Northam Road (now Jalan Sultan Ahmad Shah) at a time when the European bungalows along the north beach were being replaced with 'palatial' residences of the Straits Chinese: ' . . . we enter Northam Road, one of the prettiest roads in Georgetown, notwithstanding its proximity to the business centre. It is the beginning of villadom—fine, large

The Loke Yew Mansion is the oldest towkay mansion in Kuala Lumpur. The city's famed philanthropist bought it as a modest house in a 12-acre estate in 1892 and spent the next 12 years modifying it with the help of both Chinese and European craftsmen.

residences enclosed in spacious grounds (locally called "compounds") with tropical foliage on every side.' The road was well kept, shaded with trees and lit by electric arc-lamps at night.

Western décor, Eastern decorum

Led by the Western-educated Straits born, the Chinese moved out of their shophouses in significant numbers in the late 19th century, when wealth and ambition compelled them to try out an alien lifestyle in detached residences which they called *ang-moh lau* (European villas). The older generation stayed put in their townhouses but maintained 'country villas' and stables in their plantations on the outskirts of town. The wealthiest kept bungalows on the hill and by the sea, just as their European counterparts did. While the mansions

Towkay Heah Swee Lee (1875–1924)

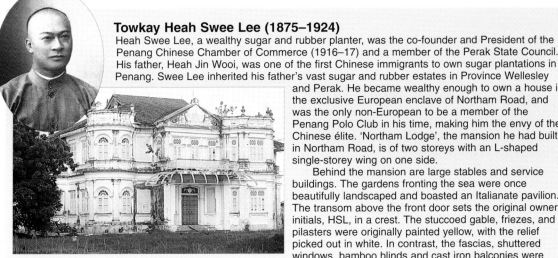

Heah Swee Lee, a wealthy sugar and rubber planter, was the co-founder and President of the Penang Chinese Chamber of Commerce (1916–17) and a member of the Perak State Council. His father, Heah Jin Wooi, was one of the first Chinese immigrants to own sugar plantations in Penang. Swee Lee inherited his father's vast sugar and rubber estates in Province Wellesley and Perak. He became wealthy enough to own a house in the exclusive European enclave of Northam Road, and was the only non-European to be a member of the Penang Polo Club in his time, making him the envy of the Chinese élite. 'Northam Lodge', the mansion he had built in Northam Road, is of two storeys with an L-shaped single-storey wing on one side.

Behind the mansion are large stables and service buildings. The gardens fronting the sea were once beautifully landscaped and boasted an Italianate pavilion. The transom above the front door sets the original owner's initials, HSL, in a crest. The stuccoed gable, friezes, and pilasters were originally painted yellow, with the relief picked out in white. In contrast, the fascias, shuttered windows, bamboo blinds and cast iron balconies were rendered in green. The mansion was later renamed 'Soonstead', after Swee Lee's son-in-law.

Heah Swee Lee's mansion, 'Northam Lodge', was built around 1910 on the site of a former European residence in Northam Road, Penang. It features a fish scale glass marquee over the front entrance.

The entrance hall of Falim House in Ipoh, Perak. The Chinese practice of prominently displaying photographs of ancestors is a mark of filial piety.

boasted English names such as 'Hardwicke' and 'Nova Scotia', or personalized names such as 'Soonstead', the hill villas tended to have European resort names like 'Tosari', 'Lausanne' and 'Mon Sejour'.

While embracing Western architectural forms, traditional principles concerning the internal organization of space were observed in the Chinese mansion. The latter sometimes featured two reception halls, one fastidiously decorated with Western furniture and fittings for receiving European guests, the other decorously furnished with staid blackwood, inlaid mother-of-pearl furniture for receiving Chinese guests. In place of the conventional I-shaped bungalow, many variations of the Chinese courtyard mansion were devised. Enclosed courtyard spaces, larger kitchens and ample veranda space were provided at the rear of the house, where the jealously guarded womenfolk spent most of their time.

Imported Chinese blackwood furniture was fashionable in towkays' homes.

Grand old mansions

The oldest surviving Straits Chinese mansion in the Eclectic style is probably the Chinese Residency built by Cheah Teik Soon in the 1880s. It reflects the culmination of several experiments in blending Eastern and Western architecture. In *Twentieth Century Impressions of British Malaya*, it is described as 'the pagoda-like residency of a wealthy Chinaman, which is four storeys in height, from the topmost balcony of which a splendid bird's-eye view of the harbour and mainland is obtained'. The dramatic appearance of this polygonal building was achieved by multi-tiered roofs, fasciated eaves, balconies and decorative cast iron rails. In the 1910s, the mansion was converted into a hotel known as 'Raffles-by-the-Sea'. Later, it housed the Pi' Joo Girls' School and the Shih Chung Branch School.

'Homestead', the stately home of Lim Mah Chye, was designed by Stark & McNeill in 1919. The wide frontage, parallel to the waterfront, comprises a colonnaded portico with a balcony on top, flanked by a pair of towers. Many of the features of these Straits Eclectic mansions were copied from fashionable neighbours who, in turn, may have got their inspiration from their travels abroad.

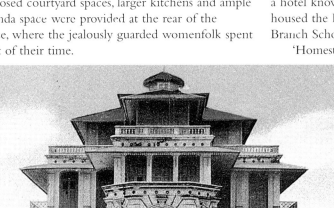

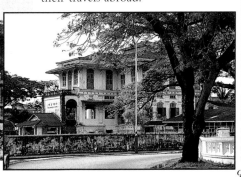

Foliated designs

A wrought iron filigree grille used as a window screen.

Columns with ornate, European-style foliated motifs were a popular feature in many Chinese mansions.

The facades of some of the Chinese villas, including the window screens and columns, were richly embellished with leaf-like motifs.

Foliated designs made from wrought iron were extensively used for architectural decoration in England from the late 18th to the 19th century as a result of the technical improvements in the production of iron, a fashion which caught on with the wealthy in Malaysia.

FAR LEFT: The Chinese Residency was the first four-storey private residence in Penang.

LEFT: After World War II, the Chinese Residency was reduced to a three-storey building, and stripped of its ornamental balconies.

The Anglo-Oriental Building (Wisma Ekran), built in 1937-40, displays a variety of Art Deco details, and represents an early break from classical and colonial architecture.

1. Parliament House, Kuala Lumpur, built to symbolize the newly independent status of the nation, incorporates an unusual sunshade cladding on its tower and podium.

2. Reinforced concrete offered increased design opportunities, such as the rounded corners of this building on Jalan Yap Ah Loy, Kuala Lumpur.

3. The Great Eastern Life Assurance Building on Jalan Ampang, Kuala Lumpur, displays a curved facade and porthole windows.

4. The repetitive floors, horizontal strip windows and round porthole windows of the Loke Yew Building in Kuala Lumpur indicate a break from the Classical and Art Deco styles in favour of Modernism.

5. The International Style, seen here in the design of Federal House, Kuala Lumpur, was adopted widely in architecture after World War II. The metal roof cladding is a recent addition to the original vault roof.

6. Government offices, such as the Bangunan Persekutuan (Federal Building) in Petaling Jaya, were constructed throughout Malaysia to cater to the nation's administrative and economic needs.

THE RISE OF MODERNISM

The rise of nationalism and the consequent aspirations to self-government that emerged in the 1920s and 1930s had significant implications for Malaysia's architectural and urban planning. The idea of a nationalist culture with the requisite visual symbolism had to be incorporated into the progressive image of a young, dynamic, multiracial country.

Adapting traditional Malay architectural forms to modern building design, seen here in the roof form of the National Museum, became widespread in the years following Independence.

Art Deco as a decorative style for buildings represents an early break from the Classical style that hitherto dominated contemporary architecture in Malaysia. However, it was not until the advent of true Modernism and the International Style in the 1950s that the country's 'modern' skyline began to take shape. Although many architectural projects were still commissioned from expatriate architects practising in Malaysia, the first generation of local architectural graduates began to make their presence felt.

Following World War II, massive migration to the cities, coupled with a squatter problem and increasing sanitary concerns, resulted in the development of new towns such as Petaling Jaya. However, Western planning methods of gridiron plans and zoning were imposed, resulting in a rapid deployment of urban development strategies at the cost of the country's vernacular heritage.

The immediate post-Independence period witnessed a flurry of activity in defining a Malaysian architectural identity, ranging from the strict Functionalist Corbusien idea of a tropical regional architecture of sunshades and bare, concrete finish, to revivalist, eclectic attempts to adapt traditional Malay vernacular architecture. An architecture of statehood, in the form of expressive monuments, was considered vital to portray the country's vernacular heritage, technological prowess and economic strength.

The post-Independence growth of commercial, recreational and administrative activities, especially in the Federal Capital Kuala Lumpur, led to the construction of many buildings which reinterpreted the Modernist styles originating in the West. Of particular importance to the growth of the country was the requirement for large numbers of government schools, clinics and offices. Similarly, the growing need to produce graduates to satisfy industrial and administrative demands, in both the private and the government sectors, then led to the establishment of numerous universities and institutes of higher education throughout the country, beginning with Universiti Malaya in Kuala Lumpur.

Petaling Jaya, a new satellite town on the outskirts of Kuala Lumpur, was created in the mid-1950s to alleviate housing problems and encourage industrial development.

Art Deco

The term Art Deco refers to a style of applied decoration made fashionable in the late 1920s in Europe and America. With its simple ornamentation, clean, rectilinear lines and geometrical forms, Art Deco can be seen as a precursor to the Modern style. It was adopted to a certain extent throughout prewar Malaysia, particularly in the design of shophouses and entertainment buildings.

A 1950s photograph showing shophouses along Jalan Tuanku Abdul Rahman dating back to the 1930s, their facades designed in Art Deco style.

The Odeon Cinema in Kuala Lumpur was one of several prewar cinemas in Malaysia built in Art Deco style.

Decorative elements

The term Art Deco is derived from the Exposition Internationale des Arts Décoratifs et Industriels Modernes (the International Exposition of Modern Decorative and Industrial Arts), held in Paris in 1925. Although the style originated in Europe, the best examples of Art Deco architecture can be seen in America, particularly in skyscrapers such as the Chrysler Building and the Empire State Building. Art Deco style was not restricted to architecture but encompassed all segments of contemporary culture, including the fine arts and the design of furniture, ceramics, textiles, glass, metalwork, jewellery and many household appliances. The homogeneous interiors, exteriors and objects served the needs of a design- and style-conscious middle class intent on showing off its newly refined taste for things modern and exotic looking.

Art Deco design was inspired by turn-of-the-century early modern furniture and object design from Glasgow and Vienna; by the Orient, ancient Egypt, pre-Columbian civilizations and tribal Africa; by Neoclassicism, Gallic Classicism and, to a lesser extent, Cubism, Futurism and Expressionism.

Art Deco in Malaysia was most commonly applied to the facades of 1930s shophouses, and good examples can be found along Jalan Tuanku Abdul Rahman, Lebuh Ampang and Jalan Bangsar in Kuala Lumpur. These shophouses feature the typical devices of Art Deco: the abstraction of a facade into strongly emphasized vertical and horizontal elements, with decorative expression reduced to patterns of abstract geometrical shapes.

Features of Art Deco buildings in Malaysia

Flagpoles

Concrete flagpoles are a common feature of Art Deco buildings in Malaysia. In the majority of cases, the flagpoles remain a purely decorative item, endorsing Art Deco architecture as an architecture of ornament. The flagpoles extend from the top of the building with bands or, occasionally, bird motifs sculptured at the base of the poles as if affixing them to the wall facade.

A bird motif anchors the flagpole on a shophouse in Jalan Tuanku Abdul Rahman in Kuala Lumpur.

A bird motif and a double band feature on another shophouse along Jalan Tuanku Abdul Rahman.

Three horizontal bands at the base of the flagpole contrast with the vertical treatment of the windows on a hotel in Jalan Tuanku Abdul Rahman.

Banding devices

The wide eaves which were common in tropical buildings to keep out the sun and rain were adapted in Art Deco buildings into horizontal banding devices, such as sunshades and ledges, which merge into the heavy horizontal articulation of the buildings. This banding device was also used to form vents above glazed window openings, hence the fine line between decorative form and practical function.

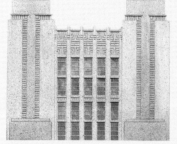

The vertically banded front elevation of the Anglo-Oriental Building, which is held between two towers, contrasts with the horizontal bands of the two side wings.

Individual concrete canopies above the first-floor windows of the Anglo-Oriental Building offset the wide banding below.

Art Deco shophouses are easily recognizable by their geometric forms and clean lines, as well as their flagpoles.

Plaster moulding

Shanghai plaster provided the same visual effect as stone but was a considerably cheaper building material. The plaster could be sculpted into the required Art Deco motifs. The finish was usually left in beige colour but was occasionally painted in the pastel colours of the period.

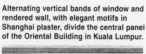

Alternating vertical bands of window and rendered wall, with elegant motifs in Shanghai plaster, divide the central panel of the Oriental Building in Kuala Lumpur.

A wide band, embellished with a fine linear design, separates the first and ground floors of the Anglo-Oriental Building. The design is modulated at the capitals of the ground-floor piers.

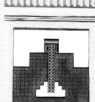

Kuala Lumpur's Central Market represents a successful rehabilitation of the city's Art Deco wet market. The original banding and window decoration have been retained.

The Oriental Building sits on the corner of Jalan Tun Perak and Jalan Melaka in Kuala Lumpur, its curved form addressing Masjid Jamek beyond.

Many buildings dating from the 1930s in town centres across Peninsular Malaysia display Art Deco features, especially in Kuala Lumpur, George Town, Ipoh, Alor Setar and Johor Bahru. Art Deco was also adopted for the private villas of the newly rich Chinese who made their fortunes from tin and rubber in the late 1920s. The decorative nature of Art Deco made it the obvious style to portray this new wealth, endorsing Art Deco as a superficial style of applied ornamentation.

Malaysianization of Art Deco

Unlike in Europe and America, where the monumentality of Art Deco was often expressed in sculptured stone, in Malaysia stone was not readily available and was therefore too expensive. Local builders looked for a finish that was more easily available but which possessed properties similar to stone: the alternative was found in Shanghai plaster, a good, cheap, external grade material which could be applied easily, by skilled craftsmen, to the finely sculptured decorative motifs of the style and which had the matt appearance of stone. This skill was brought by labourers arriving from mainland China.

Until this time, solid panel or louvred timber shutters were the most commonly used window treatment in local buildings. These were superseded in Art Deco buildings by steel-framed windows which were generally glazed in a deep green cast glass. Although it was probably the cheapest glass available, the green cast glass did possess heat resistant properties making it a sensible choice of material for the tropical Malaysian climate. The green glass also provided a colourful contrast to the beige Shanghai plaster, while the thin glazing bars of steel windows provided light counterpoise to the massive treatment of Art Deco walls.

One institutional building which displays traces of the Art Deco style is the Johor State Secretariat Building in Johor Bahru. This building departs from the international flavour of Art Deco by incorporating motifs of Moorish origin into its design to reflect the importance of Islam in Malaysia; thus Art Deco is confirmed as an architecture not only of ornament, geometry, texture and colour but also of symbolism.

Art Deco and the entertainment industry

The eight-storey Oriental Building is a fine example of the links between the new science of broadcasting and the new aesthetic of Art Deco. The composition of the facade has strong parallels with radio designs of that period; in fact, the building originally had 'Radio Malaya' advertised in large letters on its facade. The building has a heavily rusticated, arcaded base while the facade above it is held between two tower-like elements. A panel between these towers is framed by a white stucco frieze of interlocking discs.

This thematic link between the Art Deco style and the new entertainment industry was also evident in the design of many new cinemas and dance halls. The most notable of these is the Odeon Cinema on the corner of Jalan Tuanku Abdul Rahman and Jalan Dang Wangi in Kuala Lumpur. The strong vertical mullions, tower-like elements and flagpoles are all Art Deco motifs. The wide, horizontal, fluted piers in green-coloured Shanghai plaster are another interesting feature. Other examples of the Art Deco style are the Rex, Cathay and Lido cinemas in Penang, Kuala Lumpur and Ipoh, as well as numerous dance halls in the urban centres of larger towns throughout Malaysia.

Art Deco survived beyond the 1920s and 1930s in Malaysia and was used primarily in non-institutional buildings. The inventive and playful nature of this style allowed it to be easily adapted to reflect the new commercial development at that time. It also provided a departure from the Neoclassical style of government and institutional buildings of the time, creating a different idiom for a new type of building.

The sunburst motif is common in Art Deco design and is seen here on the clock tower in Medan Pasar (formerly Market Square) in Kuala Lumpur.

The memorial was erected in 1937 to commemorate the coronation of King George VI of England. The memorial plaques were removed following Independence.

The tall, first-floor windows of the Anglo-Oriental Building have individual concrete canopies, while the second floor is treated as a narrow band which appears to be receding due to the deep, continuous overhang directly above the windows and the darker shade of Shanghai plaster.

The inventive nature of Art Deco

Although Art Deco is seen generally in individual urban buildings, in the Rubber Research Institute Building it is employed for a complex of linked, single-storey buildings set in a landscaped compound. The buildings are almost modular with identical facade elements.

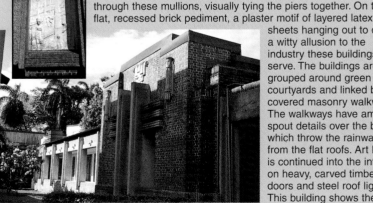

Unlike most other examples, these buildings are in facing brick, with monumental corner piers. These piers frame the window openings, which are divided into three vertical bands by two large, protruding plaster mullions. Three horizontal rendered beams appear to be threaded through these mullions, visually tying the piers together. On the flat, recessed brick pediment, a plaster motif of layered latex sheets hanging out to dry is a witty allusion to the industry these buildings serve. The buildings are grouped around green courtyards and linked by covered masonry walkways. The walkways have amusing spout details over the beams which throw the rainwater from the flat roofs. Art Deco is continued into the interior on heavy, carved timber doors and steel roof lights. This building shows the inventive, even playful, nature of the Art Deco style.

The Rubber Research Institute is one of the few building complexes designed in Art Deco style. *INSET*: Bas relief panels depict rubber tapping.

Arrival of the International Style

In 1932, a young American architect called Philip Johnson, together with historian Henry-Russell Hitchcock, organized a seminal show of architectural designs at the Museum of Modern Art in New York. The exhibition, entitled 'International Style', served to define the architectural movement emerging at that time. Although few buildings were erected during the war years in Malaysia, particularly during the Japanese Occupation, there are some buildings falling within this period which illustrate this transition from the quasi-classicism of Art Deco to true Modernism.

Located in Jalan Tuanku Abdul Rahman, the former UMNO Building is one of the most refined examples of the early Modernist style in Malaysia. Seen here is the day of its opening in 1955 by the Sultan of Selangor.

International origins

The term International Style was coined to reflect the internationalization of European 'compound' architecture, that is, the emerging modern style of work by architects living and working with other artists in a compound such as Bauhaus, through the transmigration of its principal architects and ideas into America and further afield. Such an immediate postwar Functionalist style emerged due to the need for low-cost buildings that were easy to erect yet which offered social and economic revitalization. Ironically, this style was imported and transplanted into a wealthy and flourishing America, inadvertently turning an essential postwar building form into a popular, stylistic expression.

To distinguish itself from previous architectural styles, the International Style emphasized volume rather than mass; regularity as opposed to symmetry; and dependence on the intrinsic quality of materials instead of applied decoration. Glass, curtain walling, unrelieved cubic blocks and corners left free of visible support were characteristics of the later

Designing in the International Style

The best early example of International Style architecture in Malaysia is Federal House, an eight-storey administrative building situated to the south of Dataran Merdeka (Merdeka Square) in Kuala Lumpur. The design, by B.M. Iversen, was the winning entry in an architectural competition held in 1951. The building was conceived as a slab block containing offices with an adjoining block to house other public spaces; staircases, lift lobbies and an entrance hall link the two blocks. The facade of the slab block is treated as a thin frame filled entirely with screens of metal-framed glass and green vitrolite panels, making

buildings designed in the International Style.

Rapid advances in technology were made during the war years and the globalization of international trade through improved communication technologies was beginning to break down cultural barriers between different nations. International Style buildings could soon be found on both sides of the Atlantic Ocean, in South America and Asia. Furthermore, developments in construction technology allowed completely new forms to be created which were aesthetically much lighter than anything that had been built before.

Early Modernism in Malaysia

Between the two extremes—the decorativeness of Art Deco and the austere, pure form of the International Style—a transitional form of expression was clearly visible. The former Sime Darby Building is representative of this transitional period. The facade of the small, four-storey building is broken down into two rectangular blocks. The smaller, vertical rectangle is in stone, with a thin slit window running through it. The larger rectangle is an abstract pattern of horizontal bands, with steel-framed vertical windows set in between, emphasizing its linear expression. Both of these rectangles are held together by a thin cantilevered canopy. The design's success lies in its deliberate simplicity. The flatness of these blocks contrasts with

Roots of Modernism: The Bauhaus

The Bauhaus (House of Building) was the most important school of art of the 20th century. Originating in Weimar and later moving to Dessau, both cities in Germany, the Bauhaus was an institution where artists, craftsmen and architects worked together and learned from one another. The Bauhaus attracted students from all over Europe who sought a new environment in which their designs would not be constrained by prevailing, mainstream trends.

Although Walter Gropius, the instigator of the Bauhaus, was initially influenced by Expressionism, his ideals of craftsmanship soon changed direction. By the 1920s, the design aims of the Bauhaus became more industrial and stark, and increasingly devoid of any decoration. Buildings were seen as machines: pure and functional.

Due to the unstable political climate in 1930s Germany, most of the institution's staff emigrated to America and Britain, taking with them the Bauhaus ideals. The move towards an International Style which employed new construction methods and spoke of a new, unified world was exemplified in the buildings of the Bauhaus.

The Bauhaus school in Dessau, Germany, was designed by Walter Gropius in 1925.

Federal House one of the earliest buildings to use plastic as a building material. The delightful visual quality of this facade treatment is somewhat compromised by the fact that the occupants have had to paint in many of the clear glass panels to reduce the glare from the tropical sun and the resultant heat gain.

The circulation block features stone walls and punched, round openings. The front of the block is curved and more open. Sunshading horizontal fins, which are curved in plan, protect this open element. The sunshades have been reduced to the thinnest concrete slabs.

the rustication of the Chin Woo Stadium and Oriental Building facades. By using reinforced concrete, the massiveness of the former buildings is replaced by a slender structure, the change representing a distinct advance in construction technology.

Transitional piece: The Chin Woo Stadium

The Chin Woo Stadium in Kuala Lumpur is one of the best examples of a transitional building in Kuala Lumpur. The facade displays a massiveness associated with Art Deco, but none of the geometric decorative detailing usually seen in Art Deco buildings. The curved facade is interrupted by two towers, which themselves have no markings other than two narrow, vertical window slots. The windows and wall panels between the structural piers of the facade are faced in metal-framed glass, heralding the curtain-wall facades of Modernism. Inside the stadium, the reinforced concrete structure is more blatantly expressed. Large, arched beams act as supports for the massive spans required by the stadium. Light is introduced through horizontal windows set between the layered flat slabs above the arches.

Unlike the facades of Classical and Art Deco buildings, which feature a vertical succession of differing ornamentation, each floor of the Loke Yew Building is entirely repetitive. The windows are designed in horizontal strips, a tenet of Modernism. These strips are emphasized by cantilevered ledges above the windows on each floor, and end at one corner in curved, full-length, glazed doors which in turn open onto curved balconies.

The ocean liner was a modern, attractive form of transport of the time. The curved end of the long Harrisons & Crosfield Building in Kuala Lumpur is reminiscent of a ship's prow. The third storey is rectilinear and is set back from the prow. With two mast-like flagpoles atop and an iron railing around it, this upper floor completes the maritime image by resembling the bridge of a ship.

Air-conditioned future

With the introduction of air conditioning in the late 1940s, architects were finally able to embrace fully the International Style. The tropical climate was no longer considered a determining factor in building design, paving the way for the curtain-walled glass boxes of the future. The need for natural ventilation and sunshading, still evident in buildings of the transitional style in the form of horizontal fins and recessed or open spaces, became obsolete and thus serves to distinguish buildings of this transitional period from those built in the 1960s and beyond.

Radical changes in Malaysian politics leading up to, and after, Merdeka (Independence), and an improved national economy, meant that the time was right for architects in Malaysia to leave behind the more austere functional architecture of the transitional period and adopt the luxuriant International Style generally associated with America: an architecture of pristine glass boxes, an architecture befitting a young, forward-looking nation.

Heralding the International Style

The former Sime Darby Building on Jalan Ampang, Kuala Lumpur, is an early example of Modernism in architecture in Malaysia.

The Harrisons & Crosfield Building in Kuala Lumpur exhibits many of the ocean liner characteristics associated with the International Style.

The Loke Yew Building was one of the first buildings in Kuala Lumpur to house a lift. At one end of the building, the window strips are punctuated by round porthole windows, evoking the ocean liner.

Developments in concrete technology

Pre-tensioning concrete

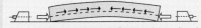

A high-strength steel strand or bar, known as a tendon, is stretched between two abutments by a hydraulic jack until a predetermined tensile force is developed. Concrete is cast in formwork around the tendon and fully cured.

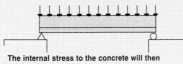

The tendon is cut and the tensile stress is transferred to the concrete through bond stresses.

The internal stress to the concrete will then counteract the stresses that will result from an applied load.

Reinforced and, later, prestressed concrete, often precast on site, became a standard building material. Concrete, which has been used as a structural building material since Roman times, is strong in compression but weak in tension. During the latter part of the 19th century, however, it was discovered that the insertion of steel mesh or rods enables concrete to withstand much greater stress.

Prestressing, which introduces internal stresses to concrete in order to counteract stresses that will result from an applied load, can be achieved in two ways. Bars or cables can be stretched with jacks which are released once concrete has been poured around them (pretensioning), or voids can be left in precast concrete elements to allow cables to be threaded through and stretched to the right level (post-tensioning).

Planning a new town: Petaling Jaya

Following World War II, a large number of 'new towns' were created in Malaysia to support a growing and increasingly urban-based population. This new town development was conceived primarily as a vehicle to expedite the housing, industrial and economic development of the country at a time of postwar economic recovery and early self-government.

TOP: Petaling Jaya New Town (Section 7 and 52) is home to the 27-storey Menara MPPJ. *BELOW LEFT*: Petaling Jaya is typified by rows of terrace housing. *BELOW RIGHT*: A typical residential street.

Location of Petaling Jaya

TOP: The first national-type school in Petaling Jaya was opened in Section 1 in 1954.

BOTTOM: A typical late 1950s house in Section 1.

New towns and villages

Some new towns in Malaysia were designed to control spasmodic, unplanned industrial development in Kuala Lumpur and to maximize the economic return from mining activities, while others were set up to protect civilians against intimidation by Communist insurgents and to provide adequate housing for squatter communities. During the Japanese Occupation, permanent building construction in Kuala Lumpur had virtually ground to a halt although temporary building work did take place on a large scale. Unsightly squatter settlements had mushroomed, rapidly deteriorating into slums.

Petaling Jaya

Petaling Jaya was the first and only new town built in the postwar, pre-Independence period, and it became a model for future new town development in Malaysia. Although Petaling Jaya, commonly referred to as PJ, was not the first new town to be built on a new site, it was, however, the first satellite town designed along proper town planning principles with an infrastructure that emulated new town development in postwar Britain.

Demand for industrial sites in the capital city had arisen in the 1930s and had intensified after World War II. The creation of a new township on the outskirts of Kuala Lumpur was intended to solve the problem of overcrowding in the city, especially through the resettlement of urban squatters occupying land earmarked for development.

In 1951, the State Government of Selangor acquired approximately 486 hectares (1,200 acres) of land planted with poor quality rubber trees from Palmlands Estate at a price of $1,200 per acre. The land was situated about 9 kilometres southwest of Kuala Lumpur along the Klang Road. Actual construction of the town did not begin until February 1953 under the auspices of the Kuala Lumpur District Officer with advice from a board whose members were nominated by the State Government of the day.

The proposed new township was originally designed to cover an area of 1 214 hectares (3,000 acres) with a target population of 70,000. The land-use components integrated the need for residence, employment and recreation in a number of connected neighbourhood units, with land specifically set aside for residential, industrial and commercial purposes, government buildings, public facilities and other uses.

From the outset, about 1,300 housing lots measuring 420 square metres (4,150 square feet)

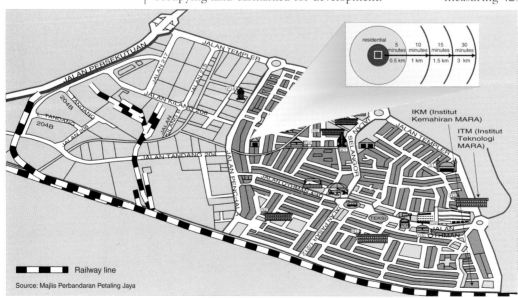

Railway line

Source: Majlis Perbandaran Petaling Jaya

Plan of Petaling Jaya Old Town

0.5 km / 5 minutes walk from house

• Kindergartens
• Local shops and hawker stalls
• Open spaces and small recreational parks

Shops are located within comfortable walking distance.

each were offered for sale at a price of $200 to the squatters originating from the Imbi Road, Kampung Pandan and Peel Road areas in Kuala Lumpur. The same year also marked the birth of the first national-type school, the Sekolah Kebangsaan Jalan 10. A year and a half later, more than 800 housing units had been completed and occupied but the demand from the affluent middle class for better quality housing kept increasing and superseded the original objective of resettling the squatters. By the end of 1957, 3,193 residential buildings had been completed with a further 322 units under construction. More than 25,000 people had been accommodated and the new town of Petaling Jaya was progressing way beyond the expectations of its instigators.

In 1954, administrative reorganization under Ordinance No. 36 led to the setting up of the Petaling Jaya Authority, empowered to raise loans for developing the satellite town and acquiring additional land for development. In 1955, the Authority was accorded certain functions of local government and a Town Section was established to deal with local government administration. The Authority also started to collect property assessment rates and issue licences to meet administrative and maintenance costs. The Petaling Jaya Authority was converted into the Petaling Jaya Development Corporation in 1958 and was accorded full local government administrative status.

Shah Alam

Proposals to shift the State Capital of Selangor out of Kuala Lumpur started as early as 1956 when G. Rudduck, a town planning adviser from Australia, recommended that a new town site be identified. However, it was not until 1964 that a new state capital, located between Kuala Lumpur and Port Swettenham (now Port Klang) on the Federal Highway, was approved by the Kuala Lumpur and Klang Valley Regional Council and named Shah Alam. Planning principles and building designs adopted by the new state capital were undoubtedly derived in part from the experiences of developing the new town of Petaling Jaya.

New Villages and the Communist insurgence

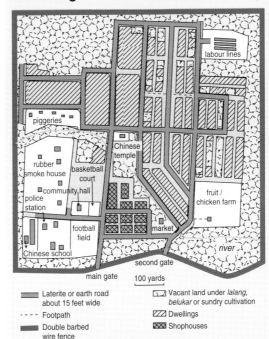

The demarcation of public and private land, as seen in this typical New Village plan, leaves little room for community development.

During the Emergency period (1948–60), nearly 10 per cent of Malaysia's population was resettled into New Villages. Seventy New Villages or townships were created with a population of more than 2,200 each. These settlements established a distinctive urban form whose features are still discernible. New villages were built in response to the Communist insurrection and the postwar sanitary problems. They were conceived as part of the British military strategy to isolate Communist guerrillas from civilian sources of support by relocating large numbers of mostly Chinese persons into 'white areas' or townships that were cut off from any contact with Communist insurgents. Little consideration was given to town planning. A number of these New Villages now have populations exceeding 30,000, and are thus self-sustaining townships.

The basic requirements of the New Villages were sanitary (open spaces and public facilities were included), security (the whole village was surrounded by barbed wire to separate the civilians from the Communist guerrillas) and social (neighbourhoods were created). However, the policy of improvisation resulted in the creation of traditional, demographically static and immobile settlements. Irrespective of location and size, these settlements were constructed based on a uniform layout following a gridiron street pattern. As security measures were often deemed more important than site planning, social and health problems often arose.

Environmental degradation and the first new town

Kuala Kubu Town, the administrative centre of Ulu Selangor District, located on the bank of the Selangor River, had been developed rapidly due to extensive mining activity. Over the years, however, the river bed slowly silted up with tailings from the hillside mines. As the river frequently burst its banks, a bund was constructed to prevent the river water from flooding the town. Realizing the precarious situation the town was in, the authorities in 1927 ordered five blocks of shophouses to be built on higher ground—a site which became known as Kuala Kubu Baru (literally 'New Kuala Kubu'). Late one afternoon in 1931, the bund burst, flooding the whole town and causing extensive damage to the buildings. The incident left the residents with no choice but to intensify the development of Kuala Kubu Baru, Malaysia's first 'new town'. The original town of Kuala Kubu is still buried under silt.

The original town of Kuala Kubu in Selangor is now buried under silt.

1 km / 10 minutes walk from house

- Primary schools and religious schools
- Local shops and hawker stalls
- Clinics

Clinics are located close to housing areas.

1.5 km / 15 minutes walk from house

- Secondary schools
- Wet markets, high street shops, hawker centres and offices
- Cultural centres

A trip to market requires only a short bus or car journey.

3 km / 30 minutes walk from house

- Colleges offering secondary and tertiary education
- Shopping complexes, high street shops, restaurants and offices
- Administrative centres and recreational parks

Parks can easily be reached by bicycle or on public transport.

Developing a modern Malaysian architecture

Internationally, the 1950s and 1960s was a period of rethinking and re-evaluating many of the fundamental principles of the International Style. With the rise of nationalism in newly independent countries and the perceived decline of Western 'Progressive' ideals, non-Western nations such as Malaysia searched their roots to identify images that would serve as models for their architectural future.

The Employees Provident Fund (EPF) Building in Petaling Jaya uses sunshading devices in the form of metal grilles which dominate the elevations.

The nationalist response

In the West, where the International Style ideals were born, criticism of its bland machine aesthetic came from architects and artists who favoured a more communicative building relating more closely to the local sociocultural and historical context. The importance of Internationalism in architecture began to ebb with national traditions coming to the fore, based on climate, natural resources, local traditions and economic concerns. These criticisms resulted in four distinct approaches towards producing a more socially and historically relevant, and nature-sensitive, design than the existing international 'glass box'.

The Geology Building of Universiti Malaya was planned along an east–west axis with floors set back for sunshading.

Climatic solutions

Examples of climatic solutions in Functionalist design by architects in Malaysia during the 1950s and 1960s can be seen in the use of energy conservation devices and strategies, such as sunshading elements and building orientation. The building is taken as a machine that is modified climatically through the sensitive design of fenestration, choice of weathered materials and spatial layout.

Sunshading devices usually take the form of metal grilles, or concrete fins and screens. The

The Penang branch of Bank Negara combines a receding facade and volume, and deep overhangs with widely spaced vertical fins for climatic relief.

Kuala Lumpur General Hospital, on the other hand, uses the 'egg crate' or concrete box shading devices made famous by Le Corbusier.

Vernacular materials in construction

Another approach in adapting modern design philosophy to the local or regional setting is the use of vernacular materials and planning concepts. On the international scene, Hassan Fathy was researching and designing villages for the poor in Egypt using vernacular adobe construction to its full extent. The vernacular approach proved to be economically, culturally and technologically successful. However, in Malaysia the use of the vernacular tended towards producing images rather than serious statements as to the potential of vernacular materials. The Kuching Catholic Cathedral was one of the earliest postwar buildings to use *belian* (ironwood) shingles as cladding material for its roof.

Traditional identity

Debates and discussions about a Malaysian architectural identity did not take place seriously until the 1970s. Although a national congress on Malay culture was held immediately after Independence, from 30 December 1957 to 2 January 1958, with the objective of defining what constituted Malay art, history and traditions, no paper was presented on the idea of a Malaysian architecture or architectural heritage. However, informal discussions about the search for a Malaysian identity in architecture had already begun, especially with the construction of strong national symbols

Sunshading devices in the early 1960s

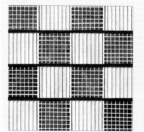 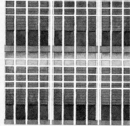 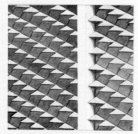

The use of concrete fins and screens on buildings can be found mostly on government buildings designed by the JKR or Public Works Department, such as the Bangunan Persekutuan (Federal Building) in Petaling Jaya.

Horizontal and vertical louvres on the Kuala Lumpur Maternity Hospital (now part of the Kuala Lumpur General Hospital) are reminiscent of colonial tropical designs and hint at a regional characteristic in tropical design.

The American International Assurance (AIA) Building in Jalan Ampang, Kuala Lumpur, employs an unusual external metal sunscreen cladding whose design inspired shading devices on many other buildings.

such as Parliament House and Muzium Negara (the National Museum). The shift towards a clearer Malaysian traditional identity was attempted in the midst of struggle between the philosophical tenets of Modernist Functionalism and mere image making.

Most buildings during the 1950s and 1960s tended to be designed within a 'Traditionalist Functionalist' approach since it was the easiest reconciliation between the nation's need to express an identifiable image and the architects' code of Functionalism. A common reference was the silhouette and forms of traditional roofs. Parliament House in Kuala Lumpur was one of the first experiments; the struggle between identity and architectural integrity is evident in the contrast between the podium roof and the highly conspicuous tower block. While the podium roof alludes to the Bugis or Melaka high pitch angle, the tower block stubbornly uses a Functionalist vocabulary with its unusual facade. In the Negeri Sembilan State Mosque, the conoid reinforced concrete roof may have been chosen from among the many long-span structural systems available as a reference to the famed Minangkabau horned roofs as the eaves are curved in a conspicuous manner. Indulgence in symbolism may have been seen as appropriate since religious architecture and buildings of a national character, such as Parliament House, were probably regarded as exceptions to the rule of regional Functionalism. A bolder and more obvious use of traditionalism in architecture can be found in the A&W Drive-In restaurant in Petaling Jaya in its suggestion of the use of the traditional *bumbung panjang* or gable roof. However, here the roof structure is extended to the ground and forms a concrete A-framed structure.

The Negeri Sembilan State Mosque represented a contemporary approach to mosque design in the 1960s.

The design of the A&W Drive-In restaurant in Petaling Jaya adopts a traditional Malay roof form within its Functionalist approach.

Muzium Negara: An example of Neotraditionalism

Muzium Negara, or the National Museum, in Kuala Lumpur is an important landmark in Malaysian architectural history as it was the first monumental work that clearly departed from the Modernist vocabulary in favour of Neotraditionalism. The museum uses the traditional Malay architecture tripartite division of *kolong*, main body and pitched gable roof. The kolong, or the underside of a Malay house which is raised on stilts, is conspicuous in this building as the ground floor walls are recessed to allow for a colonnade. However, the Functionalist rationale is still apparent in the deeply shaded glass wall on the ground floor which serves to protect the administrative offices from the destructive rays of the sun. The double-pitched gable roofs of the two side wings are almost literally adapted from Melaka, Bugis and Terengganu roof forms.

The literal adaptation of traditional elements is reinforced by the use of the double-layer gables on the central block, the main roof form inspired by the Balai Besar (the Great Hall) in Alor Setar, along with the Bugis-inspired *tebar layar*, or gable screens. Suggestion of ornamentation on the column capitals of the kolong is yet the strongest statement against the taboo of Modernist architectural principles on the use of ornament and preconceived styles. The building is truly a remarkable achievement in reinterpreting the traditional vocabulary into a new building type couched in a Classical composition.

The architecture of statehood

On 31 August 1957, the President of the United Malays National Organization, Tunku Abdul Rahman, proclaimed Malaysia's independence from Britain and in doing so became the first Prime Minister of an independent Federation of Malaya. To mark Merdeka (Independence), several large public buildings and monuments were commissioned to assert the independent status of the country.

Stadium Merdeka on the day of its opening in 1957, shortly before the declaration of Independence.

The Dewan Bahasa dan Pustaka Malaysia in Kuala Lumpur houses the nation's Institute of Language and Literature.

Parliament House
Easily recognizable by its pineapple skin cladding.

Monumental scale

Public buildings designed to commemorate Merdeka were necessarily grand in scale and stood alone as monuments to the newly independent status of the country. Stadium Merdeka (the Independence Stadium) was completed in time for the Independence celebrations of 31 August 1957. Built on a high plateau in the heart of Kuala Lumpur, the massive sporting arena was likened to the Acropolis of Athens. From its high ground, the stadium enjoys a commanding view overlooking Chinatown and the Pudu area in the city below. Stadium Merdeka was the venue for the first international football tournament in Asia, the Merdeka Tournament, which was inaugurated in 1957. It is an open stadium constructed of reinforced concrete with a thin shell roof, and arches over the grandstand. Four prestressed concrete pylons supporting the corner floodlights were cast on site and lifted into position. Later, in 1974, additional facilities were incorporated, including open and covered viewing galleries which increased the seating capacity to 40,000.

Stadium Negara (the National Stadium) was completed five years after Independence on a site next to Stadium Merdeka, in time to host the Thomas Cup badminton tournament held in 1962. The circular-plan stadium originally featured a reinforced concrete ring supporting a steel 'bicycle wheel' roof. At the time, it was one of the largest examples of a bicycle wheel roof in Southeast Asia. Due to persistent leaks, however, the roof was replaced in the early 1980s by a domed roof supported by a space-frame structure.

A statue of Malaysia's first Prime Minister, Tunku Abdul Rahman.

The tenth Yang di-Pertuan Agong, Tuanku Ja'afar, accompanied by the Raja Permaisuri Agong, opens a Parliamentary session in the Dewan Rakyat (House of Representatives). Seated on the left are Prime Minister Dato' Seri Dr Mahathir bin Mohamad, Deputy Prime Minister Dato' Seri Anwar bin Ibrahim and the Cabinet of the day.

Another monumental building of fine proportions constructed at this time was the Dewan Bahasa dan Pustaka Malaysia (the Institute of Language and Literature Malaysia). The Dewan Bahasa dan Pustaka was established in the late 1950s to develop Bahasa Malaysia as the national language and to encourage literary talent. Designed in true Modernist style, with V-shaped struts featuring on the facade, the building comprises a large block containing offices, with a concert hall extending at right angles from it. The concert hall is raised on columns or pilotis to allow for a covered entrance and through driveway. The end wall of the concert hall features a colourful mosaic mural depicting various national themes.

Local adaptations of Modernism

Parliament House was designed as a symbol of a new nation and of democracy in Malaysia. The building was expressed in the modern architectural language of the International Style with the ubiquitous composition of tower block atop a podium. In this case, the three-storey podium, housing the Senate and the Dewan Rakyat (House of Representatives), is of very large proportions. Eleven triangular concrete pinnacles, forming a sort of concertina roof, crown the podium above the Dewan Rakyat. The unusual structure is supposed to resemble the Bugis or Melaka roof form.

The most expressive, and Functionalist, part of the building is the precast concrete panelling that envelopes the 18-storey tower block. Reminiscent of the skin of a pineapple, it functions as both sunshading and aesthetic device, providing a sense of scale, texture, rhythm and form to the facade. A ceremonial square is landscaped with ornamental pools and is used for formal ceremonies.

Displaying a mixture of Islamic and Modernist design principles is Masjid Negara (the National Mosque) which was completed in 1965. The building is constructed in reinforced concrete and clad in Italian marble, with many fine decorative details. It comprises a main prayer hall surrounded by wide galleries or verandas with geometrically patterned filigree screen walls, ceremonial rooms, administrative offices, meeting rooms, library, mausoleum, ornamental landscaped pools and gardens, all within a 13-acre site.

Murals to promote statehood

Scenes from Malaysia's history are depicted in this section of the wall mural featured on Muzium Negara.

A feature popular in Malaysia is the use of murals on institutional buildings to promote statehood, a practice first adopted in immediate post-Independent Malaysia. The murals either take the form of wall paintings or mosaics made out of thousands of small, coloured tiles.

The end wall of the concert hall, which extends from the Dewan Bahasa dan Pustaka building, features a large mural by artist Ismail Mustam illustrating the unifying nature of language and literature in Malaysia. The mural depicts people from all walks of life and extols the need for a literary movement in Malaysia.

The two exhibition wings of Muzium Negara both feature murals by Cheong Lai Tong, one depicting Malaysian historical events and cultural attributes, the other illustrating the country's economic and political development. The use of murals to promote personal and national development has continued over the years, with murals particularly evident on school buildings.

The Dewan Bahasa dan Pustaka mural extols the virtues of learning the national language.

The daring design of Masjid Negara's main prayer hall eschews the traditional domed roof in favour of a unique, reinforced concrete, folded-plate roof form in the shape of an umbrella. The design has since inspired numerous miniature, metal versions covering prayer halls throughout the country. Originally light purple in colour, the folded-plate roof of the grand hall, and the similar roof structure of the mausoleum, were later renovated and now feature blue aluminium panels. An elegantly proportioned 74.4-metre-tall minaret successfully balances the horizontal massing of the architectural composition.

Set within the serene, landscaped Lake Gardens is Tugu Negara (the National Monument). The bronze sculpture comprises seven figures: five victorious soldiers bearing the Malaysian flag represent different branches of the security forces, while below them two slain enemies represent Communist terrorists. The sculpture is surrounded by water and is backed by a crescent-shaped, covered pavilion shaded from the sun by geometrically patterned screen walls, and supporting three onion-shaped domes.

Stadium Negara now sports a domed roof supported by a space-frame structure.

The decision to build Masjid Negara was made by Tunku Abdul Rahman.

Tugu Negara stands as a permanent reminder of the debt owed to those Malaysians who lost their lives defending democracy.

Building to serve a nation

With Independence (Merdeka) in 1957 came rapid development, particularly in the new Federal capital of Kuala Lumpur. There was an immediate need for a variety of infrastructure and building types to serve both the city's metropolitan requirements and those of Malaysia as a whole. As well as several massive developments, including a new international airport and a major hospital, Malaysia also required a national network of public service buildings such as schools and clinics.

Developing a regional style

As the bustling centre of business and administration in Kuala Lumpur was soon to be transformed by the many high-rises built in the decade following Independence. Most buildings were still commissioned from expatriate architects but the immediate post-Independence period also saw the first generation of Malaysian architects given more responsibility in determining the architectural landscape of the city.

Many of the buildings designed in this period attempt to achieve the optimum design and best expression of a tropical high-rise. The 13-storey Police Co-operative Building, completed in 1959, represents one of the earliest attempts to use the building's shape and vertical shading fins to produce an architecture conducive to the hot and humid Malaysian climate. The more substantial Chartered Bank, designed by the same architect, uses some of the deepest overhangs that have been seen in a Malaysian high-rise to shade the glass curtain wall. The overhang is so deep that it requires a cantilevered beam to support the floor slabs, resulting in a skeletel expression reminiscent of the traditional vernacular buildings of the past. The AIA

A typical JKR office block used to house offices of government departments.

Gateway to a nation

The Subang International Airport, renamed the Sultan Abdul Aziz Shah International Airport Subang in 1996, was opened on 30 August 1965 to serve Malaysia as its most prestigious gateway. The airport was built at a cost of RM52 million and boasted the longest runway in Southeast Asia at 3474 metres. Almost 33 years later, on 30 June 1998, the aiport was superseded by the new Kuala Lumpur International Aiport as the main gateway to the nation (see 'Mega projects').

Symbolic design features

The choice of structural system and form of the building was unique in its expression of the roots and aspirations of the new country. The use of the hyperbolic paraboloid shell roof with mushroom columns alludes to a forest canopy, a design concept that can be traced back to Frank Lloyd Wright's Johnson Wax Building. Wright was a keen proponent of both an organic style of architecture and an architecture of democracy. Inherent in this particular structural system

Mushroom columns support the hyperbolic shell roof.

Building, which was completed in 1964, utilizes the concept of sunscreening by means of a mesh of metal grilles on the facade. This may have inspired the designers of the Dayabumi Complex built almost two decades later.

Despite some attempts at a regionalist reaction to the Western models of high-rise, the architects of

JKR standard plans

Since Independence, the Jabatan Kerja Raya, or JKR (formerly known as the Public Works Department, or PWD), has been involved in a massive national development programme of public buildings, such as schools, rural government offices and health clinics. This has been carried out, for the most part, by the use of standard plans which, although repetitive and straightforward, do solve the problem of producing a large number of buildings that are not only fast to construct but

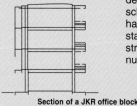

Section of a JKR office block

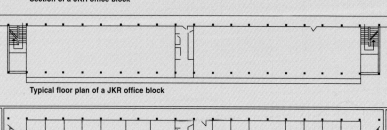

Typical floor plan of a JKR office block

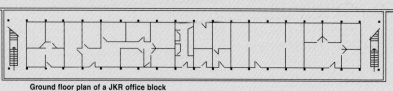

Ground floor plan of a JKR office block

also economic to build and maintain, and which respond well to the tropical climate.

The JKR standard plan for office blocks was originally designed by Ivor Shipley and took the form of a three-storey building with a single corridor, which was open to the elements on one side. On the other side were offices; the corridor was accessed by a staircase at both ends. The design was used throughout the country and was later adapted for high-rise buildings. The open corridor and staircases were naturally ventilated, which reduced the dependence on air conditioning.

When the Cawangan Kerja Pelajaran (Educational Works Branch, Ministry of Education) was absorbed into the then PWD in 1964, standard plans were developed for schools to be built all over Malaysia. As with the standard plans for office blocks, the first standard plans for schools featured one corridor with classrooms on one side. In the earlier plans, access to the first floor was often via an external concrete staircase, while for later plans, internal stairwells were incorporated.

The JKR standard plans for rural clinics were perhaps the simplest of all the standard plans and allowed for building at minimal cost in less-developed areas. Made from timber and often raised above the ground on concrete stilts, the buildings were influenced by Malay vernacular architecture. A basic rectangular plan comprised a waiting room with a shaded veranda, the main clinic and an examination room.

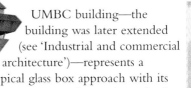

The reception desk at what was then the only departure terminal.

UMBC building—the building was later extended (see 'Industrial and commercial architecture')—represents a typical glass box approach with its tower atop a podium. The Federal Hotel, which was rushed to completion by 1957 to house the foreign dignitaries attending the Merdeka celebrations, shows an architecture that makes little attempt to respond to the tropical climate, with the slight exception of short, horizontal protrusions to protect the windows from water seeping into the window frames. The hotel is one of the few buildings from this period wholly entrusted to a Malaysian architect.

The 18-storey Lee Yan Lian Building was the tallest building in Kuala Lumpur during the early 1960s.

The departure terminal in the late 1960s.

was the message of the natural forest while the repeated columns denote the equality of men. Thus, the metaphor and symbolism of a country rich in natural resources aspiring to be a democratic state can still be associated with the airport design. The use of the inverted umbrella and openness of the complex suggest Malaysia's tropical climate. It is significant that the designers opted for this solution over that of a space-frame system or a portal structure.

Ahead of its time

When the Lee Yan Lian Building was completed in 1959, it was the tallest building in the country. An 18-storey office tower, with a podium-like feature on one facade, rises in a broken box composition and terminates at the top in a penthouse. Although the building is clothed in the usual Modernist garb of plain, undecorated walls and box-like geometry, its massing is a delightful interplay of cuboids expressing the three different functions of public, office and private space. An attempt at tropical high-rise design is evident in deeply recessed windows in box frames and a continuous horizontal sunshading device that overhangs the building's curtain wall.

most building types sought to retain the architectural expressions of the International Style. The number of undistinguished tower blocks on podiums increased considerably in every city. The original

Building for practical needs

1. The plan of the Kuala Lumpur General Hospital maximizes airflow to ensure a cool, dry environment.

2. Wisma Angkasapuri, the state broadcasting headquarters for radio and television, uses a 'pineapple skin' cladding, developed from Parliament House, for sunshading.

3. Constructed of reinforced concrete, Bank Negara (the Central Bank of Malaysia) comprises a large banking hall and tower block. The concrete is textured by bush-hammering to form rough striations, and the building is flanked by curved stair towers supporting a large cantilevered roof.

4. The design of the Police Co-operative Building in Kuala Lumpur incorporates vertical fins to shade windows from direct sunlight.

5. The Federal Hotel was one of the first buildings wholly entrusted to a Malaysian architect.

6. The Chartered Bank Building on Jalan Ampang in Kuala Lumpur features very deep overhangs.

Universities

Since 1962, when the first independent Malaysian university, Universiti Malaya, was established in Kuala Lumpur, there has been a surge in the number of institutions of higher learning throughout the country. Each university is unique in the sense that it was established to lead in a specific field related to the country's potential growth. Such distinctiveness is also evident in the architectural designs of the institutions themselves.

Designing for education

Designs for universities and other institutes of higher education differ from those of other institutional buildings in terms of scale. A university master plan has to accommodate faculty buildings and lecture halls, and communal buildings such as libraries and mosques, as well as administrative buildings and student hostels.

Traffic patterns and pedestrian movement, forming the circulation routes around academic buildings, administrative blocks and student hostels, also have to be planned. Walkways need to maximize the flow of students from hostels to other parts of the university with minimum discomfort. Distances have to be kept short, and

Universiti Kebangsaan Malaysia (UKM) has one of the more student-friendly campus plans in Malaysia. For the first time in a Malaysian university, the design of all the buildings was centrally co-ordinated. The result is an aesthetic balance between the different faculty buildings.

Vernacular Revivalism

The campuses of Universiti Teknologi Malaysia (UTM), Universiti Islam Antarabangsa (UIA) and Universiti Utara Malaysia (UUM) speak of an era when a Malaysian identity in architecture was frequently sought, often based upon a revivalism of eclectic traditional Malay vernacular architecture.

Concessions to traditional Kedahan architecture are seen in the roof forms and the generous verandas of the Mu'adzam Shah Great Hall in UUM, while UTM opts for east coast architectural elements in its rendition of the house with large fascia boards on gable ends. The main administration building at UTM (above) uses a blend of roof forms for shading in a fresh modern interpretation of vernacular architecture.

protection provided against harsh sun and heavy rain. Efficiency within an individual building is also vital as good circulation allows for large numbers of people to enter and move through the buildings with optimum ease.

Academic buildings must also be relatively economical to build and maintain. Site and building plans need to allow for extensions and other additions as the university population grows.

Corbusien traditions in Malaysia

Le Corbusier's work in Chandigarh (the Punjab capital in India), during the late 1950s, was a major source of inspiration to 1970s Malaysian architects. The Kuala Lumpur General Hospital, the Academic Building at Institut Teknologi Mara (ITM) in Shah Alam, and the Dewan Tunku Canselor at Universiti Malaya are all testimony to the philosophy of the Swiss-French master, the most revolutionary architect of the 20th century. These buildings are bold enough to be recognized as modern in line with the country's new spirit, while the mechanics of the architecture truthfully respond to the tropical climate.

The Expressionist idiom is carried through in the design of academic buildings, such as the Faculty of Arts building at Universiti Malaya and the Administration Block at Universiti Kebangsaan Malaysia. The latter uses exposed, fairfaced brick walls within a slender reinforced concrete frame. Both buildings are typical of institutional buildings of their time which did not seek to identify with cultural and religious typologies. Their architecture is pure and raw, with aesthetics born out of rationalization instead of pretentious, cosmetic treatment.

In the Faculty of Arts extension building at Universiti Malaya, the concrete has been employed expressively through angular planning, resulting in a pattern of shadows cast on the walls.

The Dewan Tunku Canselor, which serves as the Great Hall for Universiti Malaya, closely resembles the Chandigarh High Court in the sunshading elements and off-form concrete finish. It embodies the new aesthetics that emerged from the brutalist expressions of concrete as a new-technology material. It is an icon of an era when new architecture was symbolized by form, function and materials, instead of colour, stylism or novelty. A state of equilibrium was achieved by softening the concrete with void spaces and water elements. *INSET:* The Chandigarh High Court in Chandigarh, India, exemplifies Le Corbusier's use of concrete and sunshading devices.

Moreover, buildings must provide a pleasant environment for learning and teaching. Designing hostels demands a balance between a student's need for privacy to study and the communal facilities shared with other students. Hostels must provide a range of private, semi-public to largely public spaces that reflect a student's life both as an individual and as a member of the hostel community and of the university at large.

Malaysian planning concepts

With the exception of the new Universiti Islam Antarabangsa (the International Islamic University), or UIA, campus, the planning concept of most universities in Malaysia is fairly uniform. Student hostels are isolated from one another and scattered over campus sites. These hostels are located far from the faculties, which are found mainly around the central parts of the campus. Such planning concepts mirror the old Modernist cities and the Asian modern metropolis where dependence on vehicular transport is unquestioned. The absence of shaded linkages, coupled with a tendency to choose hilly locations for campuses, does not facilitate walking and cycling around campus.

Another feature lacking in Malaysian universities is student plazas for outdoor interaction, shaded by walkways and trees. Although many of the university grounds are filled with well-manicured lawns and landscaped gardens, little provision is made for students simply resting or waiting for classes. When plazas do exist, they are often too exposed to the sun to be of practical use to the students.

Architectural forms and images

University architecture in Malaysia can be divided into fairly distinct periods, beginning with the late Modernist designs common to Universiti Malaya, Universiti Putra Malaysia (formerly Universiti Pertanian Malaysia) and Universiti Kebangsaan Malaysia (the National University of Malaysia). This style stems from the idea that the building is a machine that responds to the local climate, achieved by the use of Le Corbusier's brise-soleil or egg crate constructions, vertical and horizontal fins or louvres, and twisted window angles. In the Corbusien architectural tradition, a chunky mass of *béton brut* concrete (concrete displaying a rough and raw finish) is the main construction material.

Several of the newer universities, such as Universiti Tenaga Nasional and the proposed Cyberjaya campus of Universiti Telekom (to be called University Multimedia), have opted for a Modernist approach but give the buildings a new sleek form of aluminium cladding and tinted glazing. The style alludes to today's sophisticated high-tech era and

Post-Modern design appeal

The School of Art and Design Annex at the Institut Teknologi Mara campus in Shah Alam, Selangor, is a fine example of a contemporary building environment that is inspirational and conducive to studying and teaching, while providing sufficient order. The design successfully embodies the energetic, adventurous and creative spirit of the School of Art and Design, at the same time overcoming and blending in with its difficult site: a steep embankment lush with greenery. Different-coloured horizontal and vertical circulation paths intersect at open courtyards which act as meeting places with natural light and ventilation.

The Post-Modern design of the School of Art and Design Annex at the Institut Teknologi Mara campus in Shah Alam offers an environment conducive to creative study. LEFT: Post-Modernism meets Le Corbusier in the design of the various campus buildings.

speaks of a forward-looking international vision but the designs make few concessions to the local tropical climate.

Designed within a framework that resembles an Arab city, with close proximity of buildings and a multitude of courtyards, the UIA campus is laid out along a central spine which connects the faculty buildings and student hostels.

Building reuse

Universiti Sains Malaysia (the Science University of Malaysia), formerly known as Universiti Pulau Pinang, was established in 1969. Soon after, the campus was moved from the Malayan Teachers Training College at Gelugor, Penang, to its present site at the former British army base in Minden, Penang. Architecturally, the university is remarkably homogeneous despite the varied styles of the buildings, many of which were taken over from the British. The schools used by children of army personnel were converted into more comfortable accommodation while the labour lines were converted into undergraduate accommodation. The army's former laundry was turned into the staff kitchen and the cold stores became the *surau* (prayer room). Later buildings are characterized by hipped roofs, exposed columns and deeply shaded arcades. The use of low-rise structures, that sit snugly behind small hills, creates a human scale such as can be found in Penang's famed city streets.

The buildings and layout of the Universiti Sains Malaysia complex reflect its origins as a British army base.

The design of the Universiti Islam Antarabangsa campus features courtyards (top) and covered walkways (middle).
Buildings, such as the main administration building (bottom), display an eclectic mixture of Middle Eastern proportions and traditional Malay vernacular elements to create a Muslim-Malay identity.

1. Kuala Lumpur's skyline is dominated by tall buildings. In the centre of the picture is Menara Kuala Lumpur and on the right, the Petronas Twin Towers, recognized as the tallest building in the world in 1996.

2. The bamboo shoot design of the Telekom Tower alludes to the building's Southeast Asian locale while making concessions to the tropical climate and incorporating 'smart' features.

3. The avant-garde design of the Bank Negara Disaster Recovery Centre in Shah Alam synthesizes forms, spaces, ideas and materials in what is one of the few examples of deconstruction in Malaysian architecture.

4. Vernacular revivalism as seen in the Sabah Museum in Kota Kinabalu, Sabah. The lines of the building are based on the design of a traditional Rungus longhouse, which has outward-sloping walls underneath a broad, sloping roof.

5. Modern buildings are once again incorporating tropical features into their designs in an effort to conserve finite energy resources. Residential houses, such as the Nilly House in Petaling Jaya, use natural timber, open atriums and wide, overhanging eaves to encourage natural ventilation and sunshading.

6. The towering, white Dayabumi Complex represents a landmark design in the search for a local, modern Islamic architectural identity. In the foreground is part of the Post-Modern Central Square.

MODERN ARCHITECTURE

The IBM Plaza attempts a high-rise solution to tropical architecture.

The rather dormant architectural activity of the 1970s, typified by utilitarian designs and iconic concrete monuments, was to be largely eclipsed in the following two decades when the country's economy grew beyond expectation. The simultaneous awakening of the development sector saw the emergence of new building types such as condominiums, resort hotels and shopping centres and, with it, an ever-changing urban skyline.

With the arrival of the shopping centre and office complex, urban dwellers were presented with a new alternative to the existing shophouse environment. Centralized facilities such as car parks, air conditioning and food outlets further hastened the decline of the shophouse. Corporate and private clients began to desire a more 'global' look for their projects, and architects became more aggressive in their approach to form, function and imagery: glass towers made their appearance and curtain walling became fashionable.

Increased urban migration and a rising middle class resulted in a great demand for mass residential housing throughout the country. Large housing estates, characterized by endless rows of linkhouses, became the residential norm despite criticism of their insensitive designs. Condominium living became the sought-after option for the more affluent section of the community, resulting in high-rise designs led more by marketing than by architectural principles.

In the ongoing search for a Malaysian architectural identity, vernacular revivalism, Islamic symbolism and tropical design have all entered the vocabulary. The adaptation of vernacular architecture to modern building design is most evident in resort hotels which strive to offer guests an environment that reflects the surrounding cultural heritage but has yet to find its place in commercial or residential architecture. Designing for the tropical climate is again at the fore, set against a global call for energy conservation.

Rapid economic growth during the 1980s and much of the 1990s triggered several monumental building projects. These mega projects include the Petronas Twin Towers, for a time the tallest building in the world, the Kuala Lumpur International Airport, and the new garden city of Putrajaya. Such icons will undoubtedly remain as architectural landmarks well into the 21st century.

Parallel with the growth in political stability and economic status, political patronage and corporate image became direct influences on the ultimate form of architecture. The symbolism of these buildings is clear, even to the man on the street. The pure Modernism that had arrived in the late 1960s was moulded and synthesized into the mutations and variants that now characterize the fabric and appeal of Malaysian cities.

Menara UMNO towers above its prewar neighbours and radically changes the Penang cityscape.

New landmarks

The 1970s marked a fresh beginning for Malaysia, the nation having recuperated from the Emergency period, armed confrontation with Indonesia and the pressures of interracial conflict during the late 1960s. Many building designs of the 1970s and 1980s began to show an enthusiasm and optimism in spirit, reflecting attempts by architects of the time to develop a 'new' architecture for Malaysia.

Vernacular Malay architecture is incorporated into a high-rise environment at the Pusat Dagangan Dunia Putra (Putra World Trade Centre). In the foreground is the Pan Pacific Hotel Kuala Lumpur.

Early high-rise building in Malaysia

The late 1970s and early 1980s saw the skyline of Kuala Lumpur change from one dominated by two-storey shophouses to one dotted with high-rise buildings.

With few examples of tall buildings in the region at that time, several early attempts at high-rise building were far from inspiring. Gradually, however, architects in Malaysia acquired the necessary skills and high-rise became commonplace.

As was the norm elsewhere, early high-rise buildings in Malaysia were designed in the modern International Style, some of the more elegant examples in Kuala Lumpur being Bangunan Pernas, Wisma PHIP and Wisma Hamzah Kwong-Hing.

Other buildings aimed to express corporate and commercial success. Covered in reflective glass curtain walling, these towering edifices were designed to show off a bold, corporate image, and are located in prestigious urban centres. Examples in Kuala Lumpur include Bangunan LTAT, Wisma Selangor Dredging, Bangunan MAS, Wisma Genting and Menara Lion. Some high-rise buildings of this period display more regional character than previously in their design,

whether in the use of sunshading devices or traditional elements to emphasize their national character. Menara Maybank, Bank Bumiputra and the Pusat Dagangan Dunia Putra (the Putra World Trade Centre) are good examples of this type.

Islamic symbolism

The 1980s witnessed more development in the search for an independent Malaysian Islamic architectural identity, particularly within high-rise building. One of the most notable landmarks in Kuala Lumpur is the Dayabumi Complex, housing a 35-storey office tower, the Kuala Lumpur General Post Office and a two-storey shopping arcade. Modern Islamic reference was introduced to the design in the form of geometrically patterned grilles, which function as a sunshading device, and pointed arches below the main tower block.

The Lembaga Urusan Tabung Haji (LUTH) Building, commonly referred to as the Tabung Haji Building, is home to the offices of the Malaysian Muslim Pilgrim's Fund. The elegant tower represents the architect's search for a sculptural model that continues the traditions of Islamic architectural forms in a modern building. Contemporary Islamic elements in the design include the use of a circular floor plan, hinting at continuity, and the use of geometric patterns, a common feature of Islamic design. More overt symbols of Islam were achieved with inscriptions of Allah (god) on the facade and a minaret for the *surau* (prayer room).

Perhaps fortuitously, the best structural solution to the unusual form of the Tabung Haji Building was found to be the use of five pillars, an allusion to the five pillars of faith in Islam. Likewise, the most economical way to bridge the gaps between the five pillars was to use shallow arches, themselves recognizable symbols of Islam.

Dayabumi Complex
This notable landmark was constructed in 1984 as part of a government-sponsored urban development project.

1 Islamic-style arches at the base of the tower.

2 Islamic motifs on the grille design.

Curtain walling

The building boom in Malaysia was greatly fuelled by the growing range of new technical developments in the construction industry, such as reinforced and pre–stressed concrete, often precast on site, and curtain walling.

The introduction of curtain walling led to the continuous steel and tinted glass facades common to commercial skyscrapers worldwide. A curtain wall is a non-load-bearing wall which can be applied to the front of a framed structure so that structure and cladding are mutually distinct.

Stick system

anchor
curtain wall
vision glass
spandrel
spandrel glass
spandrel beam

A system of curtain walling where tubular metal mullions and rails are assembled and attached to the building exterior. Vision glass and spandrel units are then fitted to the frame.

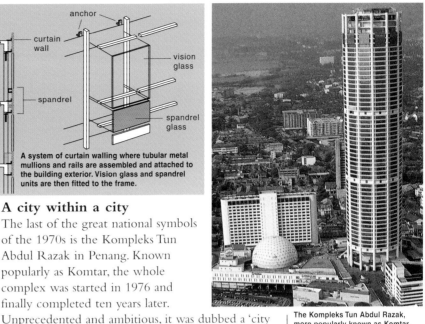

The Kompleks Tun Abdul Razak, more popularly known as Komtar, remains the most distinctive landmark in Penang.

The tower and the hut

The transposition of cultural references (particularly the Malay vernacular house) into contemporary settings was attempted during this period with varying degrees of success. Architects experimented with the use of abstract forms, colours and patterns in the search for a Malaysian architecture. Two rather controversial buildings in Kuala Lumpur, combining indigenous elements with high–rise, are the new Bank Bumiputra headquarters and the Putra World Trade Centre. Both buildings feature oversize Malay roofs over their respective podiums and have provoked much discussion as to whether such vernacular expression is suitable or indeed necessary.

A city within a city

The last of the great national symbols of the 1970s is the Kompleks Tun Abdul Razak in Penang. Known popularly as Komtar, the whole complex was started in 1976 and finally completed ten years later. Unprecedented and ambitious, it was dubbed a 'city within a city', with a 65-storey tower which was at that time the tallest building in the country. However, its sheer size and scale prompted public debate on the conflicts between development and conservation, between sensitivity and naivety, and between creation and destruction.

Imagery in 1980s high-rise buildings

Cultural symbolism
The design of Menara Maybank in Kuala Lumpur is a slightly modified version of the winning entry in an international competition organized by Pertubuhan Akitek Malaysia (the Malaysian Institute of Architects) in 1979. The building is considered to resemble a *keris* (a traditional Malay dagger).

Islamic symbolism
The LUTH Building in Kuala Lumpur is easily recognizable for its unusual waisted form and Islamic features, such as a *surau* (prayer room) with a minaret, and inscriptions of Allah (God) in Jawi script on the upper section of the tower facade. The structural use of the building's five pillars alludes to the five pillars of faith in Islam.

Corporate image making
The Sabah Foundation Building in Kota Kinabalu, Sabah, one of four 'hanging' structures in the world, is an architectural and engineering feat. The 30-storey glass shrouded building is supported by high tensile steel rods from a central core and continues to be one of the most widely accepted symbols of dynamism and corporate success.

Regional Modernism
The sleek, octagonal Pernas Building in Kuala Lumpur is home to the offices of Bank Islam. The building displays concessions to its regional setting by recessing windows to shade them from direct sunlight. Contemporary Malaysian and Islamic motifs are displayed on the facade of the building at street level.

Industrial and commercial architecture

With the opening of Malaysia's first combined retail, office and residential outlets in the early 1970s, residents of Kuala Lumpur were presented with a new alternative to the existing main street shophouse environment. The challenge for architects since then has been to design complexes which meet their users' needs efficiently and which offer an intelligent response to the cultural context in which they are built.

Completed in 1965, the Colgate-Palmolive factory features a barrel-vaulted roof to provide an uninterrupted work space below.

The Century Batteries factory in Petaling Jaya was one of the first to offer a column-free interior.

Industrial architecture

Some of Malaysia's more distinctive factories were built in the decade following Independence, a time of confidence in the future development of the country. Design briefs of the day demanded large, uninterrupted work spaces, free of columns. The Century Batteries factory, built in 1962 in Petaling Jaya, uses a hyperbolic paraboloid roof made from non-corrosive, reinforced concrete to cover over 1300 square metres of column-free internal space. The same roof design, permitting a column-free interior, was used five years later in the construction of the Setapak Roman Catholic Church. The Guinness Brewery factory in Petaling Jaya opted for a continuous, folded, plate roof with the use of simple construction material as infill.

Factory construction increased rapidly in the 1970s and 1980s with the boom in manufacturing, but few of these buildings stand out for their architectural merit having been designed primarily as simple shelters for the machinery within. It was not until the 1990s that architects were invited to play a greater role in the design of industrial buildings, to give factories definitive images, to create buildings that responded to the demands and desires of the client, and to create a sense of well-being among the factory workforce.

The George Kent Technology Centre in Sepang, Selangor, is a good example of late 1990s office building and factory design. The main entrance atrium, used for corporate functions, features large, tubular steel structures, a core lift tower and a steel staircase. The building enjoys natural ventilation in the form of horizontal openings within the depths of the vertical truss, and natural lighting.

BOTTOM: For the George Kent Technology Centre, a progressive and dynamic image has been successfully projected through the use of the company's corporate colours and by deliberately exposed steel building structures. MIDDLE AND TOP: Interior views of the George Kent Technology Centre.

The decline of the shophouse

The first one-stop shopping centres and high-rise office blocks began to appear in the late 1960s and early 1970s as developers rode the wave of the building boom that continued unabated into the early 1980s. As larger companies demanded their own office blocks next to high-end retail complexes and prestigious hotels in downtown Kuala Lumpur, the so-called Golden Triangle began to take shape.

For the person in the street, the self-contained retail and commercial complex, with the comforts of a cool, air-conditioned shopping environment, represented a distinct step up from traditional main street shopping. Early examples such as Wisma Central, Ampang Park and Pertama Complex, all in Kuala Lumpur, fascinated consumers, luring them away from the high street shops that hitherto had represented the only retail option.

Similarly, most private offices were located in traditional shophouses until the construction of new medium- and high-rise office complexes enticed owners out of their normal environment and into modern, air-conditioned offices with facilities and

Shopping complexes

1970s: Ampang Park Shopping Complex

The Ampang Park Shopping Complex is interesting due to its central, street-like plan which functions as circulation. The wide 'street' is designed to be used for exhibitions and product demonstrations and links to a 'square' in the centre, creating an airy and pleasant space. It allows visibility from the interior to the exterior, providing continuity between them, thus avoiding the effect of being sealed in. While still popular, the complex does not have the great visibility of contemporary shopping centres.

Mixed-use complexes

1970s: Wisma Central

The plan of Wisma Central, the first mixed-use complex in Kuala Lumpur offering retail outlets, offices and residential units under one roof, is considered innovative and complex for its time, despite the banal exterior. Shop lots occupy the lower floors; apartments occupy the upper floors; while the floors in between house offices, which surround a central cavity with a badminton court. Today, however, the corridors on the lower and middle floors have a warren-like feel about them and most of the apartments have been turned into offices.

amenities such as restaurants, ample parking space and round-the-clock security.

Many of the early designs of commercial complexes from the 1970s were dependent on imported Western models and showed little consideration to either the local, tropical climate (glass panels were exposed to the sun), or to the cultural context in which they were placed.

It was not until the 1980s that architects in Malaysia began to demonstrate a greater confidence in experimenting with multi-use complexes and high-rise buildings. Architects began to experiment with the visual aesthetic of the building, adopting a Post-Modern style of design, using mechanisms and ornamentation to draw attention to their projects.

By the 1990s, a crisper architectural identity could be observed. Sunshading devices and natural ventilation are present in many office blocks of this period, culminating in buildings such as Menara Mesiniaga, Menara UMNO and Central Plaza (see 'Tropical architecture'). Even the traditional shophouse was given a modern interpretation at

Then and now

An early tall office complex in Kuala Lumpur, the United Malayan Banking Corporation (UMBC) Building was constructed in two phases by two different architects, which explains the mixture of styles used. The 28-storey block was built in 1971 and incorporates curtain walling for a sleek, Modernist look. The second phase is an assortment of shapes: a tall slab, a conspicuous octagonal tower topped with a circular crown, and a podium block with a pitched roof, and hooded sunshading on the facade.

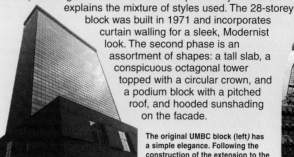

The original UMBC block (left) has a simple elegance. Following the construction of the extension to the building (right), the colour maroon was applied to all the facades to link all the blocks together.

Tai Pan Crest Shophouses where designers introduced a high-tech facade of steel brise-soleil. Shopping centres designed in the 1990s avoid the maze-like corridors common to their 1970s predecessors and opt for sophisticated designs that afford shops greater visibility and shoppers greater mobility.

1980s: Wilayah Shopping Complex

The facade of the Post-Modern Wilayah Shopping Complex, which is situated on the corner of Jalan Dang Wangi and Jalan Munshi Abdullah in Kuala Lumpur, is a thin layer that seems detached from the structure of the building. It wraps itself around the curved building, and has large cutouts to highlight the main entrances. On the ground level, the facade becomes a colonnade that takes inspiration from the traditional covered five-foot way.

1990s: Lot 10

The inside of Lot 10 in Kuala Lumpur bears little relation to the outside. The plan is sophisticated and simple. There are three parts: a curvilinear, covered atrium, an inner ring of walkways around this, and an outer ring of shops and boutiques. The inner ring of circulation acts like an interface between the courtyard and the shops. Spectators can watch shows in the courtyard from the wide balconies of the walkways. The plan avoids dingy corridors and creates easy access and visibility for all shops.

1980s: Nagaria Complex

Instead of incorporating everything under one roof, this Post-Modern complex is made up of three parts, each displaying a totally different facade. Folded horizontal bands run along the five-storey shopping mall giving it a staggered rhythm, with planting spilling over the top of the wall. The 16-storey office block is a bland exercise in curtain walling, while the 10-storey apartment block creates interest with its facade, a play on grids (see detail). Horizontal bands project out to form balconies or shading devices and recess to create the effect of peeling away from the grid facade.

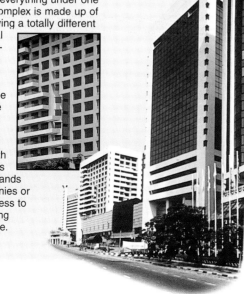

1990s: UE3

This integrated, 11-acre development on Jalan Cheras in Kuala Lumpur comprises a shopping centre, four 14-storey office blocks and one block of serviced apartments. Architecturally distinct, and possessing separate entrances, the various units are, however, linked by secondary routes for ease of access. The main shopping centre features a naturally lit, central atrium which leads to the entrance rotunda in one direction and the anchor tenant in the other.

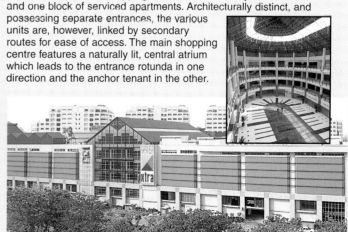

Large-scale housing and high-rise development

During the early 1980s, increasing urban migration to the cities and a rising middle-class population resulted in an extraordinary demand for mass residential housing in Malaysia, ranging from low-cost houses and flats to medium-cost linkhouses and apartments, to high-end bungalows and luxury condominiums. Not only did the population of Kuala Lumpur pass one million, but outside the capital residential development expanded rapidly to cope with the demand for housing.

Bukit Bangsar (Bangsar Hill) in Kuala Lumpur supports a cluster of upmarket condominiums of every shape, size and architectural style.

PUBLIC AND PRIVATE SECTOR HOUSING TARGETS AND ACHIEVEMENT (1991–1995) (house units)

	SIXTH PLAN TARGET	COMPLETED 1991–1995	% OF TARGET
Low-cost	343,800	261,386	76.0
Medium-cost	200,500	282,436	140.9
High-cost	28,700	103,638	361.1

The linkhouse

The ubiquitous form of housing in Malaysia is the linear linkhouse, or terrace house, which is either single- or double-storey. Each house unit occupies a rectangular lot with a land area between 130 and 170 square metres. The choicest unit, located on a corner lot, is usually twice as large as the intermediate lots. With such spatial constraints, the planning of these houses is usually predictable and mundane: deep living spaces, a small rear kitchen, and bedrooms with toilets on the upper floors are the norm. Nevertheless, this typology remains the mainstay of the country's mass housing strategy.

A typical housing estate is made up of a grid-like network of infrastructure, comprising a main ring road and several feeder roads. The house lots are linearly arranged back-to-back (with a service lane in between), with both end/corner lots fetching the highest prices depending on the size of the land available. Several reserve areas (for schools, civic buildings and mosques) and open areas (such as children's playgrounds and playing fields) may be allocated as directed by the local authorities. Despite the adequate infrastructure provided, the design of many housing estates does not always conform to the practical needs of the average resident.

Shortcomings in the design of the average linkhouse are often the result of factors such as by-law limitations and restrictive land codes. The car porch is not always large enough to fulfil its function due to setback rules; the small, dry kitchen space often necessitates ad hoc extensions, and the garden space in front usually leaves little room for soft landscaping. Poor workmanship further detracts from the attractiveness of such homes.

Late 1960s linkhouses at Taman Seputeh in Kuala Lumpur feature central courtyards and remain as landmarks of early linkhouse typology.

1970s semidetached houses in Petaling Jaya cater mostly to middle-income house buyers.

1980s semidetached houses at Taman Tun Dr Ismail in Kuala Lumpur offer an unusual blend of pitched roof forms.

Housing estates in the Klang Valley

Since the late 1970s, housing developments have mushroomed in all parts of the country but particularly in the Klang Valley. Housing projects in Subang Jaya, Taman Tun Dr Ismail, Taman TAR (Tunku Abdul Rahman), Bandar Utama, Bandar Sunway and Cheras are all home to tens of thousands of people who either work in the surrounding areas or who commute daily to the nation's capital, Kuala Lumpur. The self-contained Subang Jaya township (together with the adjacent USJ), one of the largest housing estates in the country, was first developed in the 1970s, and is a showcase of the many different types of linkhouses that exist.

Even though the design and planning of houses built in the many townships across the country are fairly standard and similar, the typologies are not necessarily moulded by the social and economic needs of a typical Malaysian family. Derived from the planning of the 18th-century shophouses in Penang and Melaka, the deep designs of the typical units often result in a lack of adequate daylight and natural ventilation in the inner spaces. Various regulations were imposed under the 1984 Uniform Building By-laws to ensure that clerestory windows and high-volume spaces were incorporated in the design to circumvent these inadequacies. Most, however, were implemented purely to satisfy the by-law requirements without any serious thought to the practicality and workability of such elements.

Rows of identical houses are a common sight in Klang Valley housing estates.

Low-cost housing

The provision of low-cost housing has long been an important factor in residential development in Malaysia. However, because of the relatively low profits to be gained, developers have not put as much effort into this sector as into the medium and high-end sectors. Consequently, the search is still on for a solution which meets the need for cheap houses which are, at the same time, socially acceptable.

Early solutions

The Cheras Low-cost Cluster Link Housing Project, completed in the mid-1970s, is one of the earliest attempts to solve the low-cost housing dilemma. Instead of offering high-rise flats, the architects favoured clusters, or groupings, of four double-storey units. Each unit comprises kitchen/dining and living areas on the ground floor and two bedrooms on the first floor. A breezeway passes through all four units at the ground level in an attempt to encourage interaction between neighbours. The concept of cultivating a neighbourhood spirit is common to most low-cost housing projects as the end users are often perceived as newcomers to the city who are more in tune with the kampong way of life.

Low-cost, high-rise flats still represent the only housing option for many low-income families in Malaysia.

Designs submitted for low-cost housing competitions have favoured two forms of housing: cluster and terrace. Cluster housing is still thought of by many to be the best means of achieving high density without the repetitiveness of flats. Clusters made up of different numbers of houses help to break the monotony. They are also preferred as a means of maintaining community spirit. Terrace houses are preferred by designers who believe that house owners will eventually want to extend their house and park their cars close to the house, which is not always possible with a cluster arrangement. Natural cross ventilation is encouraged in all designs to supplement ceiling fans, while locally sourced building materials and simple construction patterns are favoured to minimize costs.

Bedroom 1

Bedroom 2

Dining

Living

Garden

An axonometric drawing of the Cheras low-cost cluster house developed in the mid-1970s.

Contemporary solutions

In 1982, a ceiling price of RM25,000 was set for the construction of low-cost housing units. This necessitated innovative house designs that would use simple materials while offering a pleasant and functional place in which to live. In mid-1998, the ceiling price was raised in three stages to a maximum of RM42,000 depending on the type and location of the house.

PRICES FOR LOW-COST HOUSING UNITS (POST-JUNE 1998)

LOCATION/AREA (price per sq metre land)	PRICE OF EACH UNIT (RM)	MONTHLY INCOME OF TARGET GROUP (RM)	TYPES OF HOUSES
Small towns and rural areas (RM14 and below)	30,000 and below	850–1,200	Terrace
Big towns and suburban areas (RM15–44)	35,000	1,000–1,350	Flats (five floors without lifts)
Major towns/cities (RM45 and above)	42,000	1,200–1,500	Flats (above five floors with lifts)

Condominium living

An ever-increasing number of affluent, urban Malaysians are attracted to condominium living because of such factors as privacy, quiet surroundings, security and exclusivity. Especially favoured are private, low- or high-rise apartment units with recreational facilities, security surveillance and choice-address locations. During the late 1980s and 1990s, the purchase of condominiums reached fever pitch despite their high prices.

Condominiums are marketed on the basis of their design styles, which are purported to reflect different architectural periods in the West. Many designs, however, appear cosmetic and many are inappropriate in the Malaysian context. Moreover, the imposition of such a Western concept on the Malaysian way of life inevitably takes its toll. The drying of laundry has to be done on a balcony designed as living space, while the wall-mounted air-conditioning compressor units appear like pimples on building facades.

The most common type of condominium development comprises clusters of low-rise buildings, usually 3–4 storeys, within a heavily landscaped ground. Where land area is limited, a high-rise tower solution is adopted, making the panoramic view the main selling point. Situations frequently arise, however, where a new high-rise condominium block overlooks the gardens and bedrooms of existing low-rise units or detached houses adjacent to it.

The concern of architects and developers to provide a healthy social setting for condominium dwellers, with maximum interaction between residents, has resulted in designs which feature apartments clustered around swimming pools, barbecue pits and tennis courts.

Pangsa Murni in Wangsa Maju, Kuala Lumpur, was one of the earliest condominium projects in Malaysia, based upon the winning entry in an 'Alternative forms of housing competition' held in 1984 whose rationale was to provide community living within an apartment setting.

Large-scale housing developments in sensitive, natural locations have aroused concern about their impact on the environment. Construction work for apartments in hilly areas has resulted in the polluting of water catchment areas and the siltation of hill stations and, in the worst cases, has caused buildings to collapse. Nevertheless, condominium living is likely to increase to cater to Malaysia's ever-growing middle-class population.

The glossy brochure is an effective marketing tool to sell condominiums.

The design of Pangsa Murni Condominium in Wangsa Maju won the 'Alternative forms of housing competition' in 1984.

Despite showing its age, the condominium still offers residents a swimming pool and gymnasium facilities, a jogging track that circles the perimeter fence and a good community spirit.

Resort hotels and architecture for tourism

Designing resorts which reflect the country's cultural heritage has been the preoccupation of architects in Malaysia since the boom in local and international tourism began in the early 1980s. Some architects have incorporated indigenous design elements into resort architecture while others have attempted to recreate the kampong setting or have tried to design buildings in response to the local, tropical climate.

Malay-style buildings facing the pool at Club Méditerranée, Pahang.

Vernacular traditions

Two of the earliest international resorts which in their external form went far in recreating indigenous rural architecture are the Club Méditerranée and the Tanjong Jara Beach Resort, located on the east coast of Malaysia. Both resorts take their cue from local construction methods, craft work and materials as seen in the use of local timber. Existing site conditions were respected, and by raising the buildings on stilts, the architects successfully minimized damage to the surrounding environment. At the Tanjong Jara Beach Resort, the stilts are more functional as they also safeguard the resort against high sea levels during the monsoon.

Pelangi Beach Resort, in Langkawi, comprises single- and double-storey chalets raised half a metre above the ground and located in apparent random fashion around a lake and gardens with no chalet directly facing another. The chalet roofs are exposed internally, allowing the roof system to breathe by dissipating warm air through the roof. Louvred windows and large balconies provide ventilation and shade and reduce the need for air conditioning. Of particular note is a pyramidal roof with another roof stacked on top of it, located atop the pool's sunken bar pavilion. The roof form is akin to the *meru* type, of which the earliest local example is the 18th-century Masjid Kampung Laut in Kelantan (see 'The Southeast Asian Great Mosque').

Designing for ecotourism

The design and construction of the Marang Resort and Safaris, completed in the late 1990s, met three basic conditions, namely that the project be wholly Malaysian, that disruption to the environment be minimized and that local craftsmen from the surrounding area be involved. Wooden houses, set in 65 acres of mangrove riverine land near Marang in Terengganu, are situated in clusters as in a Malay village and blend in successfully with the environment. The local ecology was preserved by the use of only hand-held tools and light machinery; building material, much of it locally sourced, was transported over the river on rafts and temporary pontoon bridges. Furthermore, the layout of each chalet attempts to mirror that of the Malay house with clearly defined public, semi-public and private spaces.

At Pelangi Beach Resort in Langkawi, Malaysian *cengal* timber is used for structural purposes, especially the roof beams and trusses; other local timber used includes *kempas* and *nyatoh*. Glazed, clay tiles are used on the chalet roofs.

Fantasy destinations

The Datai Langkawi, completed in 1993, claims to be influenced by traditional Malay architecture as well as Mayan, Japanese and Tibetan architecture and falls into the category of fantasy, Neotraditional resort design. The resort was planned along axial routes and vistas, creating experiences out of visual incidences, heightened by intricate compositions of architectural forms and materials not previously experienced in Malaysian resort architecture. The resort clings to the hillside and is only just visible from sea or land; the top of the structure barely exceeds the height of the surrounding trees.

The main building features deep roof overhangs and wide verandas while the 40 villas that hug the surrounding hillside are raised on stilts to resemble Malay houses and to take advantage of the natural breeze. Local materials were used extensively in the design, including granite and *balau* timber from the island itself. *Belian* wood from Sarawak was used for the low-hanging, shingle roof of the lobby entrance.

The kampong revisited

Several hill stations are located in the mountainous region of central Peninsular Malaysia. With the exception of Genting Highlands, they were founded by the British, mainly for Europeans, as retreats from the heat of the lowlands. Recently, resorts have risen around lakes, some of which were artificially created with hydroelectric dams, such as Kenyir Lake in Terengganu and Pedu Lake in Kedah. With low density and plenty of land to build upon, these resorts usually take the form of a collection of timber chalets scattered around the lakes. Further kampong-like resorts have also emerged on smaller islands, such as Pangkor Laut in Perak and Pulau Redang off the coast of Terengganu.

Virtually uninhabited until the 1960s, when the former Sultan of Perak made his private residence there, the island of Pangkor Laut, was successfully developed into an exclusive holiday retreat in the mid-1980s. The main attraction of Pangkor Laut

The design of the Datai Langkawi allows for close communion between interior and exterior spaces. Covered walkways and viewing platforms catch the early morning and late afternoon sun but exclude the hot midday rays.

Resort are the clusters of Malay-style *rumah tiang seribu* (house on a thousand stilts)—timber houses raised on stilts above the sea. The houses are linked by wooden boardwalks and closely resemble the raised fishing villages of Peninsular Malaysia, Sabah and Sarawak.

Urban hotels and resorts

The vast majority of Malaysia's international business and resort hotels located in urban centres are modern in appearance, and wholly unrepresentative of indigenous architecture. Concessions to the tropical climate are also noticeably absent in many of the high-rise buildings, especially those completed in the 1980s and early 1990s when the imported curtain-walled, glass box design took precedence.

Relatively isolated from the mainland until the construction of the Penang Bridge in 1985, the island of Penang has largely maintained its urban scale. The majority of the larger hotels, such as the Penang

Mutiara, Shangri-La's Rasa Sayang Resort and the Equatorial Penang, have an urban scale where high density is achieved over premium land and serenity is created through attractive landscaping.

Climatic solutions

The rationalization of architecture and climate can be seen, in varying degrees, in many newer buildings in Malaysia and particularly so in resort, if not urban hotel, architecture. The Hyatt Kuantan, completed in the early 1980s, is one of the earliest examples of the application of traditional Malay building principles to a resort in terms of natural light and ventilation. The Hyatt Kuantan features a large, naturally ventilated main entrance lobby with a double-tiered *meru* roof and exposed rafters.

More recent examples include the Impiana Resort in Cherating, which also has a cavernous lobby entirely free of air conditioning. In the Hotel Equatorial Penang, a towering atrium lobby becomes the central space around which the various accommodations are located. The atrium allows for both natural lighting and ventilation, while a ground floor waterway links the interior and exterior by way of a cascading waterfall.

The Sebana Golf Clubhouse in Sebana Cove, Johor, was built primarily with trees cleared from the site. Coconut trees on concrete terraces support mangrove trusses and a deep *atap* (thatch) roof whose low overhang provides sufficient shading.

The New World Renaissance Kuala Lumpur Hotel vies with other commercial buildings for precious space in Kuala Lumpur's Golden Triangle.

The Sebana Golf Clubhouse in Johor relies on natural lighting and ventilation in its main dining room.

Replicating a fishing village: Pangkor Laut Resort

Clusters of wooden kampong-style houses, raised on stilts above the sea, at Pangkor Laut Resort, off the coast of Perak.

Tropical architecture

Repeated calls for a distinct tropical architecture are being made for the simple reason that the weather in tropical countries, such as Malaysia, is vastly different from that of countries in northern Europe and North America where the majority of today's architectural innovations and movements originate. Until the advent of air conditioning, all buildings in Malaysia had been designed with particular regard to local, tropical climatic conditions. With greater global awareness of the environment, and a renewed perspective on contemporary Malaysian architecture, architects are once again looking towards tropical solutions in building design.

Climatic design of the traditional Malay house

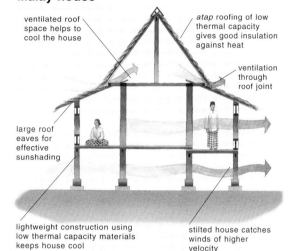

ventilated roof space helps to cool the house

atap roofing of low thermal capacity gives good insulation against heat

ventilation through roof joint

large roof eaves for effective sunshading

lightweight construction using low thermal capacity materials keeps house cool

stilted house catches winds of higher velocity

Climatic conditions

The basic tenet of tropical architecture is finding various ways and means of reacting to and/or harnessing the local tropical climate for improved living conditions.

The typical characteristics of a tropical climate include intense sunshine, resulting in high temperatures, strong glare and high radiation levels, as well as high rainfall, and consequently a risk of flooding. High humidity levels mean that evaporative cooling is greatly reduced. Furthermore, the air is often still with only light prevailing winds.

The passive approach to tropical architecture entails keeping unwanted climatic elements, such as heat and rain, out while encouraging more of the good elements, such as natural ventilation and lighting. The more active approach to tropical architecture, however, attempts to harness certain climatic elements for energy and increased efficiency, such as solar power, hydropower and wind power.

Responding to the climate

The passive response to tropical architecture has been practised for centuries by the people of Malaysia and is, today, slowly making a comeback in modern residential design. The basic concept demands that direct sunshine and heat be kept out, as must the rain. Roofs are often steeply pitched to facilitate water drainage and to provide a large, ventilated roof space below which allows warm air to dissipate and the building to keep cool. Large

1. Gaps between overlapping roof eaves, and *sobek*, or flat cutout patterns above the windows, encourage natural ventilation.

2. The absence of internal walls means increased cross ventilation.

3. No nails are used in the main structure of the house. Wooden slatted floorboards on the *anjung* (porch) allow rain dissipation to plants below.

Tropical designs for modern residential housing: The Salinger House

Designed by architect Jimmy Lim for Haji Rudin Salinger, the Salinger House received the coveted Aga Khan Award for Architecture in 1998. The house was constructed by traditional craftsmen from Malaysia's east coast and took over six years to build. No nails were used in the main structure, which is built almost entirely from *cengal* wood, and no machinery was used in the construction process. Clay roof tiles, designed in the traditional *singhorra* style, each bear the name of the house owner in Jawi.

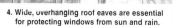

4. Wide, overhanging roof eaves are essential for protecting windows from sun and rain.

5. *Jejala*, or multi-panelled, fenestrated carvings above doors, are intricately carved on both sides and encourage ventilation between rooms.

6. Gaps between wooden slats under the roof eaves allow air to enter.

High-rise solutions in tropical architecture

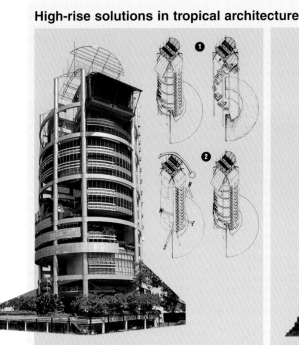

Menara Mesiniaga

This 14-storey building is an early example of high-rise tropical design in Malaysia. Lift lobbies, stairwells and toilets on all floors (1) are ventilated and lit naturally. Plants spiral up the side via a succession of recessed terraces.

Windows on the east and west sides, which face the sun, have external louvres as sunshading (2). The north and south sides, not directly facing the sun, have unshielded, glazed curtain walling to encourage natural lighting. A skeletal roof provides the frame for solar panelling.

Central Plaza

This 27-storey building is located in the heart of Kuala Lumpur's Golden Triangle. Cool air is introduced through a system of louvres and balconies on the hot, west facade. The east and west facades, which both face the sun, feature glazing that is recessed from the main structure for sunshading.

The lift lobby, stairwells and toilets, located on the south side of the building, are all naturally lit and ventilated. Vertical planting is introduced to the north face of the building in a series of diagonally rising steps which culminate at the rooftop pool.

Menara UMNO

The futuristic-looking, 21-storey Menara UMNO in the central business district of Penang features 14 floors of office space which, although designed to be air conditioned, can be naturally ventilated and lit.

No desk is located more than 6 metres from an openable window, while specially designed wing walls direct wind to balconies that act as airlocks with adjustable doors and panels for natural ventilation.

All the lift lobbies, stairwells and toilets are lit by sunlight and can be naturally ventilated in the event of a power failure.

overhangs prevent rain from entering, offer shading, and reduce unwanted glare.

Maximizing natural ventilation in a building is essential and can be accomplished by a variety of methods. Wind speed increases with altitude so building a house on stilts, or incorporating openings in the walls of tall buildings, encourages airflow. The use of large windows and air vents in the roof or walls has a similar effect, but designs must also prevent rain from entering. Orientating a particular building towards the direction of the prevailing wind is important. Airflow can be increased by arranging houses in random order as opposed to the regular patterns seen in most housing estates which trap air and prevent adequate ventilation.

Rooms with outside walls and a large roof space will remain cooler than rooms enclosed by other rooms. Designing large open spaces within the house and minimizing the number of room partitions encourages air flow and cooling.

While the choice of construction materials is also paramount to tropical architecture, modern building design, particularly high–rise, may severely limit that choice. Timber is not only abundant locally but also possesses low thermal mass, meaning that less heat is retained and transmitted into the building. Bricks, concrete and glass, on the other hand, tend to radiate heat into a building.

A protoype house: The Roof-roof House

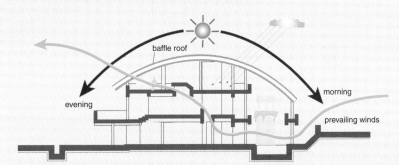

The Roof-roof House is designed as a life-size working prototype of the bioclimatic design ideas of architect Kenneth Yeang. The design attempts to harness climatic elements to shape the building's enclosure, configuration and spatial organization. The building's enclosures are intended to work as a valve, filtering out undesirable solar radiation, and filtering in natural ventilation.

As the name of the house implies, the emphasis of the design is on the roof. The baffle roof (a roof designed to regulate the flow of light and wind) covers the flat roof of the first floor and extends over the pool and terrace below. The sectional design of the roof aims to block the west and noon sun while letting in the morning sun. The baffle roof is also intended to direct cooling breezes onto the lower floors. In addition to this filtering device, there is a system of sliding grilles and panels, and adjustable blinds, which can be operated by the occupants for maximum cross ventilation.

The building's north–south orientation protects the main living areas from the direct sun. Ground floor living spaces face east and open onto the pool, thus taking advantage of the prevailing southeasterly wind.

A future for the past: Conservation and reuse

Since the building boom of the 1970s, many of Malaysia's historic buildings have been demolished. Recent large-scale urban redevelopment continues to threaten prewar buildings, while other heritage buildings are simply deteriorating due to age and neglect. To lose these buildings, however, is effectively to obliterate historical memories, and there is now increasing pressure from various segments of the community to conserve the nation's architectural heritage.

This *rumah kutai* (a rare type of traditional Malay house from central Perak), located in Kuala Kangsar and known as the Bamboo House, was restored to its original state and awarded a Jurors Award by Pertubuhan Akitek Malaysia in 1995.

The conservation issue

Conservation is the action taken to prevent decay, embracing all acts that prolong the life of cultural and natural heritage. Building conservation relates specifically to the processes of maintenance, repair and restoration of historic buildings which aim to prolong a building's life and function.

Laws for historic building conservation are established through legislation whereby a national inventory of historic buildings includes lists and

Causes of building decay

- **Structural**: Decay resulting from the natural pull of gravity over time.
- **Man-made**: Damage caused by neglect, vandalism, fire and nearby construction work.
- **Climatic**: Decay caused by solar radiation, temperature, moisture in the air and wind.
- **Botanical**: Disintegration of masonry caused by the roots of creepers and other plants.
- **Biological**: Collapse due to acid produced by bacteria and lichens which react chemically with structural material.
- **Fungi**: Damage to organic materials such as timber by fungi, mildew and yeasts that do not require any sunlight to survive.
- **Fauna**: Weakened structural timbers due to insects such as termites, greater risk of fire due to rats' nests and the corrosive effects of bird droppings.
- **Economic**: Destruction of buildings to make way for new developments.

ABOVE AND RIGHT: Rumah Bomoh, a traditional house in Cangkat Jering, was successfully restored despite structural damage by termites.

Methods of building conservation

- **Prevention of deterioration**: Controlling the surrounding environment to minimize air pollution from local industry, humidity and light, fire, theft and vandalism, and vibrations from traffic or construction work.

ABOVE AND RIGHT: No. 25 Jalan Pudu Lama in Kuala Lumpur is a 1920s terraced Chinese townhouse. Now fully restored, the building houses the Malaysian office of Sotheby's.

- **Preservation**: Undertaking regular checks and repairs.
- **Consolidation**: Adding supportive materials to ensure structural integrity.
- **Restoration**: Restoring a building using original parts wherever possible, based upon archaeological and historical evidence.
- **Rehabilitation**: Returning an otherwise functionally, and therefore economically, defunct building to a state of utility in the hope of ensuring its continued existence, while preserving the significant portions and features at the same time.
- **Reproduction**: Copying artefacts and decorative elements that are scarce or threatened and maintaining aesthetic harmony.
- **Reconstruction**: As a last resort, moving an entire building to a safer location or reconstructing an irreparable building with new materials.

Preserving Kuala Terengganu's waterfront

The historic waterfront entrepôt, or trading port, of Kuala Terengganu has occupied the same spot at the mouth of the Terengganu River (Sungai Terengganu) since the 2nd century when Greek maps of the ancient world called it Perimoula. The present-day buildings (which encompass Kampung Cina, Kampung Lorong Haji Jamil and parts of Kampung Tiong and Kampung Banggol) were built at the end of the 19th century following a fire

schedules of old buildings for protection. Conservation zones can be created through town planning action, with guidelines for redevelopment and the integration of new and old buildings. Alternatively, financial incentives should be provided to owners to reuse their historic properties; others could be compensated. Conservation of heritage buildings is important for a country to understand its cultural past, to serve as a resource pool of traditional building techniques, and to enrich urban life generally.

Inevitably, building conservation necessitates a certain degree of intervention and it is the golden rule of conservation that this intervention be kept to a minimum, preserving as much as possible of the original fabric of the building. Historical evidence should not be destroyed, falsified or removed, and complete documentation of all materials and construction methods is encouraged prior to, and during, intervention.

Selecting buildings for conservation

Malaysian buildings deemed worthy of conservation fall into three groups: those buildings with historical significance, buildings with architectural significance, and buildings possessing other significant cultural or social values.

Historic buildings include those connected with significant events in Malaysia's cultural, political, economic, military and social history. They also include homes or meeting places for notable personages or activities. Historic buildings also represent historical development patterns such as ports, agricultural settlements and railways, and include institutional buildings such as schools, jails, town halls, markets and places of worship.

Malaysian buildings of architectural significance are those displaying a particular, or an unusual, style or construction technique. They represent an important work of an architect or craftsman, or are particularly rich in details reflective of their time. Buildings of architectural significance can have an

in 1880 which razed the town to the ground. The buildings, mostly shophouses, display a variety of styles. Decorative features include wooden carvings, plaster renditions of Terengganu Malay carvings, classical European pilasters, imported tiles and timber fretwork over the windows. Kampung Cina was listed in World Monuments Watch's 100 Most Endangered Sites 1998–1999.

important influence on the character of the surrounding environment, or may simply be aesthetically pleasing to the eye. Furthermore, buildings not architecturally significant in themselves may nevertheless be vital for maintaining an area's scale and continuity.

Ultimately, even old buildings in Malaysia which were sturdily built, with a high degree of design integrity, usually need upgrading to meet current building bylaws, including the provision of essential services and safety requirements.

The present-day headquarters of PAM was built in 1903 as a residence for Loke Chow Kit. It later became the Empire Hotel and then the Peninsula Hotel.

Early building conservation in Malaysia
The earliest call for a national building conservation movement appeared in a 1976 issue of *Majallah Akitek* (Architecture Malaysia), the official mouthpiece of Pertubuhan Akitek Malaysia (PAM), or Malaysian Institute of Architects. A far-sighted proposal was made for the creation of a Kuala Lumpur Conservation Area around Dataran Merdeka (Merdeka Square). The paper also called for increased public awareness, the enactment of laws,

the listing of buildings and the greater involvement of architects and planners in this endeavour. Thankfully, the heritage buildings around Dataran Merdeka were eventually conserved, reused and today house the nation's law courts. However, an important factor in their survival is the fact that they were government buildings; in order to safeguard the thousands of privately owned heritage properties in Malaysia, one single law is needed.

In early 1983, public disquiet came to the fore with the imminent threat of destruction of one of Kuala Lumpur's most well-known historical buildings, the former Loke Chow Kit residence, and headquarters of PAM. At that time, a group of concerned Malaysians and expatriates were in the process of forming the country's first non-governmental organization for the conservation of heritage buildings, to be called Badan Warisan Malaysia (Heritage of Malaysia Trust). The main objective of Badan Warisan Malaysia is to promote the preservation of those buildings deemed by the council of the Badan to be part of the heritage of the country for the benefit and education of Malaysians. Badan Warisan Malaysia also initiated a national inventory of historic buildings recording nearly 30,000 prewar buildings in 247 towns.

A comprehensive Building Conservation Act has still to be realized in Malaysia despite much preparatory work on a draft Act in the early 1990s. The recommendations call for a conservation fund, for means to offer financial incentives to owners of historic properties, and for the training of government officials in the appropriate legislation. Existing laws that do involve building conservation include the Antiquities Act, which applies to buildings that are 'reasonably believed to be at least 100 years old', the Local Government Act, the Land Acquisition Act and the Town and Country Planning Act. One law which inadvertently protected buildings was the Rent Control Act but this was repealed in 1997.

Reconstructing a Malay timber house
In the mid-1990s, the Badan Warisan Malaysia purchased a Rumah Penghulu (headman's house) in Kedah, reconstructing and restoring it in the grounds of its office in Kuala Lumpur.

1. The original house was in a state of disrepair due to lack of resources for restoration.

2. A 1916 Straits Settlements coin, found under the *tiang seri* (main column), effectively dates the house, which was originally located in Kedah. A 1996 one ringgit coin was added before the tiang seri was raised again.

3. Original timber was used in the restored house while damaged parts such as the windows were rebuilt in exactly the same form.

4. Old Chinese-style roof tiles were sourced as the house required about 31,000 tiles and only 15,000 had been salvaged from the original site.

The rehabilitation of Central Market
Towards the end of the 1980s building boom, the then 50-year-old Kuala Lumpur wet market was saved from demolition at the last minute and converted into a cultural market. Pasar Seni, or Central Market as it is called, is one of the earliest examples of a private developer obtaining the lease of a large, state-owned property, retaining it and reusing it for commercial purposes.

The facades, no two alike, were glazed by a blue-green, heat-resistant calorex, and linked by a moulded frieze or 'sweat-band'. Twenty-four step-headed entrances with metal grilles open out to the surroundings with two main entrances at either end of the central mall. Typical Art Deco colours were chosen for the restored building while the original friezes and decoration were left intact.

To retain the spatial quality of the large single-storey box, the new shops were arranged in discrete clusters, away from the surrounding walls and roof. Upper level

Kuala Lumpur's Pasar Seni, or Central Market, is the result of a successful rehabilitation of the city's wet market which was destined for demolition.

shops and restaurants were linked by three bridges, and a hydraulic lift was introduced in the centre of the mall. Small kiosks selling arts and crafts reused the old wet market concrete stalls on the ground floor and artists were invited to set up their easels.

127

The Petronas Twin Towers

Reaching a height of 451.9 metres, the Petronas Twin Towers was acknowledged in 1996 as the tallest building in the world by the Council on Tall Buildings and Urban Habitat. It is the most advanced building ever erected in Malaysia, and an icon for the 21st century.

The KLCC occupies the site of the former Selangor Turf Club.

Design history

In 1991, Petronas, Malaysia's national oil company, invited leading architectural firms from around the world to submit a design concept for its new headquarters at the Kuala Lumpur City Centre site. The winning entry, two 88-storey-high towers linked 170 metres above street level by a sky bridge with two 44-storey side towers, was submitted by Cesar Pelli & Associates Inc., an internationally renowned firm of architects based in Boston, USA.

The project was launched in 1992, and in May 1993 piling and foundation work began. In April 1996, three years after the first construction work began, the pinnacles were put in place on top of the towers, bringing the height of the Petronas Twin Towers to its full 451.9 metres.

A national icon for Malaysia

Although the design of the Petronas Twin Towers projects an image of a dynamic, rapidly industrializing country, it also responds to the tropical climate and to Islamic architectural traditions, all within a Malaysian cultural context.

Contemporary Malaysian motifs, adapted from *pandan* weaving and *bertam* palm wall matting patterns, feature on the marble floor of the entrance lobby to each tower, while the wall motifs are inspired by *songket* weaving patterns and timber carving.

The form of the towers reflects the importance of geometry in Islamic architectural tradition. The shape of the towers' floor plate is based upon two

The construction process

The towers stand on a 4.5-metre-thick raft containing 13 200 cubic metres of grade 60 reinforced concrete, weighing approximately 32 550 tonnes, and supported by 104 barrette piles varying in length from 60 to 115 metres. The raft was cast in a single pour lasting 54 hours, the largest pour in the history of Malaysia's construction industry.

Up until the 73rd storey, floor levels were completed four at a time, taking 4–5 days per floor. The concrete core walls were cast in place first, followed by the 16 columns, the ring beams joining the columns, and then the concrete cantilevered slabs which form the geometric shape. The steel beams and composite floor were then put in place before, finally, the concrete stairway was cast in place.

In order to keep the site free of debris, teams spent two hours every night checking each floor. Every morning, 5–10 lorry loads of debris were removed.

Two main cranes per tower, and one per annex tower were made to operate continuously for 24 hours a day, 7 days a week. Six crane operators were allocated to

each crane. The cranes were equipped with television cameras and monitors to provide the operators with unobstructed views of the lifting hook.

ABOVE LEFT: Almost 80 000 cubic metres of concrete reinforced with 16 000 tonnes of steel were required for the concrete core and frame of each tower.
LEFT: A total of 36 910 tonnes of steel were used in the Petronas Twin Towers for beams, trusses and reinforcement.

Design features of the Petronas Twin Towers

1. The exterior is organized in horizontal ribbons of vision glass and stainless steel panels. In all, there are 65 000 square metres of stainless steel cladding and 77 000 square metres of vision glass.

2. The towers are connected 170 metres above street level by a 58.4-metre-long, 750-tonne, two-storey sky bridge.

3. The sky bridge has rotational pins at the end of each leg and at the top of the crown of the arch, which act as a centering device equalizing joint movement at both towers. The girders are pinned to the crown of the arch which stays centred between the towers while both girder end blocks slide on pads. As the towers move together or apart, the legs change slope, the spherical bearings rotate at spring points and the legs flex at their top end.

4. Horizontal 'bull noses' and vertical 'teardrop' sunscreen brackets provide shading to the windows.

5. The Petronas Concert Hall is designed in the shape of a 19th-century European concert hall.

6. The unitized curtain wall panel system comprises 33 000 panels.

interlocking squares forming an eight–pointed star; eight semicircles are inserted into the re-entrant corners or angles.

Although the windows run in continuous horizontal ribbons to offer occupants unrivalled views, they are protected from the glare of the sun by projecting shades. Tinted, laminated glass also helps to reduce heat gain from the sunlight as well as ultraviolet (UV) transmission.

Unique design features

Each tower tapers inwards in six intervals with the walls at the upper levels tilting gently towards the centre. Both towers are topped by a 73.5-metre-high, 176-tonne structural steel pinnacle comprising a mast, a ring ball and, at the very top, a spire ball. The ring ball, located about a third of the way up the mast, is made up of 14 circular tubes of varying diameter and conceals tracks for equipment to wash the external facade above the 88th floor.

The Petronas Twin Towers has the highest concentration of double-deck lifts of any building in the world to transport the expected 6,000-strong office population. Double-deck lifts carry more people, reduce waiting time and require less hoist way. Passengers reach the lower office floors via lifts at street level. An escalator in the lobby takes people to a mezzanine level where they may enter the upper deck of the lift. A computer-controlled system optimizes efficiency during peak hours, such as the early morning, by only allowing upper deck passengers to stop at odd floors and lower deck passengers even floors. During off-peak times, both decks may stop at any floor. To reach the upper floors, passengers take different high-speed, double-deck, shuttle lifts directly to the sky lobbies, located at the sky bridge, where they change to other lifts.

The shape of the Petronas Twin Towers' floor plate attempts to incorporate Islamic geometric principles by superimposing two rotated squares with small, circular infills.

Kuala Lumpur City Centre

The Petronas Twin Towers is the jewel in the crown of the new Kuala Lumpur City Centre (KLCC). The Petronas Twin Towers' podium houses the 864-seat Petronas Concert Hall, the Petronas Art Gallery, a reference library on energy, petroleum, petro-chemical and related industries and Petrosains, an interactive petroleum discovery centre. The base of the towers is also home to a 6-storey shopping and entertainment complex known as Suria KLCC (1). The complex is anchored by several large retail stores and a 13-screen cineplex.

In addition to the Petronas Twin Towers, the KLCC comprises the 50-storey Menara Maxis (Maxis Tower) (2), a *surau* (prayer room) (4), the 30-storey Menara Esso (Esso Tower) (5) and the 38-storey Mandarin Oriental Kuala Lumpur (6), all set on the fringe of a park. The 20-hectare public park, designed by landscape artist Roberto Burle Marx, includes a fountain pool, a 0.8-hectare children's playground, a bird sanctuary and a jogging track. More than 1,700 trees have been planted in the park, among which 74 species of indigenous trees can be identified.

The District Cooling Centre (3) houses a central chilled water production facility which provides chilled water for air conditioning to all buildings in the KLCC. The setup is powered by natural gas and employs a non-CFC (chlorofluorocarbon), environmentally friendly refrigerant.

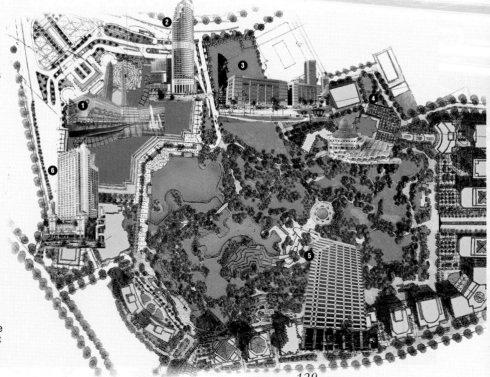

Mega projects

During the early 1990s, impressive economic growth triggered some notable building projects in Malaysia that were monumental in both size and influence. These mega projects were important not only in projecting an image of a dynamic, rapidly industrializing country, but also in promoting the transfer of technology within the construction industry.

The skyline of Kuala Lumpur has undergone many changes in the final decade of the 20th century.

1. The roof of the new National Art Gallery evokes the overlapping *bumbung panjang* (long ridge roof) of a *gajah menyusu* house (a traditional Malay house whose design resembles a suckling elephant).

2. The design of the National Library in Kuala Lumpur alludes to the *songket tengkolok* (traditional Malay folded brocade headgear).

3. The roof of Kuala Lumpur's new National Theatre is inspired by the *sirih junjung*, a cone-shaped arrangement of betel leaves on a pedestal tray.

4. The National Science Centre in Damansara with its distinctive geodesic dome atop a circular base.

The Multimedia Super Corridor

The Multimedia Super Corridor (MSC) is a strategic initiative by the public and private sectors to transform Malaysia into a world leader in information technology development and application. Geographically, the MSC is a 50-kilometre-long, 15-kilometre-wide stretch of land that extends south from the Kuala Lumpur City Centre and the Menara KL to the new Kuala Lumpur International Airport in Sepang.

Key components of the MSC include two new purpose-built cities: Putrajaya and Cyberjaya. Putrajaya is intended to be the new Federal political and administrative centre, supporting a population of over 500,000, while Cyberjaya will be a centre of information technology development to service domestic, regional and global markets and will be home to the Multimedia University, the proposed new campus of Universiti Telekom.

Not since Brasilia and Canberra were designed and built has such a plan for a city been unveiled. Putrajaya's design is that of a garden city with emphasis on a green environment. The birth of Putrajaya represents the pinnacle of Malaysia's mega project development that can be traced back to the construction of the Dayabumi Complex in the early 1980s (see 'New landmarks').

Reaching for the sky

Towards the end of the 1990s, three mammoth projects were completed that radically transformed the skyline of Kuala Lumpur. The tallest and most impressive was the Petronas Twin Towers (see 'The Petronas Twin Towers'), the most identifiable icon of the new Kuala Lumpur City Centre(KLCC). The Petronas Twin Towers building was recognized by the International Council on Tall Buildings and Urban Habitat in 1996 as the tallest building in the world. In addition to the Petronas Twin Towers, which rises to 88 storeys, or 451.9 metres, the KLCC comprises the 50-storey Ampang Tower, the 38-storey Mandarin Oriental Hotel and the 30-storey Menara Esso (Esso Tower), all set on the fringe of a large, landscaped public park.

Two other skyscrapers that appeared in the mid-to late 1990s are Menara Kuala Lumpur (Kuala Lumpur Tower) and Menara Telekom (Telekom Tower). The Kuala Lumpur Tower, which houses telecommunication equipment, is the tallest tower (as opposed to a building) in Southeast Asia and the third tallest in the world, rising to 421 metres. A

The vision of Cyberjaya promises a modern, eco-friendly centre of information technology development, home to the Multimedia University (Universiti Telekom) and Multimedia Super Corridor companies.

circular concrete tower shaft, with vertical ribs on the surface, fans out into a tower head, almost 50 metres in diameter, with painted aluminium Islamic patterns, and glass arranged in the form of Islamic *muqarnas*.

One of the last mega projects to be completed in the 20th century is Menara Telekom, located on the border of Kuala Lumpur and Petaling Jaya. The building's design was influenced by Malaysian sculptor and painter Latiff Mohidin's sketch of the *pucuk rebung*, or bamboo shoot. The elegant tower, whose design brief demanded 'intelligent' building features, is functional, aesthetic and people friendly. Sky gardens, located at three-floor intervals, offer office workers a garden view instead of the usual 'toy car' perspective, and a green retreat during breaks. Double-deck lifts and sophisticated telecommunications systems are just some of the advanced features of Menara Telekom.

A new gateway to Malaysia

A new chapter in Malaysia's aviation history became reality in 1998 with the opening of the Kuala Lumpur International Airport (KLIA). Located 50 kilometres south of Kuala Lumpur, in Sepang, the new airport is one of the most advanced in Asia, and boasts the tallest control tower, the longest conveyor belt system and, during the building stage, the largest airport construction site. Even the three-storey kitchen, which prepares in-flight meals, uses a 5.38-kilometre-long internal track to transport food items to the respective areas within the airport.

Putrajaya will become Malaysia's new Federal administrative capital and will house the Prime Minister's office, ambassadors' residences and Dataran Putra (People's Square).

The interior design of the Kuala Lumpur International Airport (KLIA) resembles a futuristic forest canopy.

An arboretum, located in the departure terminal of the KLIA, showcases Malaysia's natural heritage.

KLIA's design was conceptualized by eminent Japanese architect Kisho Kurokawa, and attempts to incorporate Malaysian cultural characteristics within a Functionalist approach. The main terminal building, with its futuristic design of glass and steel, is covered by a state-of-the-art hyperbolic paraboloid shell roof inspired by the domes of Islamic architecture. The airport is surrounded by a man-made forest. The saplings are expected to reach a height of 30 metres within 20 years. An arboretum, located at the satellite building where planes depart, contains many indigenous plant species in an attempt to showcase Malaysia's natural rainforest heritage. Sensors built into the viewing glass automatically control sunshading blinds.

Avant-garde design

Hidden from public view is the Bank Negara Disaster Recovery Centre in Shah Alam, one of the few examples of deconstruction in Malaysian architecture. Forms, spaces, ideas and materials are synthesized in a haphazard-looking building comprising four distinct parts. A copper drum at the entrance, housing lifts and a spiral staircase, is the tallest element and ends in a slanting, sky-lit roof. This connects to a long, curved building housing offices which is fronted by a glass-clad wall leaning 10 degrees forward. A rectilinear spine wall uses different-sized windows for visual interest while the final part of the complex is an oval end building.

1990s mega projects

1. The Sultan Salahuddin Abdul Aziz Shah Mosque in Shah Alam.

2. The Shah Alam Stadium.

3. The Bank Negara Disaster Recovery Centre, Shah Alam.

4. The design of Menara Telekom (Telekom Tower) was influenced by a sketch of a bamboo shoot.

5. The Petronas Twin Towers, recognized as the tallest building in the world in 1996.

6. Menara Kuala Lumpur (KL Tower).

7. An artist's impression of the Government precinct in Putrajaya.

8. An artist's impression of the Multimedia University (Universiti Telekom) in Cyberjaya.

9. The Kuala Lumpur International Airport.

Glossary

Italicized words are in Bahasa Malaysia except where indicated. (Ch.) Chinese, (Hi.) Hindi, (La.) Latin.
Page numbers in brackets refer to illustrations in the volume.

A

Airwell: Courtyard within a house, open to the sky (p. 91).

Anglo-Indian style: Combination of European and Asian building traditions developed by Europeans in India from the 17th century, characterized by European-style symmetrical facades with wide verandas and high ceilings (p. 94).

Anglo-Straits style: see Straits Eclectic style (p. 80).

Anjung: Covered entrance porch where guests are greeted and male guests often entertained, and where family members can relax. Built as an extension to the front of a Malay house, the *anjung* is accessed by steps and leads to the *serambi*, or reception area (p. 20).

Arabesque decoration: Ornate style of decoration using flowers, foliage and, less often, animal and geometric figures to produce an intricate pattern of interlaced lines (p. 95).

Arcade: Series of arches supported on piers or columns.

Arch: Curved structure of wedge-shaped blocks spanning an opening which support each other, and the load above, by mutual compression (p. 82).

Architrave: Main beam or lowest part of an entablature immediately resting on a column (p. 81); also used for a moulded frame round a door or window.

Art Deco: Style of decorative art made popular in the late 1920s in Europe and America, characterized by geometric motifs and streamlined and curvilinear forms (p. 100).

Atap: Lightweight yet insulating roof thatch, often made from *nipah*, *rumbia* or *bertam* palm leaves (pp. 12–13).

B

Baffle roof: Louvred roof designed to shield the house from direct sunlight (p. 125).

Bakau: Species of timber used to make stilts for houses, especially those built on water.

Balau: (La.) Durable hardwood of the genus *Shorea*.

Balustrade: Horizontal railing supported by vertical balusters.

Bangunan: Building.

Baroque style: Originating in Italy in the early 17th century; characterized by free and sculptural use of the Classical orders and by the dramatic combined effects of architecture, sculpture, painting and the decorative arts.

Barrel-vaulted roof: Design of roof where the vault, or arched structure, has a semicircular cross section (see illustration below).

Bas relief: Sculptural relief which protrudes only slightly from the background surface (p. 101).

Base: Lowest part of any architectural structure or element (p. 81).

Bay window: Window projecting out from the main wall of a building forming an alcove in the room.

Beam: Rigid structural member designed to carry a load across a space, transferring the weight to supporting elements (see illustration below).

Belian: *Eusideroxylon zwagerii* (La.), ironwood; a highly durable timber species indigenous to Sabah and Sarawak.

Bertam: *Eugeissona tristis* (La.), a local palm species whose leaves are used to make *atap*, or roof thatch.

Béton brut: Concrete left in its natural state after formwork is removed (see illustration below).

Bilik: Room, apartment in a longhouse.

Bomoh: Malay traditional medicine man or spirit healer.

Bracket: Support for corners or fixtures (p. 13).

Brise soleil: Louvred screen or fins designed to shield windows or walls from direct sunlight.

British 'Raj' style: Combination of Gothic architecture and the decorative features of buildings of Muslim India and the Middle East, evolved by the British in India in the late 19th century.

Buluh picap: Flattened bamboo, laid over floor joists as flooring material (p. 13).

Bumbung lima: 'Five ridge roof', hipped roof comprising four sloping roofs (p. 25).

Bumbung panjang: 'Long ridge roof', gable roof comprising two sloping roofs (p. 24).

Bumbung Perak: Gambrel roof, or a hipped roof with gable-like ends (p. 25).

Bumbung potongan Belanda: 'Dutch-style roof ridge', another term for *bumbung Perak*.

Butan: Finial.

Buttress: External support, often built onto or against the outside of a wall, designed to stabilize a structure by opposing its outward thrust.

C

Canopy: Awning or roof structure projecting out from a building or wall to offer shelter beneath.

Cantilever: Part of a structure that extends beyond its supporting element (see illustration below).

Capital: Top of a column, pillar or pier (p. 81).

Cengal: *Neobalanocarpus heimii* (La.), a very durable hardwood.

Chatri: (Hi.) Pillared pavilion crowned with an umbrella-shaped dome (see illustration below).

Chien nien: (Ch.) 'Cut and paste', mosaic technique using broken pieces of glazed porcelain (p. 47).

Chik: (Hi.) Bamboo blind laced with twine (p. 80).

Circulation: Movement, not just of people but also of elements, e.g. water, air, around a building.

Classical style: Architectural principles and styles of ancient Greece and Rome.

Clerestory: Opening or window in a portion of interior, such as a jack roof, that rises above adjacent rooftops (pp. 90–1).

Colonial style: Architectural style transplanted from the colonizing country and adapted to suit the local climate.

Colonnade: Series or row of columns supporting a beam.

Column: Vertical support comprising a base, circular shaft and capital (p. 81).

Conoid: Geometric surface created by rotating a parabola, ellipse or hyperbola about one axis.

Corinthian: Third and last of the Classical Greek orders, characterized by richly ornamented entablatures with a deep cornice.

Cornice: Crowning projection and uppermost portion of the entablature in Classical architecture (p. 81).

Courtyard: Open court within or adjacent to a building (p. 91).

Cupola: Spherical roof or small dome forming or adorning the superstructure of a buliding.

Curtain walling: Non-load-bearing wall attached to the structure of a building (p. 117).

D

Dome: Vaulted, spherical roof (p. 82).

Doric: First order of Greek architecture (p. 81).

E

Eave: Lower part of a roof overhang (p. 95).

Entablature: Upper part of an order of architecture comprising an architrave, frieze and cornice, supported by a colonnade (p. 81).

Expressionism: Style of architecture popular in the 1920s, characterized by dramatic forms and arches.

F

Facade: Face or front of a building.

Fanlight: Semicircular window with sash bars arranged like the ribs of a fan (p. 79).

Fascia board: Horizontal, carved board covering the eaves (p. 95).

Fenestration: Arrangement of windows in a building facade.

Feng shui: (Ch.) 'Wind and water', Chinese geomancy (pp. 48–9).

Festoon: Ornamental carved ribbon or garland of flowers suspended in a curve between two points.

Filigree: Ornamental lattice-like work of intricate design.

Finial: Ornament that tops a spire, pinnacle, or each corner of a tower or roof (p. 38).

Five-foot way: Deep, open veranda built into the front of townhouses and shophouses forming a continuous, covered passage (p. 91).

Foundation: Lowest part of any building, often below the surface of the ground, designed to support the building and transfer its load to the ground.

Fretwork: Timber work decorated by cutting with a fretsaw.

Frieze: Part of an entablature (p. 81).

Functionalism: Architectural belief that form follows function, i.e. the form of a building should respond to the physical requirements of its users.

G

Gable: Triangular portion of an end wall on a gable-roofed structure (see illustration below).

Gable horn: Rafters extended skywards at the gable end of a *bumbung panjang* house to resemble crossed horns (p. 14).

Gable roof: Roof sloping down in two parts from a central ridge, thus forming a gable at each end (p. 24).

Gajah menyusu: Variation on the two-structure form of gable roof, resembling a suckling elephant (p. 24).

Gambrel roof: Shallower slope above a steeper slope on a ridged roof (p. 25).

Georgian period: Originating in the early 18th century, characterized by plain interior decoration.

Girder: Principal beam intended to support loads at various points along its length.

Glass box: Glass curtain-walled buildings of the International Style.

Gothic style: Style of pointed medieval architecture developed between the 13th and 15th centuries in Western Europe.

Grecian: Architecture of ancient Greece characterized by a strict adherence to form and proportion.

Grille: Perforated screen for covering an opening.

H

Half-door: Door of half height placed in front of the main door to afford privacy when the main door is open but to allow for ventilation, usually decorated and able to swing in both directions (p. 92).

High-rise: Tall building with a large number of storeys and equipped with elevators.

Hipped roof: Roof with sloping ends and sides, and no gables (p. 25).

Hoist way: Vertical, enclosed space in which elevators travel.

Horseshoe arch: Arch in the shape of a horseshoe (see illustration below).

Hyperbolic paraboloid: Surface made by sliding a parabola with downward curvature along a parabola with upward curvature (see illustration below).

I

International Style: Devoid of regional characteristics, typified by simple geometric forms, glass curtain walling, and steel or reinforced concrete construction.

Ionic: Second order of Greek architecture characterized by slender columns, spiral scroll capitals and a simplified entablature (p. 81).

Istana: Palace.

J

Jack roof: Raised turret roof separated from the main roof by a clerestory opening (p. 90).

Jejala: Multi-panelled, fenestrated carvings above doors which encourage ventilation between rooms (p. 124).

Jelutong: *Dyera costulata* (La.), a non-durable timber species.

Joist: One of a series of small, parallel beams to support a floor, ceiling or flat roof (p. 13).

K

Kampung: Village.

Kampung air: Village built on water.

Keyhole arch: Arch designed in the shape of a keyhole (see illustration below).

Kolong: Underside of a Malay house raised on stilts.

Kongsi: (Ch.) Chinese clan house (pp. 52–3).

Kubur: Cemetery.

Kukut tupai: Wooden wedge or bracket, resembling a squirrel, used to reinforce the main structure of an Orang Asli dwelling.

L

Lambor: Unroofed platform projecting from the side door of a traditional Malay house in Kelantan or Terengganu with steps leading down to the ground (p. 27).

Laminated glass: Safety glass comprising two or more layers of glass bonded to interlayers of polyvinyl butyral resin that retains fragments if the glass is broken.

Lansaran: Dance platform, unique to Murut longhouses (p. 32).

Lantai: Floor.

Latticework: Structure of crossed strips arranged to form a regular pattern of open spaces.

Lepau: Room to receive and entertain guests in the anterior part of a traditional Malay house in Kedah, Perak, Kelantan and Terengganu (p. 20).

Linkhouse: One of a row of uniform houses, sharing at least one side wall with the neighbouring house (p. 120).

Lintel: Beam supporting the weight above a door or opening (see illustration below).

Loggia: Open-sided gallery or arcade, often with an upper storey and attached to a larger structure (p. 81).

Longhouse: Long structure raised on stilts comprising common areas and separate family apartments (p. 32).

Loteng: Attic.

Louvre: Fixed or movable inclined boards which allow air circulation, control light and prevent rain from entering (see illustration below).

M

Makam: Malay tomb.

Masjid: Mosque.

Masonry: Stonework or brickwork.

Mengkuang: Screwpine, a plant species whose leaves are used for wall panels.

Meranti: Moderately durable timber of the genus *Shorea* (La.).

Merbau: *Intsia palembanica* (La.), a species of durable timber.

Mihrab: Decorative panel or niche in a mosque designating the *qiblat* (p. 86).

Minaret: Tall, slender tower attached to a mosque from which the call to prayer is made (p. 84).

Mock Tudor style: Decorative rather than structural imitation of Tudor style, characterized by half-timber frame 'black and white' houses.

Modern style: Style emerging in the early 20th century but only becoming widespread following World War II, culminating in glass, concrete and steel module construction.

Modernism: 20th century movement within architecture and the arts representing a deliberate break from the past.

Mogul style: Architecture of the Mogul Dynasty (1526–1857), Indo-Islamic in origin, characterized by highly decorative mosques and palaces.

Mortise: Rectangular hole cut into a piece to receive a tenon of the same size (p. 23).

Moulding: Contoured ornamental band to decorate a wall or other surface.

Mullion: Vertical member dividing precast panels on a curtain wall (p. 117).

Multifoil arch: Ornamentation of an archway with foliation having more than five foils (see illustration below).

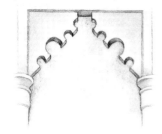

Muqarna: Stone or plaster stalactite ornamentation in Islamic architecture.

Mural: Large picture painted on, or applied to, a wall or ceiling.

N

Neoclassical style: Characterized by the widespread use of Greek and Roman orders and decorative motifs, and of strong, simple, geometric compositions.

Neogothic style: Late 18th and 19th century revival of the Gothic style, characterized by stained glass windows, spires and pointed arches.

Neotraditional: Reviving forms and styles of traditional architecture in a modern context.

Nibong: *Oncosperma tigillarium* (La.), a local palm species whose trunks are used as stilts for houses built on water.

Nipah: *Nypa fruticans* (La.), a variety of creeping palm whose fronds are used for roof thatch.

Nyatoh: Timber species of the genus *Palaquium* (La.).

O

Ogee arch: Pointed arch, each side of which is a double curve with the concave side uppermost (see illustration below).

Onion dome: Bulbous, ribbed dome common in Islamic architecture (see illustration below).

P

Padang: Village green, field or central clearing.

Palladiansim: Style imitating Roman architecture developed by Palladio, the 16th-century Italian architect from Vicenza.

Pandan: Plant of the genus *Pandanus* (La.) whose leaves may be used as a temporary roofing material.

Pantile: S-shaped roof tile, laid so that the downturn of one overlaps the upturn of the next.

Parapet: Part of a wall extending above the roof; sometimes acting as a balustrade (see illustration below).

Partition: Interior wall dividing all or part of a room.

Pavilion: Light, decorative structure with open sides, detached or part of a building.

Pediment: Decorative gable end of a Classical building supported by the entablature (p. 81).

Pelantar: Raised platform at the rear of a Malay house used for washing and drying (p. 21).

Peles: Gable end (p. 27).

Perabong: Thatch capping to cover the peak of the roof (p. 13).

Petaling: *Ochanostachys amentacea* (La.), moderately durable timber species.

Pier: Solid masonry support, more massive than a column.

Pilaster: Shallow pier or column attached to, or part of, a wall (see illustration below).

Pilotis: Stilts, columns or pillars supporting a raised building.

Pinnacle: Decorative vertical structure ending in a pyramid or spire, often crowning a buttress or gable.

Pintu pagar: 'Fence door'; see 'half-door' (p. 92).

Pitched roof: Sloping roof.

Plinth: Lowest square member of the base of a column; also projecting, stepped or moulded base of a building.

Podium: Continuous base on which a temple or other structure is built.

Porte-cochere: Porch large enough for vehicles to pass through (p. 81).

Portico: Colonnaded entrance vestibule or porch with a roof supported on at least one side by columns.

Post-and-beam: System of construction using a framework of posts and beams.

Post-Modernism: Reaction to Modernism and, within architecture, to the International Style; characterized by the introduction of vernacular elements and playful illusion and decoration.

Precast concrete: Concrete cast in a place other than where it is to be installed in the structure.

Prestressed concrete: Concrete with internal stresses introduced by pre- or post-tensioning in order to counteract the stresses that will result from an applied load (p. 103).

Purlin: Horizontal roof beam resting on principal rafters and supporting subsidiary ones (p. 13).

Pyramid roof: Roof in the shape of a pyramid (pp. 42–3).

Q

Qiblat: Orientation of Mecca indicating the direction in which to pray.

R

Rafter: One of a series of parallel beams for supporting the roofing material on a sloping roof (p. 13).

Railing: Barrier comprising one or more horizontal rails supported by balusters.

Reinforced concrete: Concrete strengthened by the insertion of steel rods (p. 103).

Renaissance style: Term applied to the reintroduction of Classical architecture all over Europe from Italy in the 15th and 16th centuries.

Rib: Ridge or projecting piece of stronger or thicker material across the surface or through a structure serving to support, strengthen or adorn as in a vault.

Ridge: Top of a roof where two sloping planes meet.

Ridge piece: Timber running the length of a roof ridge to which the upper ends of the rafters are attached (p. 13).

Ridge pole: Another term for ridge piece (p. 13).

Ruai: Gallery in a longhouse.

Rumah bujang: 'Bachelor house', another term for *rumah tiang enam*, or house with six posts (p. 27).

Rumah dangau: Vernacular dwelling comprising one single house unit.

Rumah dapur: Kitchen of a Malay house; also the place where women congregate and where a family may dine, seated on mats on the floor (pp. 20–1).

Rumah ibu: Core area, and the most private part, of a Malay house in which occupants pray, sleep and perform household chores such as sewing and ironing (pp. 20–1).

Rumah kutai: Central Perak variation on the long ridge roof house whose walls, and sometimes floors, are made entirely of bamboo matting; the roof is made from *atap* (p. 25).

Rumah lepau: Traditional house in Kedah or Perlis which has been extended with a *lepau* at the front (p. 20).

Rumah penghulu: Headman's house (p. 10).

Rumah rakit: House built on a raft above water (p. 28).

Rumah selang: House comprising two *bumbung panjang* structures connected by a covered passageway.

Rumah serambi: 'Veranda house', another term for *rumah tiang duabelas* (p. 27).

Rumah tiang duabelas: House with twelve tiang, or posts (p. 27).

Rumah tiang enam: House with six tiang, or posts (p. 27).

Rumah tiang seribu: House built on stilts above water (pp. 28–9).

Rumbia: *Metroxylon rumphii* (La.), a species of palm whose leaves are used to make *atap*, or roof thatch.

S

Saddle roof: Ridge joining two higher elevations of a roof.

Screen: Frame covering an opening in a wall.

Selang: Covered passageway linking the main part of a Malay house to the kitchen, or linking two *bumbung panjang* to form one house, or *rumah selang* (p. 21).

Selasar: Roofed structure, or veranda, built along one side of a traditional Malay house in Kelantan or Terengganu.

Semangat rumah: Spirit of a Malay house that must be appeased for the home to be peaceful.

Serambi: Long, narrow reception area, or veranda, where social and religious functions involving non-family members take place (p. 21).

Serambi gantung: 'Hanging' veranda in front of a house.

Shell roof: Roof constructed from thin, curved plate structures (pp. 110–11).

Shophouse: Two-storey urban house with a ground floor shop open to the road and living quarters upstairs (pp. 90–1).

Shutter: Protection for windows and other wall openings (p. 23).

Silang gantung: 'Open scissors', gable horns formed by extending rafters skywards at the gable ends of a *bumbung panjang* house (p. 14).

Singhorra **tile**: Brittle, clay roof tile from Singhorra (Songkhla) in southern Thailand (p. 27).

Skyscraper: Exceptionally tall building with many storeys, supported by a steel or concrete framework from which the walls are suspended.

Sobek: Filigree-like woodcarving placed above a window to encourage natural ventilation (p. 124).

Solar power: Heat from the sun converted into electrical power.

Songket: Gold thread cloth.

Space-frame: Three-dimensional structural frame based on interconnected triangle frames (see illustration below)

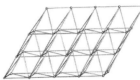

Span: Space between two supports of a structure; also the structure supported.

Stilt: Post or pile supporting a raised structure above land or water (p. 29).

Straits Eclectic style: Blend of Chinese, Malay, Indian and European architectural styles common to 19th- and early 20th-houses in the Straits Settlements (Penang, Melaka and Singapore).

Stucco: Plaster applied to a building facade to give it the appearance of stone; low relief plaster or cement decoration on ceilings and walls (p. 94).

Stud: Slender, structural timber in a wall frame.

Sunshade: Any form of exterior device comprising vertical or horizontal fins so angled as to shield a wall or window from direct sunlight.

Surau: Prayer room.

Swag: Classical festoon of flowers, fruit and foliage carved in stone or modelled in plaster (p. 79)

T

Tangga: Ladder, steps or stairway.

Tanju: Open deck on a long-house.

Tebar layar: Triangular gable ends of a Malay house, angled to encourage ventilation of the roof space and keep the house cool.

Tebuk separuh: Semi-piercing, with regard to carved wall panels.

Tebuk terus: Direct piercing, with regard to carved wall panels (p. 36).

Tebuk timbul: Embossed piercing, with regard to carved wall panels (p. 36).

Terrace house: One of a row of connected houses situated on a terraced site.

Thatch: Material for covering a roof, such as palm leaves fastened together.

Tiang: Post supporting the roof structure of a main house (p. 27).

Tiang seri: Central post (p. 22).

Tie beam: Horizontal timber for connecting two structural members to prevent them from spreading apart.

Tongkat: Intermediate post supporting a house floor (p. 27).

Tou-kung: (Ch.) Bracket system used in Chinese temples to support roof beams and project eaves outward (p. 51).

Tower: Tall building or structure that is high in proportion to its lateral dimensions.

Townhouse: Urban house in a row or terrace.

Truss: Triangular structural frame with internal, linear members connecting the upper and lower chords (p. 51).

Tudor style: Developed in England in the late 16th century, characterized by the Tudor arch and half-timber frame.

U

Undan-undan: Gable ledge (p. 27).

V

Vault: Arched roof or covering over a building.

Vent: Opening in a wall or roof that acts as an outlet for air and smoke.

Veranda: Open porch, enclosed by only a railing and usually roofed (pp. 20–1).

Vernacular architecture: Style of architecture utilizing building techniques and/or materials common to a particular area or ethnic group, from any particular historical period.

W

Western Classical style: Architecture of ancient Greece and Rome.

Wrought iron: Malleable yet tough iron that is easily forged and welded.

Main Buildings

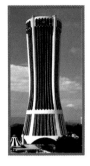

Only 20th-century buildings are listed. All are in Kuala Lumpur except where indicated.

Prewar

1908–9: **Jamek Mosque**, Public Works Department (PWD) (A. B. Hubback)

1911: **Kuala Lumpur Railway Station** (present), PWD (A. B. Hubback)

1929: **Victoria Institution** (present), PWD (A. C. Norman)

1936: **Anglo-Oriental Building**, A. O. Coltman, Booty & Edwards

1936: **Central Market**, T.Y. Lee (renovated 1986; Chen Voon Fee & William Lim)

1937: **Rubber Research Institute**, A. O. Coltman, Booty & Edwards

1939: **Johor State Secretariat, Johor Baru**, Palmer & Turner

Harrisons & Crosfield Building, A. O. Coltman, Booty & Edwards

Odeon Cinema, A. O. Coltman, Booty & Edwards

Oriental Building, A. O. Coltman, Booty & Edwards

1950s

1953: **Chin Woo Stadium**, Y. T. Lee

1954: **Federal House**, Iversen

1955: **UMNO Building, Jalan Tuanku Abdul Rahman**, Y. T. Lee

1956: **Dewan Bahasa dan Pustaka**, Y. T. Lee

1957: **Federal Hotel**, Goh Hock Guan

1957: **Stadium Merdeka**, Jabatan Kerja Raya (JKR)

1958: **Bangunan Persekutuan, Petaling Jaya**, JKR

1959: **Lee Yan Lian Building**, E. S. Cooke

1959: **Police Co-operative Building**, BEP Akitek

1960s

1960: **Kuala Lumpur Maternity Hospital**, JKR (K. C. Duncan)

1962: **Century Batteries Factory, Petaling Jaya**, BEP Akitek

1962: **EPF Building**, BEP Akitek

1962: **Stadium Negara**, JKR (S. E. Jewkes)

1963: **Muzium Negara**, Ho Kwong Yew & Sons

1963: **Parliament House**, JKR (Ivor Shipley)

1964: **AIA Building**, Palmer & Turner with John Graham & Co.

1964: **Chartered Bank Building**, BEP Akitek

1965: **Colgate-Palmolive Factory, Selangor**, BEP Akitek

1965: **Guinness Brewery, Selangor**, BEP Akitek

1965: **Masjid Negara**, JKR

1965: **Subang International Airport, Selangor**, BEP Akitek

1966–74: **Kuala Lumpur General Hospital**, Wells & Joyce Architects

1967: **A&W Drive-In, Petaling Jaya**, Malayan Architects Co-partnership; succeeded by Chen Voon Fee & Rakan Rakan

1967: **Negri Sembilan State Mosque, Seremban**, Malayan Architects Co-partnership; succeeded by Jurubena Bertiga International

1967: **Setapak Roman Catholic Church, Selangor**, BEP Akitek

1968: **Geology Building, Universiti Malaya**, Malayan Architects Co-partnership; succeeded by Chen Voon Fee & Rakan Rakan

1968: **Kuching Catholic Cathedral, Kuching**, BEP Akitek

1968: **Taman Seputeh linkhouses**, Arkitek MAA

1969: **Bank Negara, Penang**, Malayan Architects Co-partnership; succeeded by Jurubena Bertiga International

1970s

1970: **Bank Negara**, JKR (Nik Mohammed)

1971: **Arts Faculty Extension Building, Universiti Malaya**, Akitek Berakan

1971: **UMBC Building**, Eric Taylor (original building); Goh Hock Guan (additions)

1972: **Dewan Tunku Canselor, Universiti Malaya**, BEP Akitek

1973: **Ampang Park Shopping Complex**, Design Partnership with S. P. Chow & Rakan Rakan

1976–87: **Komtar, Penang**, Jurubena Bertiga International

1976: **Cheras Low Cost Cluster Link Housing**, Akitek Tenggara

1979: **Hyatt Kuantan Hotel, Kuantan**, Kumpulan Akitek

1979: **Sabah Foundation Building, Kota Kinabalu**, Wisma Akitek & James Ferrie

1980s

1980: **Bangunan Bank Bumiputra**, Kumpulan Akitek

1980: **Club Mediterranée, Pahang**, Hijjas Kasturi Associates

1980: **Tanjong Jara Beach Resort, Terengganu**, Wimberely, Wisenand, Tong & Goo with Akitek Bersekutu

1982: **Wilayah Complex**, ABC Akitek with DP Architects

1984: **Dayabumi Complex**, BEP & Arkitek MAA

1984: **Roof-roof House**, T. R. Hamzah & Yeang

1985: **IBM Plaza**, T. R. Hamzah & Yeang

1985: **Pan Pacific Hotel Kuala Lumpur**, Kumpulan Akitek

1985: **Putra World Trade Centre**, Kumpulan Akitek

1985: **Wisma Selangor-Dredging**, Kumpulan Akitek

1986: **LUTH Building**, Hijjas Kasturi Associates

1986: **Nagaria Complex**, Pakatan Reka

1986: **Pangsa Murni Condominium**, Nik James Ferrie Arkitek

1987: **Sultan Salahuddin Abdul Aziz Shah Mosque, Shah Alam**, Jurubena Bertiga International

1987: **Menara MPPJ**, Hijjas Kasturi Associates

1987: **Menara Maybank**, Hijjas Kasturi Associates

1990s

1991: **Lot 10 Shopping Centre**, Hijjas Kasturi Associates

1992: **Menara Mesiniaga**, T. R. Hamzah & Yeang

1992: **National Library**, Kumpulan Akitek

1992: **Salinger House**, CSL Associates

1993: **Impiana Resort**, CSL Associates

1993: **The Datai Langkawi**, Akitek Jururancang with Kerry Hill Architects

1993: **Wisma Genting**, CSL Associates

1994: **Shah Alam Stadium**, Hijjas Kasturi Associates

1995: **Sri Duta I Condominium**, GDP Architects

1996: **School of Art and Design Annex, ITM, Shah Alam**, Veritas Architects

1996: **Bank Negara Disaster Recovery Centre, Shah Alam**, Garis Architects

1996: **Central Plaza**, T. R. Hamzah & Yeang.

1996: **Geroge Kent Technology Centre, Sepang**, GDP Architects

1996: **Marang Resort & Safaris, Terengganu**, AsSaffa Design Practice & Bahar Omar Architect

1996: **Menara Kuala Lumpur**, Kumpulan Senireka

1997: **Menara UMNO, Penang**, T. R. Hamzah & Yeang

1997: **UE3**, Pakatan Reka

1998: **Kuala Lumpur International Airport, Sepang**, Akitek Jururancang with Dr Kurokawa

1998: **Mandarin Oriental Kuala Lumpur Hotel**, Wimberly, Allison, Tong & Goo with GDP Architects

1998: **Menara Maxis**, Kevin Roche, John Dinkeloo & Associates (USA) & NR Associates

1998: **Petronas Twin Towers**, Cesar Pelli & Associates (US) with KLCC Architects

1999 (projected): **Telekom Tower**, Hijjas Kasturi Associates

Bibliography

Abdul Halim Nasir (1984), *Mosques of Peninsular Malaysia*, Kuala Lumpur: Berita Publishing.
—— (1985), *Pengenalan Rumah Tradisional Melayu Semenanjung Malaysia*, Kuala Lumpur: Darul Fikir.
—— (1987), *Traditional Malay Wood Carving*, Kuala Lumpur: Dewan Bahasa dan Pustaka.
—— (1995), *Seni Bina Masjid di Dunia Melayu–Nusantara*, Bangi: Penerbit Universiti Kebangsaan Malaysia.
Abdul Halim Nasir and Wan Hashim Wan Teh (1996), *The Traditional Malay House*, Shah Alam: Penerbit Fajar Bakti.
—— (1997), *Warisan Seni Bina Melayu*, Bangi: Penerbit Universiti Kebangsaan Malaysia.
Aiken, S. Robert (1994), *Imperial Belvederes: The Hill Stations of Malaya*, Kuala Lumpur: Oxford University Press.
Andaya, Barbara Watson and Andaya, Leonard (1982), *A History of Malaysia*, London: Macmillan.
Annadale, N. (1903), 'Religion and Magic among the Malays of the Patani States', in N. Annadale and H. Robinson, *Fasciculi Malayenses: Anthropological and Zoological Results of an Expedition to Perak and the Siamese Malay States, 1901–1902*, Part 1, London: Longman, Green and Co.
Askandar, Adela N. N. (1997), 'The Role of the "Mother House" within the Regenerative Meaning of Tengku Putri Palace, Kota Bharu, Malaysia', dissertation, Cambridge University.
Auboyer, Jeannine et al. (1979), *Oriental Art: A Handbook of Styles and Forms*, London: Faber and Faber.
Badan Warisan Malaysia (Heritage of Malaysia Trust) (1986), *Strategi Pemiliharaan Nasional*, Kuala Lumpur: Badan Warisan Malaysia.
—— (1990), *Malaysian Architectural Heritage Survey: A Handbook*, Kuala Lumpur: Badan Warisan Malaysia.
Beamish, Jane and Ferguson, Jane (1985), *A History of Singapore Architecture: The Making of a City*, Singapore: Graham Brash.
Bellwood, Peter (1997), *Prehistory of the Indo-Malaysian Archipelago*, rev. edn, Honolulu: University of Hawaii Press; first published 1985.
Bellwood, P.; Fox, J. and Tyron, D. (eds.) (1995), *The Austronesians*, Canberra: Department of Anthropology, Australian National University.
Bird, Isabella (1990), *The Golden Chersonese: The Malayan Travels of a Victorian Lady*, Singapore: Oxford University Press; first published 1883.
Butcher, John G. (1979), *The British in Malaya, 1880–1941: The Social History of a European Community in Colonial South-East Asia*, Kuala Lumpur: Oxford University Press.
Cardon, R. (1934), 'Portuguese Malacca', *Journal of the Malayan Branch of the Royal Asiatic Society*, 12 (2): 1–23.
Carey, Iskandar (1976), *Orang Asli: The Aboriginal Tribes of Peninsular Malaysia*, Kuala Lumpur: Oxford University Press.
Chan Chee Yoong (ed.) (1987), *Post-Merdeka Architecture Malaysia, 1957–1987*, Kuala Lumpur: Pertubuhan Akitek Malaysia.
Chen Voon Fee (1983), 'Buildings for Education: A Retrospective', *Majallah Akitek*, 2: 57–61.
—— (1991), 'The Conservation of Traditional Values in Urban Development', *Majalah Arkitek*, 3 (1) and 3 (2).
Ching, Francis D. K. (1995), *A Visual Dictionary of Architecture*, New York: Van Nostrand Reinhold.
The Crafts of Malaysia (1994), Singapore: Archipelago Press.
Crain, Jay and Pearson-Rounds, Vicki (1996), 'From *Bang Tetel* to *Bawang*: Patterns of Transformation and Coherence in Lundayeh/Lun Bawang Architecture', paper presented at the Borneo Research Council's Fourth Biennial Meetings, Brunei Darussalam.
Domenig, Gaudenz (1980), *Tektonik im Primitiven Dachbau* (Tectonics in Primitive Roof Construction), Zurich: Institut ETH.
Dumarçay, Jacques (1987), *The House in South-East Asia*, Singapore: Oxford University Press.
—— (1991), *The Palaces of South-East Asia: Architecture and Customs*, Singapore: Oxford University Press.
1890–1990: 100 Years Kuala Lumpur Architecture (1990), Kuala Lumpur: Pertubuhan Akitek Malaysia.
Emrick, Michael (1976), 'Vanishing Kuala Lumpur: The Shophouse', *Majallah Akitek*, 2.
Erzigkeit, K. (1988), *Malaysia: Housing and Urban Development*, Darmstadt.
Evers, Hans-Dieter (1979), 'The Culture of Malaysian Urbanization: Malay and Chinese Conceptions of Space', University of Bielefeld and Centre for Policy Research, Universiti Sains Malaysia, mimeograph.
Falconer, John (1987), *A Vision of the Past: A History of Early Photography in Singapore and Malaya; The Photographs of G. R. Lambert & Co., 1880–1910*, Singapore: Times Editions.
Fauconnier, Henri (1931), *The Soul of Malaya*, London: Mathews and Marrot; reprinted Singapore: Oxford University Press, 1990; first published as *Malaise*, Paris: Delamain et Boutelle, 1930.
Fox, James J. (ed.) (1993), *Inside Austronesian Houses: Perspectives on Domestic Designs for Living*, Canberra: Department of Anthropology, Australian National University.
Gibbs, Phillip (1987), *Building a Malay House*, Singapore: Oxford University Press.
Guide to Kuala Lumpur Notable Buildings (1976), Kuala Lumpur: Pertubuhan Akitek Malaysia.
Gullick, J. M. (1955), *Kuala Lumpur, 1880–1895: A City in the Making*, Petaling Jaya: Pelanduk Publications.
—— (1983), *The Story of Kuala Lumpur, 1857–1939*, Singapore: Eastern Universities Press.
—— (1992), 'Bangunan Sultan Abdul Samad', *Journal of the Malaysian Branch of the Royal Asiatic Society*, 45 (1): 27–38.
—— (1994), *Old Kuala Lumpur*, Kuala Lumpur: Oxford University Press.
Hajeedar bin Hj Abdul Majid (1976/77), 'Towards a Conservation Movement in Malaysia', *Majallah Akitek*, 1 (3) and 2 (2).
Hamzah Jumiran (1979), 'Senibina Tradisional Negeri Sembilan Di Dalam Aspek Sejarah, Sosio-budaya, Reka Bentuk dan Pembinaan', MA thesis, Universiti Teknologi Malaysia.
Hashim, David Mizan (1990), 'Typology and the Evolution of the Malaysian Mosque', *Majalah Arkitek*, 2 (6): 70–82.
Hilton, R. N. (1956), 'The Basic Malay House', *Journal of the Malayan Branch of the Royal Asiatic Society*, 29 (3): 134–55.
Hooker, M. B. (1968), 'Semai House Construction in Ulu Slim, Perak', *Federation Museums Journal*, 12.
Hoyt, Sarnia Hayes (1991), *Old Penang*, Singapore: Oxford University Press.
—— (1993), *Old Malacca*, Kuala Lumpur: Oxford University Press.
Ipoh: The Town That Tin Built (1962), Ipoh: Phoenix Communications.
Izikowitz, K. G. and Sorenson, P. (1982), *The House in East and Southeast Asia: Anthropological*

and Architectural Aspects, London: Curzon Press.

Kamaruddin Mohd Ali (1983), 'The Vanishing Heritage: The Old Traditional Malay House', MA thesis, University of York.

Kelbling, S. (1983), 'Longhouses at the Baluy River', *Sarawak Museum Journal*, 32 (53): 133–58.

Khoo Kay Kim (1991), 'Taiping (Larut): The Early History of a Mining Settlement', *Journal of the Malaysian Branch of the Royal Asiatic Society*, 44 (1): 1–32.

Khoo Su Nin (1994), *Streets of George Town, Penang*, 2nd edn, Penang; first published 1993.

Killmann, Wulf; Sickinger, Tom and Hong Lay Thong (1994), *Restoring and Reconstructing the Malay Timber House*, Kuala Lumpur: Forest Research Institute Malaysia (FRIM).

King, Anthony D. (1976), *Colonial Urban Development: Culture, Social Power and Environment*, London: Routledge and Kegan Paul.

—— (1984), *The Bungalow: The Production of a Global Culture*, London: Routledge and Kegan Paul.

Kleingrothe, C. J. (c. 1907), *Malay Peninsula (Straits Settlements and Federated Malay States)*, Singapore: Kelly and Walsh.

Koenigsberger, O. H. et al. (1974), *Manual of Tropical Housing and Building. Part 1: Climatic Design*, London: Longman.

Kohl, David G. (1984), *Chinese Architecture in the Straits Settlements and Western Malaya: Temples, Kongsis and Houses*, Kuala Lumpur: Heinemann Educational Books.

Laurence Loh Akitek (1996), 'Penang: Facets of a Collective Flavour', *Majalah Arkitek*, 8 (1).

Lim Chong Keat (1986), *Penang Views, 1770–1860*, Singapore: Summer Times Publishing.

Lim Jee Yuan (1979), 'Relief of Climatic Stress in Housing in Malaysia', *Majallah Akitek*, 4.

—— (1987), *The Malay House: Rediscovering Malaysia's Indigenous Shelter System*, Pulau Pinang: Institut Masyarakat.

Lim, Jon S. H. (1993), 'The "Shophouse Rafflesia": An Outline of Its Malaysian Pedigree and Its Subsequent Diffusion in Asia', *Journal of the Malaysian Branch of the Royal*

Asiatic Society, 46 (1): 47–66.

Lip, Evelyn (1981), *Chinese Temples and Deities*, Singapore: Times Books International.

Malaysia Airports Berhad (1997), *Gateway Kuala Lumpur: Building Today to Serve You Tomorrow, Yearbook and Directory 1997*, Liverpool, United Kingdom: Mediafine.

Measured drawings of Malay houses, palaces, mosques, tombs, colonial bungalows, civic buildings, etc., Collection of the Centre for the Study of Built Environment in the Malay World (KALAM), Universiti Teknologi Malaysia, Johor.

Morris, Jan with Winchester, Simon (1983), *Stones of Empire: Buildings of the Raj*, Oxford: Oxford University Press.

Multimedia Super Corridor, Cyberjaya: The Model Intelligent City in the Making (n.d.), Kuala Lumpur: Multimedia Development Corporation.

Ng, C. L. (1995), 'Feng Shui and the Ancient Art of Siting', *Majalah Arkitek*, 7 (5): 48–53.

Ng, David (1983), *Malaya: A Retrospect of the Country through Postcards*, Petaling Jaya: Star Publications.

—— (1986), *Penang: The City and Suburbs in the Early Twentieth Century*, Penang.

Noone, R. O. (1948), 'Notes on the Kampong, Compounds, and Houses of the Patani Malay Village of Banggul Ara, in the Mukim of Batu Kurau, Northern Perak', *Journal of the Malayan Branch of the Royal Asiatic Society*, 21 (1): 124–41.

Oliver, Paul (ed.) (1976), *Shelter and Society*, London: Barrie and Jenkins.

Panduan PAM 1997/98 (1997), Kuala Lumpur: Pertubuhan Akitek Malaysia.

Ponniah, S. M. (1988), 'The Hindu Temple and Its Significance', *Rasah Sri Maha Mariamman Temple Souvenir Publication*, Seremban, pp. 105–7.

Putrajaya: An Intelligent Investment (n.d.), Kuala Lumpur: Putrajaya Holdings.

Raja Bahrin Shah bin Raja Ahmad Shah (1988), *The Terengganu Timber Malay House*, Kuala Lumpur: Badan Warisan Malaysia.

Rajathurai, R. (1983), 'The

Temple: Its Growth and Purpose', *Sri Seripagar Vinayagar Temple, Maha Kumbabishega Malar Souvenir Publication*, Singapore.

Ramanathan, K. (1995), 'Hindu Religion in an Islamic State: The Case of Malaysia', Ph.D dissertation, University of Amsterdam.

Sather, Clifford (1993), 'Posts, Hearths and Thresholds: The Iban Longhouse as a Ritual Structure', in James J. Fox (ed.), *Inside Austronesian Houses: Perspectives on Domestic Designs for Living*, Canberra: Department of Anthropology, Australian National University.

—— (1997), *The Bajau Laut: Adaptation, History and Fate in a Maritime Fishing Society of Southeastern Sabah*, Kuala Lumpur: Oxford University Press.

Sculpting the Sky: Petronas Twin Towers–KLCC (1998), Kuala Lumpur: Al Hilal Publishing (Far East).

Sheppard, Mubin (1962), 'Four Historic Malay Timber Buildings', *Federation Museums Journal*, 7.

—— (1969), 'Traditional Malay House Forms in Trengganu and Kelantan', *Journal of the Malaysian Branch of the Royal Asiatic Society*, 42 (2): 1–29.

—— (1972), *Taman Indera: Malay Decorative Arts and Pastimes*, Kuala Lumpur: Oxford University Press.

St John, Spenser (1863), *Life in the Forests of the Far East; or Travels in Northern Borneo*, 2 vols., London: Smith, Elder and Co.

Sternau, Susan A. (1997), *Art Deco: Flights of Artistic Fantasy*, London: Tiger Books International.

Syed Zainol Abidin Idid (c. 1995), *Pemeliharaan Warisan Rupa Bandar*, Kuala Lumpur: Badan Warisan Malaysia.

Tan Beng Kay (1992), 'The Tall Building Urbanistically Considered: Sense or Nonsense of Place', *Majalah Arkitek*, 4 (3) and 4 (4).

Tan Soo Hai and Hamzah Sendut (eds.) (1979), *Public and Private Housing in Malaysia*, Kuala Lumpur: Heinemann.

Tate, Muzaffar D. J. (1987), *Kuala Lumpur in Postcards, 1900–1939*, From the Collection of Major

David Ng (Rtd) and Steven Tan, Petaling Jaya: Penerbit Fajar Bakti.

Teoh Ghin Soon (1994), 'Development of Petaling Jaya: Malaysia's First New Town', *Majalah Arkitek*, Monograph '94, pp. 37–51.

Thum, M. C. (1985), *The Evolution of the Urban System in Malaya*, Kuala Lumpur: Penerbit Universiti Malaya.

Tong Kok Mau, Alan (1996), 'Meeting Demand for the Nation's Housing Needs', *Majalah Arkitek*, September/ October, pp. 40–2.

Too, Lilian (1996), *The Complete Illustrated Guide to Feng Shui*, Shaftesbury, Dorset: Element Books.

'Transactions and Translations: Fascinated by Architecture' (1996), *Majalah Arkitek*, 8 (4): 14–20.

Vlatseas, S. (1990), *A History of Malaysian Architecture*, Singapore: Longman.

Waterson, Roxana (1990), *The Living House: An Anthropology of Architecture in South-East Asia*, Singapore: Oxford University Press.

Wong, Chris (1992), 'A Historical Account of the Establishment of the Prestigious Old Schools of Malaya'. *Majalah Arkitek*, 4 (1).

Wright, Arnold and Cartwright, H. A. (eds.) (1908), *Twentieth Century Impressions of British Malaya: Its History, People, Commerce, Industries, and Resources*, London: Lloyd's Greater Britain Publishing Company.

Yarwood, Doreen (1985), *Encyclopaedia of Architecture*, London: B. T. Batsford.

Yeang, Ken (1987), *The Tropical Verandah City: Some Urban Design Ideas for Kuala Lumpur*, Kuala Lumpur: Longman.

—— (1992a), *The Architecture of Malaysia*, Amsterdam: Pepin Press.

—— (1992b), 'The Skyscraper: A Consideration of Its Planning and Builtform Implications', *Majalah Arkitek*, 4 (3).

—— (1992c), 'The Tropical Skyscraper: Design Principles and Agenda for Designing Tall Buildings in the Hot-Humid Tropics', *Majalah Arkitek*, 4 (6).

Index

Picture Credits

Abdul Halim Nasir, p. 11, bamboo and timber house; p. 20, Malay house. **Antiques of the Orient**, p. 58, view of Pekan, Melaka (from Kleingrothe, c. 1907); p. 60, 'Malaye proas'; pp. 60–1, view of Kuala Terengganu; p. 63, Town Square in Melaka (from Valliant, 1852); p. 64, Fort Cornwallis (1853); p. 74, 'official quarter' in Kuala Lumpur (1890). **Anuar bin Abdul Rahim**, p. 5, Mesiniaga Building; p. 13, roof and floor construction; p. 15, outrigger craft; p. 34, cutaway of Iban longhouse; p. 42, 7th-century stone; pp. 84–5, Ubudiah Mosque; p. 91, window with columns. **Arcaid**: Niall Clutton, p. 77, 'Red House'. **Architectural Association Photo Library**: Petra Hodgson, p. 102, Bauhaus school; John Winter, p. 112, Chandigarh High Court. **Arkib Negara Malaysia**, p. 62, map of Melaka (c. 1613); p. 100, Odeon Cinema, Jalan Tuanku Abdul Rahman shophouses; p. 108, Stadium Merdeka. **Badan Warisan Malaysia**, p. 126, Rumah Bomoh; p. 127, Rumah Penghulu (1–3); Lara Ariffin, p. 126, termite damage; Gerald Lopez, p. 127, completed Rumah Penghulu. **Bellwood, Peter**, p. 14, stubs of house posts. **Brunton, John**, p. 26, Kelantanese house. **Cassio, Alberto**, p. 120, roofs of terrace houses (top left, box). **Centre for the Study of Built Environment in the Malay World (KALAM), Universiti Teknologi Malaysia, Johor**, p. 38, Istana Sri Menanti, carvings on posts; p. 39, Istana Hinggap; p. 97, Heah Swee Lee's mansion. **Chai Kah Yune**, p. 27, Terengganu and Kelantan houses, Pahang house, locking device; p. 28, *rumah rakit*; p. 29, beach houses, *rumah tiang seribu*, Orang Kuala houses; p. 31, longhouse orientation; p. 32, cutaway of Murut longhouse; p. 33, Bajau, Lotud, bamboo and Bonggi houses, *londukng*; p. 39, central tower of palace; p. 43, Masjid Al' Azim; p. 45, Makam Pahlawan; p. 48, *pa kua, lo shu*; p. 58, background to photos; p. 100, features of Art Deco buildings; p. 101, Odeon sign; pp. 102–3, Federal House; p. 106, sunshading devices; p. 113, UIA; p. 116, Dayabumi arches and grillwork. **Chan Kim Lay**, p. 97, Chinese blackwood furniture. **Chang,**

Margaret, p. 72, Taiping Convent. **Chang, Tommy**, p. 14, Illanun houses; p. 16, Rungus house; p. 28, Bajau Laut houseboat; p. 30, Mount Kinabalu; p. 31, Lundayeh village; p. 32, Rungus house, *lansaran*. **Cheah, Michael**, p. 97, portrait of Heah Swee Lee. **Cheah, Walter**, p. 126, interior of No. 25 Jalan Pudu Lama. **Chen Voon Fee**, p. 107, A&W Drive-In; p. 126, Rumah Kutai. **Chye, Andrew**, p. 89, Light Street Convent. **CSL Associates**, p. 114, Nilly House. **Datai Langkawi**, p. 123, Datai Langkawi. **Davison, Julian**, p. 6, Kelantan and Terengganu houses; p. 7, Chinese shophouse; p. 24, Negeri Sembilan roof, *bumbung panjang* west coast roof, *gajah menyusu* house; p. 25, *bumbung lima* house, Melakan courtyard house; pp. 36 and 43, Terengkera Mosque; p. 43, Masjid Lama in Nilai. **Dew, Stephen**, p. 62, map of Melaka; p. 64, map of Georgetown; p. 67, map of Kuching. **Dewan Bahasa dan Pustaka**, p. 108, Dewan Bahasa dan Pustaka. **Dumarçay, Jacques**, p. 41, remains of Istana Seri Akar. **Edifice**: Darley, p. 77, 15th-century house; p. 81, Doric temple; Knight, p. 80, Villa Saraceno. **Elias-Moore, Kerry**, p. 17, house posts from tree, cloth on post; pp. 18–19, layout of kampong; pp. 20–1, cutaway of Malay house; pp. 22–3, constructing a house; p. 23, methods of construction; p. 48, Kek Lok Temple (after Tan Yeow Wooi); p. 49, animal symbolism. **Falconer, John**, p. 58, Penang Padang and City Hall (from Kleingrothe, c. 1907); p. 67, 'Mr Brooke's First Residence' (from St John, 1863); p. 68, opencast mining, Padang Rengas Pass (both from Kleingrothe, c. 1907); pp. 74–5, view of Kuala Lumpur (1884). **Garis Architects**, p. 115, Bank Negara Disaster Recovery Centre. **GDP Architects**, p. 118, exterior, interior and detail of staircase of George Kent Technology Centre; p. 123, Sebana Golf Clubhouse. **Gerster, George**, p. 120, housing estates (middle left and right, bottom left and right, box). **Government of India Tourist Office, Singapore**, p. 85, Moti Masjid. **Hashim, David Mizan**, p. 43, modular mosque; p. 86, Sultan

Sulaiman Mosque; p. 87, Negeri Sembilan State Mosque. **Héron-Huge, Domitille**, pp. 14–15, bronze sarcophagus; pp. 38–9, cutaway of Istana Sri Menanti; p. 40, entrance gate; pp. 40–1, reconstruction of Istana Seri Akar; p. 41, wall panels in *balai besar*; pp. 42–3, Kampung Laut Mosque; pp. 52–3, Khoo Kongsi complex; p. 56, artisan at Sri Kandasamy Temple, *vimana*; pp. 56–7, cutaway of Sri Markendeshvarar Temple; p. 57, *thuara palaka*; pp. 82–3, Bangunan Sultan Abdul Samad; pp. 86–7, cutaway of Masjid Negara; p. 87, main entrance, covered passageway, classrooms; pp. 90–1, cutaway of Chinese shophouses. **Hijjas Kasturi Associates**, p. 114, Telekom Tower; p. 119, Lot 10 interior and exterior; p. 122, Club Mediterranée. **Ishak bin Hashim**, p. 32, map of Sabah houses; p. 34, map of longhouse communities; p. 74, map of Kuala Lumpur; p. 76, map of hill stations; p. 103, concrete technology; p. 104, plan of Petaling Jaya Old Town; p. 105, plan of New Village; p. 110, JKR office block plans; p. 117, detail of curtain walling. **Jabatan Penerangan**, p. 101, Oriental Building; p. 110–11, Subang International Airport exterior and interior, reception and check-in; p. 119, former UMBC Building. **Jacobs, Joseph**, p. 6, Petronas Twin Towers; p. 10, *rumah penghulu*; p. 25, *rumah kutai*; p. 50, Cheng Hoon Teng Temple; p. 68, clearing land for rubber (from Wright and Cartwright, 1908); p. 69, estate bungalow (from Wright and Cartwright, 1908); p. 70, Taiping Station, opencast tin mining (both from Wright and Cartwright, 1908); p. 71, workers carrying latex, planter's bungalow, Negeri Sembilan Miners' Association (all from Wright and Cartwright, 1908); p. 85, Jamek Mosque; p. 86, Sultan Abu Bakar Mosque; p. 87, Penang State Mosque; p. 114, Kuala Lumpur skyline. **Jenkins, Waveney**, p. 21, kitchen. **Khang, Peter**, p. 43, southern China pagoda. **Khoo Salma Nasution**, p. 65, shophouses in Carnavon Street, half-brick half-timber house, plaster-work on Noordin family tomb; p. 95, interior of Syed Alatas Mansion, Indo-

Malay house; p. 96, Tye Kee Mansion, Loke Yew Mansion; p. 97, post-war Chinese Residency. **KLCC (Holdings)**, pp. 128–9, all pictures. **Lau, Dennis**, p. 10, riverine houses; p. 11, Dusun bamboo house, veranda of longhouse; p. 31, Iban longhouse, Melanau river bank village, Penan shelters; p. 32, loft in Murut longhouse; p. 34, longhouse near river; p. 67, Sarawak Museum; p. 80, Post Office in Kuching. **Lim Suan Imm**, p. 124, interior and exterior details of Salinger House. **Loo, Ruby**, p. 101, Rubber Research Institute Building, bas relief panel. **Lueras, Leonard**, p. 34, log steps to longhouse. **Lim Teng Ngiom**, p. 76, bungalow on Fraser's Hill; p. 77, 'The Lakehouse' in Cameron Highlands. **Loh Kwong Yu, Laurence/Loh-Lim Lin Lee**, p. 49, drainage system of Cheong Fatt Tze Mansion, motifs on wall; p. 51, diagram of traditional roof truss system. **Lloyd, Arthur**, p. 26, Cambodian timber house. **Malaysian Airports Berhad**, p. 131, interior of KLIA main building and departure terminal. **Museum and Art Gallery, Penang**, p. 76, Convalescent Bungalow; p. 94, Francis Light's 'Suffolk House'. **National Heritage Board, Singapore**, p. 61, Terengganu market scene. **New Straits Times Press (Malaysia) Berhad**, p. 102, UMNO Building; p. 103, Sime Darby Building; p. 108, Dewan Rakyat interior; p. 111, Lee Yan Lian Building; p. 118, Century Batteries factory, Colgate-Palmolive factory; p. 131. interior of KLIA, arboreteum of KLIA. **Marang Resort and Safaris**, p. 122, wooden house. **Nicholas, Colin**, p. 4, Orang Asli dwelling; p. 10, traditional Orang Asli dwelling; p. 11, weaving *bertam* leaves; p. 12, Proto-Malay village, Negrito making roof, interior of house; pp. 12–13, Semai houses; p. 13, Semai man making *atap* roof. **Pakatan Reka Arkitek**, p. 119, Nagaria Complex exterior and facade detail, UE3 interior. **Pelangi Beach Resort**, p. 122, Pelangi Beach Resort exterior, details of roof forms. **Photobank**, p. 26, gable ends on Thai house; p. 35, *tanju*, corner of gallery, mural on chief's apartment, centre of head-

Picture Credits

house; p. 58, Kuching (c. 1900); p. 66, Astana, Fort Margherita, Court House; p. 67, villa; p. 90, timber shophouses; p. 92, window with fanlight and shutters. **Picture Library**, p. 6, woodcarving; p. 23, shuttered windows; p. 29, *kampung air* in Kota Kinabalu, fishing village in Perlis; p. 60, Kota Bharu market; p. 79, door on Kuching townhouse; p. 87, Sultan Salahuddin Abdul Aziz Shah Mosque; p. 96, Nam Hoe villa; p. 98, Parliament House; p. 108, statue of Tunku Abdu Rahman. **Putrajaya Holdings**, p.130, Cyberjaya; p. 131, Putrajaya. **Quirk, Brian**, p. 79, Dutch-style windows. **Radin Mohd Noh Saleh**, p. 6, Ubudiah Mosque; p. 16, foreign influences; p.19, houses in paddy-growing area, fishing village, Quariah Mosque; p. 21, *serambi*; p. 22, timber and iron house; p. 23, gable screen; p. 24, joined *bumbung panjang* structures; p. 25, staircase of Melakan house, Bugis-style house; p. 27, *bangau* on boat; p. 37, Istana Kenangan; p. 39, Istana Kenangan, detail of timber supports and woven walls; p. 42, Hindu–Buddhist sculpture; p. 43, Candi Bukit Batu Pahat; p. 44, Royal Mausoleum at Kuala Kangsar; p. 45, grave of Hang Kasturi, Balai Nobat; p. 46, Teochew Association Temple, main hall of Sri Markendeshvarar Temple, statue of Lakshmi, 'OM' symbol, *gopuram* at Mahamariamman Temple; p. 49, lion guardian; p. 50, *chien nien* barge, entrance to courtyard of Cheng Hoon Teng Temple, prayer pavilion; p. 51, 'cat crawling' ridge, 'swallow's tail' ridge, Tua Pek Kong Temple, pillars in temple; p. 52, gable on Chan Shih Shu Yuen, *shek wan* frieze, Loo Pan Hong, woodcarving on beam; p. 53, row houses; p. 54, Ambal Temple; p. 55, *vaganam* image; p. 56, *ghana*; p. 57, *gopuram*, main door, *garbagraham*; p. 61, Istana Besar in Johor, Kuala Terengganu's Chinatown; p. 62, Santiago Gate; p. 65, St George's Church; p. 72, shophouses in Papan, City Hall in Ipoh; p. 73, district courthouse in Batu Gajah, Kuala Lipis Rest House; p. 75, 'Carcosa'; p. 77, Gap Resthouse; p. 78, arches of Sultan Abdul Samad Building; p. 79, tiles on steps; p. 85, detail of chatri; p. 86, mihrab; p. 87, main prayer hall, ablution area; p. 89, courtyard of Light Street Convent; p. 94, Christian Brothers' Retreat; p. 95, Syed Alatas Mansion; p. 96, 'Homestead'; p. 97, filligree grille, motifs on column. **Rosnawati Othman**, p. 40, Istana Balai Besar. **Rossi, Guido Alberto**, p. 117, Kompleks Tun Abdul Razak, Sabah Foundation Building. **Royal**

Commonwealth Society, p. 73, view of Taiping. **Sabah Museum**, p. 33, artwork references for Sabah houses. **Sarawak Museum**, p. 66, Charles Brooke; p. 67, view of Kuching, Main Bazaar, Pavilion; p. 87, Sarawak State Mosque. **Sather, Clifford**, p. 30, Bajau Laut village. **Shekar, S. C.**, p. 6, four-storey shophouse; p. 11, shingle roof; p. 21, Chinese shophouse; p. 25, Johor-style house; p. 36, panelled walls; p. 37, tomb of Hang Kasturi; p. 41, Istana Tengku Nik, wood-panelled walls; p. 44, simple and elaborate tombs in the Royal Mausoleum in Kelantan, Sultan Mahmud Mausoleum, tomb of Tok Pelam; p. 45, grave of Sheikh Ibrahim; p. 46, main doors of Cheong Fatt Tze Mansion, circular opening in front wall; p. 47, roof of Kuan Yin Temple; p. 48, aerial view of Kuala Lumpur; p. 49, Cheong Fatt Tze Mansion, courtyard of mansion; p. 51, Kwan Yin Temple, Cheng Leong Keng Temple, Teochew Association Temple; p. 52, King Street, ancestral tablets; p. 53, Khoo Kongsi temple, gable decoration on theatre; p. 54, orphan temple, rubber plantation shrine, *gopuram* of Sri Kandasamy Temple; p. 55, Chitti Temple, Nattukottai Temple, Patthar temple, domes of Chitti temple, Kunj Bihari Temple, Lakshmi Narayan Temple; p. 60, gates of Istana Balai Besar, Istana Jahar, Muhammadiah Mosque; p. 62, St Paul's Church; p. 63, central courtyard of Stadthuys, Melaka Club, door of Christ Church, Chee Mansion; p. 65, Acheen Street Mosque; p. 71, present 'Maison des Palmes', Socfin Estate house; p. 72, Padang in Ipoh, bungalow in Taiping; p. 73, market, administrative office, Taiping Museum, Taiping Lake Gardens, Batu Gajah; p. 75, Hotel Majestic, Sanitary Board, Suleiman Club; p. 76, bungalow on Maxwell's Hill; p. 77, 'Ye Olde Smokehouse', public square at Fraser's Hill, clock tower at Fraser's Hill, Silver Park Condominium; p. 78, Sultan Abdul Samad Building; p. 79, stained glass window, facade of townhouse; p. 80, Ipoh Railway Station, interior of station; p. 81, State Assembly Building, City Hall in Georgetown, Hong Kong and Shanghai Bank in Ipoh (two views); p. 82, semi-dome and horseshoe arches; p. 83, Railway Administration Building, Kuala Lumpur; p. 84, Kapitan Kling Mosque, minaret on Masjid India; p. 85, Syed Alwi Mosque, Zahir Mosque and interior; p. 86, Jamek Mosque in Muar, Jamek Mosque in Mersing;

p. 88, St John's Institution; p. 89, Victoria Institution, Malay College, St Michael's Institution, JKR school; p. 92, back, facade and side views of Melakan townhouse, ventilation openings, half-doors, glazed tiles, floral plasterwork, designs on tiles; p. 93, kitchen, spiral staircase, landing, bridal bedroom, sitting room, formal sitting room; p. 94, bungalow in Perak; p. 95, bungalow in Ladang Changkat Kinding, bedroom, staircase; p. 97, entrance of Falim House; p. 98, Anglo-Oriental Building, building in Jalan Yap Ah Loy, Great Eastern Life Assurance Building, Loke Yew Building, Federal House, Federal Building; p. 99, houses in PJ; p. 101, clock tower, Anglo-Oriental Building; p. 103, Chin Woo Stadium, Harrisons & Crossfield Building, Loke Yew Building; p. 104, National-type school, Section 1 house, residential street, row of shops; p. 105, clinics, wet market; 106, Geology Building, Bank Negara in Penang, EPF Building; p. 107, Negeri Sembilan State Mosque; p. 109, murals on Muzium Negara and Dewan Bahasa dan Pustaka; p. 110, JKR office block; p. 111, Kuala Lumpur General Hospital, Wisma Angkasapuri, Bank Negara, Police Co-operative Building, Federal Hotel, Chartered Bank; p. 112, UTM administrative building, DTC at Universiti Malaya, detail of DTC, Faculty of Arts building; p. 113, USM, UIA block and walkway; p. 116, Dayabumi Complex, Putra World Trade Centre; p. 118, Ampang Park Shopping Complex exterior and interior; p. 119, modern UMBC Building, Wilayah Shopping Complex interior, UE3 exterior; p. 120, Taman Seputeh linkhouses, semidetached houses in Petaling Jaya and Taman Tun Dr Ismail; p. 121, low-cost flats, low-cost terraced houses; p. 125, Menara Mesiniaga; p. 126, exterior of No. 25 Jalan Pudu Lama; p. 127, PAM headquarters, Central Market interior and exterior; p. 130, National Art Gallery, National Theatre, National Science Centre. **Sheldon, Garth**, p. 15, hill tribe house in North Vietnam. **Star Publications (M) Berhad**, p. 46, *kirin*; p. 48, Phillip Cheong; p. 88, four vernacular schools; p. 89, Minister of Education viewing model of 'smart school'. **Sui Chen Choi**, p. 13, building materials from the forest. **R. Sundrammorthy**, p. 15, patterns on Dongson bronze drums. **Syed Iskandar Ariffin**, p. 44, Muslim cemetery, Royal Mausoleum at Kampung Langgar. **Tam Hoe Yen**,

pp. 16–17, house-building ritual. **Tan Hong Yew**, p. 17, common roof styles; p. 25, *bumbung Perak* house; pp. 28–9, coastal and riverine settlements; p. 29, methods of keeping houses above water; p. 30, settlement zones in Sabah; p. 31, Melanau cosmos; p. 35, Iban, Melanau, Orang Ulu and Bidayuh houses; p. 36, three woodcarvings; p. 39, cross section of Minangkabau house; p. 43, Terengganu Stone; p. 50, temple facade; p. 51, traditional roof truss system; p. 60, plan of Kota Bharu; pp. 72–3, plan of present-day Taiping; p. 81, Ionic order, pediment, bay; p. 88, standard plan of national-type schools; pp. 130–1, mega projects composite. **Tan Yeow Wooi**, p. 48, *luo pan*; p. 50, plan of Cheng Hoon Teng Temple; p. 53, entrance to Khoo Kongsi complex. **Tara Sosrowardoyo**, p. 7, aerial view of housing estates; p. 61, Balai Besar; p. 86, aerial view of Masjid Negara; p. 104, aerial view of terrace housing; p. 108, Parliament House; p. 109, Stadium Negara, Masjid Negara, Tugu Negara; p. 112, aerial view of UKM; p. 114, Sabah Museum; p. 117, Menara Maybank, LUTH Building, Pernas Building; p. 120, Bukit Bangsar, housing estate (top right, box); p. 123, buildings in Golden Triangle; p. 130, National Library. **Tatham, Philip**, p. 118, Wisma Central exterior and interior; p. 119, Wilayah Shopping Complex exterior; p. 121, Pangsa Murni Condominium. **Teng, Arthur**, p. 19, coconut palms shading house; **Tengku Ismail bin Tengku Su**, p. 22, erecting a Malay house; p. 27, panelled walls; p. 45, *nobat* players. **Tin Industry (Research and Development Board)**, p. 70, *palong*, tin dredge. **T. R. Hamzah and Yeang**, p. 115, IBM Plaza, Menara UMNO; p. 125, plans of Menara Mesiniaga, Central Plaza, Menara UMNO, Roof-roof House and section plan. **Veritas Architects**, p. 113, School of Art and Design Annex at ITM, ITM campus. **Wee Siew Hock**, p. 124, climatic design of traditional Malay house. **Wong Swee Fatt**, p. 82, 'Raj'-style details; p. 90, shophouse styles; p. 91, five-foot way. **Yahaya Ahmad**, p. 21, *pelantar*; p. 22, bamboo and thatch house; p. 23, arrangement of wallboards. **Yeap Kok Chien**, p. 107, Muzium Negara; p. 124, Salinger House. **YTL Corporation Berhad**, p. 121, condominium brochures; p. 123, aerial view of Pangkor Laut and detail of houses. **Yu-Chee Chong Fine Art, London**, p. 63, view of Melaka.